FIELDS OF COMBAT

A volume in the series
The Culture and Politics of Health Care Work
edited by Suzanne Gordon and Sioban Nelson

A list of titles in this series is available at
www.cornellpress.cornell.edu.

FIELDS OF COMBAT

Understanding PTSD among Veterans of Iraq and Afghanistan

Erin P. Finley

ILR PRESS
AN IMPRINT OF
CORNELL UNIVERSITY PRESS
ITHACA AND LONDON

First published 2011 by Cornell University Press
First printing, Cornell Paperbacks, 2012
Printed in the United States of America

Library of Congress Cataloging-in-Publication Data

Finley, Erin P., 1977–
    Fields of combat : understanding PTSD among veterans of Iraq and Afghanistan /
Erin P. Finley.
        p. cm. — (The culture and politics of health care work)
    Includes bibliographical references and index.
    ISBN 978-0-8014-4980-2 (cloth : alk. paper)
    ISBN 978-0-8014-7840-6 (paper : alk. paper)
    1. Post-traumatic stress disorder—United States.   2. Iraq War, 2003-—
Veterans—Mental health.   3. Afghan War, 2001-—Veterans—Mental
health.   I. Title.   II. Series: Culture and politics of health care work.
    RC552.P67F545   2011
    616.85'212—dc22   2010044491

Cornell University Press strives to use environmentally responsible suppliers and
materials to the fullest extent possible in the publishing of its books. Such materials
include vegetable-based, low-VOC inks and acid-free papers that are recycled,
totally chlorine-free, or partly composed of nonwood fibers. For further information,
visit our website at www.cornellpress.cornell.edu.

Cloth printing   10 9 8 7 6 5 4 3 2 1
Paperback printing   10 9 8 7 6 5 4 3 2 1

*To my mother, A. J. Finley-McRee, and to my grandfathers,
Dale C. Finley, Jr., and Ben Pushard, veterans who served
their country in war and their families in peace*

Contents

Acknowledgments

There is no way to convey the sum of my gratitude for all those who have been part of this endeavor.

The research could not have been completed without financial support from the National Science Foundation and the Emory Center for Myth and Ritual in American Life (MARIAL). Deborah Winslow, Sybil Bridges, and Sally Pattison-Cisna made grant application and management navigable. Bradd Shore and the MARIAL faculty, including Marshall Duke and Robyn Fivush, provided important intellectual and methodological insights and critiques along the way. The Frederic C. Bartter General Clinical Research Center provided an office and logistical support for the clinical portion of the study. All the nurses and staff there were wonderful; Sharon Pryor and Terri Barnett, in particular, were patient and wise and kept a sense of humor throughout. The South Texas Veterans Health Care System (STVHCS) provided a home for this research, and a long list of people aided in pulling the necessary pieces together. Mary Jo Pugh, Michael Parchman, and Polly Noel of the STVHCS Veterans Evidence-Based Research Dissemination and Implementation Center (VERDICT) gave me space and motivation to work through the last half of the writing and have, over the course of the past year, taught me an enormous amount about collaboration and research. Needless to say, the views expressed in this work are mine alone and do not reflect the position or policy of the Department of Veterans Affairs or the United States government.

The Emory University Department of Anthropology was my scholarly home for more than a decade, and its faculty and staff deserve my thanks for their continual support. Carol Worthman, Mel Konner, and Don Seeman were educators and mentors throughout and made me grateful to have a doctoral committee who gave so generously to the process. I still marvel at my good fortune in getting to work with my graduate adviser, Peter J. Brown. His accumulated knowledge and intellectual curiosity are matched only by his great and wonderful humanity.

Sarah Willen provided the eureka moment that set me on the course to this book. Tricia Fogarty, Michelle Parsons, Elizabeth Milewicz, and Daniel Lende all read and provided invaluable feedback on early drafts of material that became part of the book, as did participants in a 2008 Cornell workshop led by Stefan Senders and Chip Gagnon on medicalization in postconflict societies. Jen Kuzara offered patient guidance on managing statistical data. Svea Closser was my rock throughout, doggedly reading every chapter at least once and cutting through excess and obfuscation with an unerring eye (what remains is entirely my fault). The tactful editing of Suzanne Gordon and Jamie Fuller have much improved my writing. An anonymous reviewer offered extremely helpful critiques and advice, for which I am most appreciative. Jill Fleuriet and Emily Mendenhall both provided vital input at a key moment. My sister, Christine Hamlin, not only furnished moral support at every stage but also read and revised several drafts in record time.

None of this would have been possible without the veterans and family members who shared so much of their time and experience in working with me on this research. Many of them expressed a hope that their participation would make a difference for other veterans. I was and am humbled by their generosity and grace.

My appreciation goes out, too, to all the clinicians who were so patient with my many questions. I am awed by the work you do.

My family and friends are my teachers and cheerleaders, and I carry them with me always.

My husband has been a source of unending support throughout this project, in more ways than I can count. For all his encouragement, I am a happier and better thinker, researcher, writer, and human being. Hector, I am grateful for you every day.

Thank you.

Abbreviations

APA	American Psychiatric Association
BAMC	Brooke Army Medical Center
CBT	cognitive behavioral therapy
CDP	Center for Deployment Psychology
C&P	Compensation and Pension Service of the VA
COSC	Combat and Operational Stress Control
CSC	combat stress control
DOD	Department of Defense
DSM	*Diagnostic and Statistical Manual of Mental Disorders*
EMDR	Eye Movement Desensitization and Reprocessing
ESTs	evidence-supported treatments
FOB	forward operating base
HR	human remains
IED	improvised explosive device
MHAT	Mental Health Advisory Team
MRE	meals ready to eat
NCO	Noncommissioned officer
NIMH	National Institute of Mental Health
OEF/OIF	Operation Enduring Freedom/Operation Iraqi Freedom
PCL-M	PTSD Checklist, Military Version
PDHA/PDHRA	Post-Deployment Health Assessment, Post-Deployment Health Reassessment
PDS study	Post-Deployment Stress study
PE	prolonged exposure therapy
PFT	physical fitness test
PT	physical training
PTSD	post-traumatic stress disorder
RPG	rocket-propelled grenade
SAMMC	San Antonio Military Medical Center
SSRI	selective serotonin reuptake inhibitor

TBI   traumatic brain injury
VA   Department of Veterans Affairs
VBA   Veterans Benefits Administration
VFW   Veterans of Foreign Wars of the United States
VHA   Veterans Health Administration

Characters

All names, except those of public figures, have been changed.*

Adam Baldwin is a veteran of the marine reserves who served one seven-month tour in Iraq. He and his wife were married just before his deployment. He now owns an independent construction and contracting company and does volunteer work helping other veterans prepare their disability claims for the VA.

Brian O'Neil is a funny, wise-cracking veteran in his midforties. He served as a combat medic with active-duty and reserve army units in the Gulf War, Iraq, and Afghanistan. He and his wife live in San Antonio with their daughter and two sons.

Chris Monroe is an air force computer specialist who served two tours in Afghanistan in support of army units before being sent home unexpectedly. He is now medically retired from the military, and he and his wife have two children.

Derek Johnson is an army veteran who lost his leg in an improvised explosive device (IED) blast in Iraq. After his injury, he spent a year undergoing multiple surgeries and rehabilitation at Brooke Army Medical Center. He and his wife, Laticia, have two children, and he is completing a college degree in advertising.

Jesse Caldera is an air force veteran in his midtwenties who served two deployments in Iraq, volunteering for extra duty whenever he could. Like Derek, he has gone back to school since separating from the military.

Tony Sandoval is a former marine who served in both Afghanistan and Iraq, including during heavy combat in the battle of Fallujah. He now lives and works in San Antonio.

---

*All of the veterans listed here represent composites of several individuals who participated in the research. These composites were intended to disguise the identity of veterans who shared their stories while honoring the themes and integrity of their original narratives.

FIELDS OF COMBAT

INTRODUCTION

Stocky, jovial, and a master of the wry grin, Brian O'Neil served two tours as a combat medic for the U.S. Army Reserves. When his ten months in Afghanistan were up, he and his unit climbed into their vehicles and drove five hours from their fire base to Bagram Airfield. Upon reaching Bagram, they waited fifteen hours for their plane to arrive, then climbed aboard for the ten-hour flight to Germany. There was another ten-hour flight to Atlanta and then three days at Fort Benning, Georgia, before the last flight brought him home to San Antonio, Texas. "So in seven days," Brian concludes, "I went from getting shot at to sitting in my recliner. And pardon my language, but that's called the Afghanistan mind-fuck. Because you come from, 'I'm here,' to 'What the hell do I do now?'"

Like many of the more than 1.6 million U.S. service members who have served in Iraq and Afghanistan since September 11, 2001, Brian found that his long trip home was only the beginning of his journey. Veterans often talk about the normal process of "readjustment," that awkward period after long deployments during which service members reacclimate to life outside a combat zone, slowly relaxing the vigilance they have maintained through their months in unsafe territory. But for a minority of veterans, the challenges of readjustment go awry and begin to bleed into something else. They may find themselves drinking too much, unable to sleep, waking when they do sleep from unspeakable dreams, or lashing out violently at friends and loved ones. Their emotional response to the world may have changed, subtle shadings of love and concern morphing into a bleaker landscape of numbness and anger. They may find it impossible to reconnect with a family who does not know what it is to live with fear, danger, and death. They may come, over time, to struggle so profoundly with the rites of everyday life that they eventually are given a diagnosis of post-traumatic stress disorder (PTSD).[1] This book is about that journey, and that diagnosis.

Since shortly after the invasion of Iraq in 2003, the mental health of America's most recent veterans has been the focus of intense national interest. In excess of thirty thousand Americans have been wounded in action, but nearly four times that many—some 120,000 men and women—have returned home to be diagnosed with the most common and least visible of wounds: the psychological injury of PTSD.[2] News stories have vividly recounted the horrors of war and its psychological aftermath. The problem of providing adequate health care has at times become the source of public outrage, as in the media maelstrom surrounding the 2007 Walter Reed scandal. Returning veterans have engaged in a highly public battle with the Department of Veterans Affairs (VA) over perceived failures to provide appropriate treatment and compensation for service-related disabilities. Meanwhile, the diagnosis of PTSD itself remains hotly debated among psychiatrists, psychologists, and others who disagree about what sort of illness it is, what causes it, and how best to treat it. No mere turf war, these professional battles are in the process of revolutionizing how the VA provides trauma care to veterans, with implications for redefining the way PTSD itself is understood in the process. In the following chapters I untangle each of these conflicts and reveal the very real implications they have for veterans living with PTSD.

Drawing on twenty months of ethnographic fieldwork among recent veterans and their families and health-care providers in San Antonio, this book examines the cultural, political, and historical influences shaping experiences of combat PTSD in contemporary America. PTSD—while very much a real part of the human experience, observed in one form or another across the boundaries of history and culture—is not the monolithic biomedical category it often appears but rather something fluid and subject to interpretation. American understandings of combat PTSD prove to be heterogeneous and dynamic, differently understood across such diverse settings as the family, the military, and the VA mental-health-care system. In situating the stories of veterans like Brian within this wider terrain, my intention is simple: to examine how the American cultural context influences the emergence of PTSD and responses to it and to understand—within this context— what PTSD means for veterans and their families.

That understanding is critical not only to veterans but to the professionals and institutions who assist and care for them and to the policymakers whose decisions shape their chances. A careful examination of the issues makes it clear that the future of this generation of veterans is at a crossroads. Veterans of Iraq and Afghanistan are being diagnosed with PTSD in record numbers and show signs of struggling with all the demons experienced by veterans of earlier wars:

substance abuse, failed relationships, difficulty in maintaining work, even sui-cide. At the same time, the past few decades have taught us a great deal about PTSD, with the result that we now have effective treatments that can help vet-erans to take their lives back, as well as unprecedented resources for supporting veterans and their families. Much of the difficulty will lie in ensuring that veter-ans are aware of these options and resources and in making those options easily accessible to all. Toward this end, the conclusion of this book offers a series of recommendations for measures to support veterans and their families. Though we do not yet have all the answers, there are steps that can be taken at all levels to move toward a brighter future.

As an anthropologist, I find the web of tangled arguments over PTSD fasci-nating because these conflicts are in many ways about the nature of war-related suffering itself. The stories of struggling veterans trying to understand what has happened to their lives in the wake of their time in Iraq or Afghanistan, amid the havoc that has been wrought on their families and sense of self, also illumi-nate how deeply suffering is embedded in the political, economic, and cultural circumstances that make up the context of everyday life.[3]

Reflecting this vantage point, the book interweaves two focal points: veter-ans' personal experiences of PTSD and the cultural politics that surround and shape those experiences. In the early chapters I follow the chronology that most veterans themselves take—into the military, off to war, and returning home—in laying out how individual veterans describe their time in the service and how they make sense of what began to go wrong in the months and years after their return home. Chapter 1, "Fourth of July," starts things off by considering how young people in South Texas come to join the military. Chapter 2, "War Stories," explores the stories that veterans tell of their time in Iraq and/or Afghanistan, attending to how these stories are told and what they reveal about the nature of war trauma for these men. Chapter 3, "Home Again," describes what happened when these veterans came home from war and first noticed the phenomena that they would come to call PTSD symptoms.

Later chapters widen the analytic scope to consider how PTSD and post-de-ployment stress are understood in three cultural environments through which most PTSD-diagnosed veterans pass: within families, the U.S. military, and the VA's mental-health-care system. Observing how PTSD is debated and managed in each of these settings makes it possible to appreciate the life challenges this illness can create for recent veterans, as well as the many messages around PTSD that are available to them. In chapter 4, "Of Men and Messages," I examine how veterans and their families respond to the crises brought on by post-deployment stress and explore how cultural ideas around illness and gender shape male vet-erans' coping and care-seeking behaviors. Chapter 5, "Clinical Histories," tracks how American understandings of combat stress have evolved since the Civil War. Chapter 6, "Under Pressure," describes the social and structural pressures that help to perpetuate stigma in the military, while also examining how public uproar and media scandal have spurred the U.S. military to augment PTSD screening, prevention, and treatment programs in recent years. Chapter 7, "Embattled," illuminates the politicized world of VA services and professional mental health care that veterans enter when they seek help at a San Antonio–area VA mental health clinic.

Chapter 8, "Navigation," returns to the focus on individual veterans, exploring how they traverse the challenges of living with PTSD by drawing upon layers of experience they have acquired in their encounters with family and within the military and VA. The conclusion brings things to a close with a look at how PTSD is defined and debated in contemporary society and social science, offering an overview of how the disorder emerges from a confluence of neurobiological, psychological, social, and cultural phenomena and making a series of recommendations for treating and preventing PTSD among current and future veterans.

Along the way, this book addresses a series of questions:

- What do we know about the causes of PTSD? What social and cultural factors are implicated in its etiology? Why do some people develop PTSD while others do not?
- What is it like to live with combat PTSD?
- How do veterans and their family members understand PTSD, and how do these understandings shape care-seeking and coping behaviors? What cultural influences are at work here?
- What do clinical and institutional (e.g., VA and military) responses to veterans' problems with homecoming look like? What influences appear to be driving these responses?
- And finally, how are these social, clinical, and institutional responses shaping the current and future well-being of veterans and their families?

Even as it addresses such practical questions, however, this book is also about the stories that get told of war and its aftermath, including the kinds of war stories veterans tell (and don't tell) (chapter 2); the stories families tell about their experiences of PTSD (chapters 3–4); the stories the military tells about combat and its effect on service members (chapters 5–6); the stories the VA tells about its responsibility to veterans (chapter 7); the active debate over what kinds of trauma stories may help veterans and what kinds of stories may be dangerous (chapter 7); and the combined power of all these personal and cultural stories in shaping how modern-day veterans cope with their own experiences of war and trauma (chapter 8).

Together these stories shed light on the ambivalent relationship that America has with its veterans, who are both idolized and feared, and with PTSD, which turns out to stand for not only the personal aftermath of a nation at war but all the ways in which veterans' suffering is named, claimed, and made sense of in modern America.

PTSD is the technical name for a complex of symptoms that arise in the wake of a trauma, an experience that causes feelings of "fear, helplessness, or horror."[4] News reports on PTSD in the American media have made a habit of describing many of these symptoms: an overactive startle reflex, a sense of always being "amped up" and on edge, an intense desire to avoid reminders of war-related memories, and the uncontrolled invasion of these memories into waking and sleeping life. Although PTSD and its causes and symptoms will be discussed at length as we go along, it is helpful to lay out a few facts here at the beginning.

First of all, PTSD can result from a variety of traumas. These may include events that happen on one occasion, such as a rape, an assault, or a motor vehicle accident. They may also include experiences that reoccur periodically or are sustained over a period of time, like being in combat, living in a concentration camp or as a prisoner of war, or being submitted to ongoing physical or sexual abuse. An experience of trauma alone, though, is not enough to result in PTSD. In order to be given a formal diagnosis, a person must exhibit signs of lingering distress that fall into three categories (see table 1). The first of these categories, "reexperiencing" (also called "intrusive recollections"), includes the feeling of being haunted by recurrent memories or dreams of the event(s), or even feeling as though one is reliving the trauma. "Avoidance/numbing" symptoms reflect the attempt to avoid remembering the trauma, usually by trying to stay away from places, situations, and other phenomena that serve as a reminder of the event(s). Symptoms in this category can also include emotional distancing, resulting in a generalized feeling of numbness, a lack of emotion, a sense of isolation from loved ones, or the inability to imagine a future. The final category of symptoms, "hyperarousal," refers to a heightened responsiveness to the immediate environment, which often takes the form of irritability, the inability to sleep soundly, or keeping a vigilant eye out for potential danger at all times, even in situations that others may perceive as innocuous. A person may be diagnosed with PTSD by a mental health professional if he or she has lived through a significant trauma, is experiencing symptoms from each of these three categories, and continues to have these symptoms for more than a month. Even so, these symptoms are not considered sufficient for a formal diagnosis unless they create significant distress or an inability to function in normal life.

Table 1. Post-traumatic stress disorder (PTSD) symptoms

SYMPTOM CLUSTER	SYMPTOMS
Reexperiencing	• Recurrent and intrusive memories of the trauma
	• Recurrent and distressing dreams of the trauma
	• Feeling or acting as though the trauma is happening again, which may include hallucinations, a feeling of reliving the event, or dissociative flashbacks
	• Intense psychological distress at encountering cues that provide a reminder of the trauma
	• Physical reaction (e.g., increased pulse, sweating) at encountering cues that provide a reminder of the trauma
Avoidance/numbing	• Attempts to avoid thoughts, feelings, or discussion of the trauma
	• Attempts to avoid activities, people, or places that provide a reminder of the trauma
	• Inability to remember an important component of the trauma
	• Diminished interest and/or participation in important activities
	• Feeling detached or withdrawn from others
	• Limited range of feelings (e.g., not being able to feel love)
	• Foreshortened future (e.g., not expecting to have a long or normal life)
Hyperarousal	• Trouble falling or staying asleep
	• Irritability, anger
	• Trouble concentrating
	• Hypervigilance
	• Exaggerated startle response

Source: Adapted from American Psychiatric Association, *Diagnostic and Statistical Manual of Mental Disorders,* 4th ed., text rev. (*DSM-IV-TR*) (Washington, DC: American Psychiatric Association, 2000).

This was the illness I wanted to better understand when I set out for San Antonio on the day after Christmas, 2006, moving halfway across the country to explore the psychological consequences of the ongoing wars—Operation Enduring Freedom (OEF, Afghanistan) and Operation Iraqi Freedom (OIF, Iraq)—for the veterans who had been sent to fight them. Having previously studied the effects of violence on mental health among former combatants in Northern Ireland, heroin and cocaine users in Boston, and Sudanese refugees resettled in Atlanta, I was moved by the escalating numbers of men and women returning from combat to find their lives and selves in turmoil. I found myself asking, what does PTSD mean for veterans of Iraq and Afghanistan, and what impact is it having on their lives and their families? What is it like to live with combat PTSD?[5]

The answers I found to these questions are presented here in the form of stories and other findings, the result of research I conducted in 2007 and 2008 as part of what came to be known as the Post-Deployment Stress (PDS) study.

The study was supported by funding from the National Science Foundation and the Emory University Center for Myth and Ritual in American Life (a Sloan Foundation Center for Working Families). I chose San Antonio as a research site because it has one of the largest populations of retired service members in the nation, as well as Lackland and Randolph Air Force bases, Fort Sam Houston, the San Antonio Military Medical Center (SAMMC), where many of the wars' wounded are treated, and a heavily utilized VA health-care system.[6] A local VA clinic that specializes in providing PTSD treatment generously offered support for the project and became home base for the work that followed.[7] The sixty-two veterans who chose to participate in the study's in-depth interviews—of whom fifty were male veterans of Iraq and Afghanistan—were asked to talk not only about their own experiences with deployment and life afterward but also about how they thought about PTSD and what the illness meant to them.[8] These veterans were primarily Latino and white, and most had been diagnosed with combat-related PTSD, but they nonetheless represented a wide range of backgrounds and experiences: veterans of Vietnam as well as Iraq and Afghanistan; men and women; those who had been visibly injured or invisibly injured and those who were by all accounts whole and sound; representatives of the army, navy, air force, and marines; and those who served on active duty as well as in the National Guard and reserves.[9] Across a table in a little room within that VA, we began a long and ongoing conversation about war, trauma, and PTSD.

In the interviews themselves—which were usually long and free-ranging, although we kept roughly to a list of open-ended questions—we talked about adolescence and growing up, about military service and combat, family life, experiences with PTSD and other injuries of war, goals for the future, encounters with military and VA health-care systems, and the challenges of building a good life after leaving the military. Interviews were accompanied by survey questionnaires collecting information on known risk factors for PTSD, such as predeployment and post-deployment trauma exposure. Other measures included scales assessing physical and mental disability and the severity of PTSD, depression, and anxiety symptoms.[10] These and other survey data will be called upon at intervals throughout the book to shed light on key questions.

These interviews reveal that the greatest challenge for many returning veterans is not just dealing with PTSD but also trying to manage their suffering while striving for a normative life in American society. As is the case throughout the world, trying to create a "successful" life in the United States is a heavily gendered task, and gender proves to be a piece of the puzzle here as well. Although the current conflicts are remarkable for the growing role played by women serving in combat zones, I focus here on male veterans because being a man in America often means being "manly" in a way that may not be conducive to coping well with PTSD (a discussion I return to in chapter 4).[11] Often the ideals for men's behavior preclude expressing emotion or accepting the sense of vulnerability that accompanies illness and suffering, and so men may be less likely than women to seek out the health care and social support they need to effectively manage such distress.[12] Highlighting the experiences of men admittedly leaves us with a fairly traditional portrait of veterans and their families, of men going off to war and women marshaling the response at home, a portrait that does not represent many of the changes ongoing in how men and women engage in war on modern battlefields.[13] In an attempt to provide some balance, I asked seven female veterans who had served in Iraq and Afghanistan to also participate in this study, and working with them was a lesson in how extraordinary such women are, and how unique their needs may be (I offer a few comments on these needs in the last chapter). I am grateful to the many researchers who are working even as I write to fill in the gaps in our understanding of female service members' experiences of combat stress, for this will be an important element of treating PTSD among veterans in the decades to come, as more and more women take on combat roles in the military.

Although veterans are at the heart of this book, many other people and events are also essential to the stories told here. Over the course of the research, I interviewed dozens of VA- and community-based psychiatrists, psychologists, social workers, and local veterans' service representatives, all of whom contributed their own perspectives on veterans and PTSD. These participants helped to illuminate how even the experts in mental health continue to debate over PTSD: its symptoms and causes, and, perhaps most important, the best ways to support healing and recovery.

One of the great joys of being an anthropologist is working in a field that values the social settings of ordinary life, and so I was also able to go beyond the clinic and meet veterans' wives, girlfriends, and occasionally other family members for long discussions of their experiences with PTSD. They described how they often did not recognize their men after they came home from war, and how they made sense of their husbands' strange swings between anger, fear, grief, and withdrawal. We talked over coffee in Denny's and over chicken at Chick-Fil-A. We talked in their homes, where they could bring out pictures of "what he looked like before" and, once, could show me where he had punched a hole in the bedroom door. These women—for most were women—spoke of how they understood PTSD and the challenges it creates for maintaining personal sanity and a cohesive family life. Their stories and strategies for coping say a great deal about how they view their husbands as men, and how they make meaning amid the suffering that war has brought to their lives.

The freedom to move throughout the community also allowed me to learn from many of the other individuals and organizations who work locally with veterans and active-duty military, whether as veterans' advocates, army chaplains (most of whom had served one or more tours in Iraq, providing spiritual support for soldiers in the combat zone), or as artists and filmmakers portraying the experience of veterans as part of local history. In all, some 133 veterans, family members, clinicians, and members of the community participated in the PDS study.[14] Having access to life and research both inside and outside the clinic made it possible to witness how PTSD is talked about and lived out across a range of settings, from a psychiatrist's office at the VA to the "policy discussions" conducted at high volume during a local veterans' forum.

What the sum total of these conversations, interviews, and observations made clear is that PTSD means many different things to many different people. For veterans, it may be a profound alteration in the way they experience themselves and the world. For family members, PTSD may be seen as an explanation ("Aha! That's why he's been acting this way!") or an excuse ("He blames everything on his PTSD"). For mental-health-care providers working in this area, PTSD is a piece of specialized knowledge, a diagnosis on which they have a firm grasp, a natural occurrence whose course they hope to interrupt (although they may disagree vehemently with other clinicians on *how*). For many veterans' organizations and advocates, PTSD represents one shining fragment of the wrongs that veterans have been done by the military, by the VA system of health care and benefits, or by American society as a whole.

All of these perspectives are reflected in the individual veteran's experience of PTSD and may have an influence on what symptoms a veteran comes to associate with PTSD, whether and where he seeks treatment, and whether he greets the diagnosis of PTSD with relief or shame. This in fact proves to be the main message of this book: the myriad ways in which combat PTSD is understood in American life have a profound effect on how veterans with PTSD understand their own symptoms, feel about their diagnosis, and make what may be life-changing decisions about coping and care seeking.

I should make it clear from the beginning that not all the experiences of distress described by veterans in these pages necessarily fit a clinical definition of PTSD. I represent these experiences as veterans themselves described them, without putting too fine a focus on diagnostic distinctions, because veterans themselves rarely made a distinction between symptoms related to PTSD and those caused by other physical and psychological health problems (for example, a tendency to hyperventilate at imagined or remembered stress, a symptom of panic disorder rather than PTSD). Diagnosis tends to be a concern of clinicians, and since clinicians themselves may differ on whether certain symptoms—auditory hallucinations, for example, or blackouts—are associated with PTSD, I have chosen to focus on veterans' own ways of organizing their experiences. These stories aspire to experiential rather than clinical accuracy. In a sense, this decision reflects a distinction that anthropologists often make between *disease,* or what clinicians identify as the biological problem behind a given sickness, and *illness,* the holistic human experience of living with that sickness.[15] For the most part, this is a book about PTSD as illness rather than disease.

Even so, there are many areas in which this distinction seems to blur. For example, important questions have been raised of late regarding whether PTSD is being overdiagnosed among recent veterans. It has been argued that PTSD is being used as a blanket term to describe a wide variety of life concerns post-deployment, and that this labeling may produce chronic disability among veterans rather than encouraging a steady path toward reintegration and recovery.[16] This is an important question and one I will wait to address more fully in the last chapter, as a number of related issues—veterans' struggles post-deployment and the complexity of naming these struggles, as well as institutional efforts to manage PTSD within the military and the VA—will be illuminated in the intervening chapters. (Those who are eager to read about this and other matters of definition, construction, etc. should feel free to skip ahead and start with the conclusion.)

I should also make it clear that there will be relatively little discussion in these pages of the politics of the wars in Iraq and Afghanistan. One of my early hypotheses for the study was that veterans would describe efforts to make sense of PTSD illness in relation to their views on the merits of the "Global War on Terror" and their role within it. I remember suggesting this to an army chaplain toward the beginning of the research and the bemused look on his face as he smiled and shook his head. He was right; my hypothesis proved wrong. What I found instead was that most of these men were not deeply engaged with the larger national debate over whether the wars were wrong or right, over whether we should bring the troops back home or continue to support the ongoing missions. They never lacked opinions on the subject—they often expressed well-mulled-over views—but these opinions did not emerge as vital to their experience of the war or PTSD itself. In contrast with some veterans of Vietnam[17] or antiwar veterans of Iraq and Afghanistan in other parts of the United States,[18] these South Texas veterans rarely described weighing their own experiences of war in relation to national policy. Their stories were centered around other concerns: the well-being of buddies in the combat zone and their families back home, their dreams of a good life and efforts to move toward them. In all the hours of our conversations, the politics of war emerged only at odd moments and on the periphery of other stories, and so they have been left to the periphery here.[19]

In viewing these men's stories together, it becomes possible to see how culture writ large trickles down to affect life at the level of the individual. Large-scale forces—for example, the way that Americans understand war-related illness and the professional controversies that define contemporary mental health care—have a profound, immediate, and long-term influence on the personal experience of combat PTSD. And so, before turning to the task of examining PTSD as a fraught social phenomenon, the source of conflicts and debates that continue to rage, I begin by considering it as an illness that comes into and profoundly shapes individual lives. For all the clinical and political debates that make combat PTSD such a charged topic, it is in the private space of veterans' hearts and minds that the illness takes its toll, entering lives that were already in motion, already speeding along rapid trajectories toward an unseen but surely promising future.

FOURTH OF JULY

A Tradition of Service in San Antonio

July 4, 2007, dawned rainy in San Antonio, but the day had turned sunny and sweltering by the time I found a seat at an empty picnic table down at the local Veterans of Foreign Wars (VFW) post. An older woman in a red shirt came and joined me at the same table, sheltering under the shade of its umbrella. She introduced herself as Melissa, and we chatted for a while, laughing about the fact that we had both gotten lost on the way to the VFW.

We were both there for the same reason. As part of its Fourth of July celebration, the VFW was dedicating a new memorial to fifty-three local men and women who had been killed in the Global War on Terror, then more than five years in the making. I had at that point spent six months working with veterans of Iraq and Afghanistan out of the local Department of Veterans Affairs (VA) hospital, and it was with these men and women in mind that I ended up at the VFW that day. As it turned out, the events that afternoon hinted at something of what I had come to San Antonio seeking to understand: how war and its aftermath become part of daily life for veterans and their families, and how generations of American warriors have embarked upon military service only to find themselves faced with unexpected consequences.

In the age of the all-volunteer force, individual Americans must make the choice to join the military, and generally they do so with some at least abstract awareness that this may mean going off to war. The reasons they give for making this choice say a lot about both the worlds they are coming from and where they hope, upon enlisting, that the military will take them. More than that, their reasons reveal how the tradition of military service has remained firmly embedded in some sectors of American society, even as the 1970s shift away from compulsory military service (the draft) has resulted in a growing cultural separation between those who join the military and those who, for the most part, do not. Although all the veterans in the PDS study were living in the San Antonio area in 2007–8, only about half were born and raised in Texas. Of these, there was a roughly fifty-fifty split between those who grew up in San Antonio and those who were raised elsewhere in the state.[1] A few of the non–San Antonio Texans were from cities like Dallas, Houston, or El Paso, but mostly they came from rural towns, each about a dozen miles from nowhere. Mirroring Texas's demographic split, Latino veterans were more likely to have come from primarily Mexican-American South Texas, while white veterans were more likely to have come from the northern or eastern parts of the state.

Those who were born elsewhere came from across the United States and Puerto Rico, from Michigan, California, Oklahoma, Missouri, Louisiana, South Dakota, and so on. They came both from cities—San Juan, New Orleans, Detroit—and small towns—Ruidoso, Claremore, Rock Springs. Almost all came to San Antonio as a result of their military service, although the routes differed. Many found their way to South Texas for the first time as part of their military training at Lackland Air Force Base or Fort Sam Houston, returning later because they liked the area or thought they could find work here.[2] San Antonio Military Medical Center—which combines the hospital and clinic resources of Wilford Hall Medical Center, located on base at Lackland, and Brooke Army Medical Center, located on Fort Sam Houston—provides tertiary health care for all service personnel in the central United States, and some veterans initially came for treatment of service-related injuries or other health problems. (BAMC, in particular, is renowned for its state-of-the-art care of service members with burns or amputations.) Many of these veterans, particularly those seriously wounded while on combat duty, chose to make San Antonio their home during the long period of recuperation and rehabilitation. Others found themselves in San Antonio after following friends from the service who knew the area, hearing it was a cheap place to live or wanting to be close to their buddies.

San Antonio is often jokingly described as the "northernmost city in Mexico" because its population is majority Mexican American—the 2000 U.S. census reported that Latinos make up 58 percent of the city's population, alongside 32 percent non-Hispanic whites and 7 percent African Americans[3]—but it is better characterized as a place of vivid cultural fluidity. The city of 1.3 million people[4] incorporates influences from the conservative American South and Midwest and, closer to hand, the liberal capital of Austin to the east, the historically German Hill Country to the north, ranching and oil country to the west, and the Rio Grande Valley to the south.

Those who have grown up in San Antonio describe a city in transition. Beto, a former marine with giant shoulders and a wide gentle face, grew up on the west side, a predominantly Latino neighborhood adjacent to downtown, known for high rates of poverty and crime. Describing what it has been like to return home after ten years in the service, he says, "It's changed a lot since I've been away. The neighborhood, the city used to be more dangerous. It was more gangs, more things to be worried about. A lot more drugs, more violence out there. Since I came back, it's there, but I see more police, neighborhoods looking better, people trying to help out. The neighborhood I grew up in, I could point to each house and tell you what drugs they were selling. It's not like that anymore."[5]

Many of those who grew up in the urban world Beto describes chose the military as a way to escape poverty and, at times, to move past early forays into crime and violence. Tony, another marine, tells the story of growing up "rough" on the south side, exposed to "a lot of drinking and a lot of violence." He says, "It's a recipe for failure, you know? And I was falling into it." At twenty-one he was arrested for a DUI and was put on probation for six months. As soon as his six months was up, he signed up for the marines. "I was going in the wrong direction before I joined the marines, and that gave me more reason to get out of there."

Other veterans also described seeking out military service as an escape, and not only from violent urban environments. Jerry grew up in rural South Texas, helping out his ranch-hand father from the time he was eight years old. He worked in the family's grocery store, the center of commerce for their small town, and contributed to the family income by doing odd jobs on the side. By the time he was sixteen, he was working four jobs. He joined up in September of the year he finished high school. "I wanted to get out of that town," he says. "I wanted to do something. I always wanted to be an army guy, a soldier." It was a dream that sounded good to him, an opportunity that seemed a lot bigger than the town where he grew up, although he admits now that as a kid, "You watch movies, and [military service looks] totally different from what it actually is."

There is a strong sense of either/or in these stories, for military service was one of very few options for many of these men. I was surprised at how frequently people around the area reiterated this point, even those who had chosen other paths. One day I ended up talking to a salesman at Macy's after he commented that he couldn't place my accent. I said it came from 'moving around,' and he asked if I was in the military.

'No,' I said, 'but that's a good guess around here.'

He said that he was from San Antonio and that his whole family was military—'My Dad, uncles, cousins, everybody.' He said that he was the only one who didn't want to go that route, that he 'went to college instead.'

'A good alternative,' I said.

'Yeah,' he laughed, 'and safer.'

I heard the same thing from a local psychologist, a tall Latina who grew up down in the valley. She described the area as being hugely military precisely because it is so poor. She said that the recruiters go to all the 'sorriest' high schools, and that for a lot of those who sign up, the military is their 'only way out.' She snorted and added that she hadn't even known college was an option until she was a junior in high school.

In contrast to those who chose between military service and college, another group of veterans entered the service as a way of accessing education. Todd, a young white man from outside Dallas, volunteered right out of high school. He said he knew that his fireman father could not afford to send him to college, and he figured that between the GI Bill and the Hazlewood Act (which extends college benefits to veterans who are Texas residents), he would be able to get an education if he enlisted. Some of the veterans who had joined when they were older described a similar decision-making process, choosing a term and branch of service that would provide them with desired schooling or career training. I met one man in his late twenties who joined the marine reserves to get his degree in nursing and then signed up for the navy reserves as a way to finance a shift into dentistry.

For young men and women from poor or underprivileged backgrounds, then, joining up may represent a choice from among limited options. There is no longer a draft in the United States, but even in an all-volunteer force some volunteers are more voluntary than others. The disproportionate recruitment of service members from among low- and middle-income communities[6] and the reliance placed upon the less privileged to be willing to sacrifice their lives toward the advancement of national interests provide a classic example of what Johan Galtung called structural violence, that subtle process by which social inequalities take dramatic shape in the form of differential health and well-being.[7]

The risks and sacrifices of military service are significant enough, in fact, that to focus solely on the material benefits of enlisting would be to vastly oversimplify a decision that means giving up considerable freedom in order to commit, if necessary, to putting life and limb in jeopardy on a foreign battlefield. The navy reservist made this clear as we sat and talked about the fact that a lot of people join up to get their education paid for. He told me that he had another year before graduating, then one more year of advanced training, and then would owe the U.S. Navy four years of service. I asked if he would be eligible for combat deployment (as opposed to a noncombat deployment to somewhere like Guam or Korea), and he said yes. He listened mildly as I started doing calculations aloud that if he had two more years in school, maybe he wouldn't have to deploy. Maybe the United States would be out of Iraq by then.

He laughed at me a little, nicely enough, and said, 'Well, I didn't join the navy to avoid deployment.'

Point taken.

Toward the end of the time I know him, Beto lays out a more tangled knot of reasons for joining up, giving greater substance to his decision than in earlier-quoted comments about just wanting to get out of the barrio. I ask him again, "How did you end up in the military?"

And this time he answers, "A recruiter came to the high school, and someone said, 'You go talk to him, you can get out of class.'"

He grins at this and goes on. "I was like, well, why not? They keep hassling me at the house, I might as well get out of class. And being in the Marine Corps, being in the navy interested me a lot. That's what I wanted to do—go to other places, learn. I figured if I can't go to college, I might as well educate myself. [The recruiter] was real talkative....I liked what he was saying, his appearance. It got me thinking: if I can do the hardest branch of service, then I can do anything. Money for college, too, so I figured—I'm working, making a paycheck, learning a trade, and paying benefits. It didn't seem like there was anything bad to it." He grins again. "Until you go."

Beto's answer underscores two of the already noted reasons for enlisting: a way out of a rough neighborhood (or small town) and a series of options for education and a career that were better than anything else around. But he also hints at some glimmer of a future self that he saw reflected in the recruiter's manner and self-presentation ("I liked his appearance"). There is a sense in his words of a promise to himself, the belief that "if I can do the hardest branch of service, then I can do anything." Many veterans chuckle as they admit to an early fascination with how soldiers or marines are portrayed in the movies or to being awed by a particular uniform, but there is something seriously captivating in these images that grab them, some vision of a future that might be theirs.

We also shouldn't forget the sheer high-adrenaline fun that many young men in particular associate with joining the military.[8] Brian, a middle-aged army reservist, talks about how he had wanted to go into the military even as a little kid, irresistibly caught up in the masculine adventure of it. "They have cool uniforms, and you get to shoot things. Just very manly stuff!" He tells stories about his younger son, who at eight was already ready to sign up, falling asleep each night with the TV in his room turned to the Military Channel. "We go out and play paintball, and he'll go out there and play paintball and he's getting shot at and he thinks it's the coolest thing in the world. We go down to the farm and go shooting and he's got all the regular weapons. The.22 rifle that's his. Just one of those kids. Destined!"

Like Beto, veterans more often than not acknowledge some confluence of all these reasons in describing their decision to join up; they admit to having been drawn by both the honor and excitement of military service and its more practical aspects, the economic and educational benefits.[9] Brian was exuberant about the fun of military things for himself and his younger son (who was still ten years too young to actually enlist). But when he described his own decision to enlist—and later on in the time I knew him, his older son's—he spoke of the impossibility of raising a family on a minimum wage salary and about the military as an opportunity for career building and vocational training.

And finally, for those with family or other social ties to the military, the decision to join the service was often described in relation to those ties. Carlos's father was a marine in Vietnam before becoming an engineer. Carlos reported that his father was proud of his three sons when all of them decided to enlist; he was even more proud when he learned that Carlos had decided on the air force over the marines, as there was less chance of his "getting killed." A woman in her forties whom I met on a plane out of San Antonio—I couldn't understand why she was peering over my shoulder at an article on combat PTSD until she introduced herself as a psychiatric nurse for the air force—recited a long string of carefully considered reasons for enlisting in her late thirties: there was still time for her to serve out a full twenty years; the air force would pay for her master's degree; the benefits were good. Even so, it wasn't until she began talking about her husband, who had completed his career in the army, and her father, who was also a veteran, that she began to speak with any warmth. She said that she was the only one of her father's children who had gone into the military, and that it 'meant a lot' to him to see her do it. Speaking proudly of her husband's service, she said, 'He's the face I see in front of me and the boot in my rear,' both her inspiration and her support on this chosen path.

Family history may itself be a source of pride. Brian pointed out with some satisfaction that "there's been an O'Neil from my direct ancestry in every war that's been fought since the beginning of America." Derek, an African American soldier whose left leg was amputated after he was wounded by an improvised explosive device (IED) in Iraq, had no regrets about his service, despite his loss. He, too, felt his time in the military placed him in line with his ancestors, since "all of the males in my family as far back as you can count have served in some capacity." His words point to how profoundly military service may be embedded in social histories, reflecting both an identity as part of a family tradition and a web of valued relations.

In a time when national service is no longer the norm, it can be easy to underestimate the power of the traditions that shape attitudes to the military in a place

like San Antonio. I am no exception. Although my grandfathers served proudly
in Korea and World War II, I grew up in a small community in rural Maine where
veterans were not often visible and joining the military was a rare thing. It was
not until I attended that Fourth of July memorial at the San Antonio VFW post
that I first began to appreciate how deeply this heritage is rooted in South Texas
life. More than anything, it revealed a multigenerational parade that I found
striking—families gathered together to honor those who had lost their lives while
little boys played on the dusty ground and older veterans revisited the familiar
posture of standing at attention.

Tucked back off a side road downtown, the VFW post is built like an old
southern manor, with rounded front corners and a long white porch wrapping
the facade. The woman I met there, Melissa, and I sat talking as a sparse crowd
gathered around us. She was in her fifties and wore big sunglasses and a pendant
shaped like a tiny gold dogtag, with a man's profile engraved on one side. She
recommended the cable TV show *Army Wives* as good entertainment and spoke
of her niece's recent decision to join the army.

In the area around us, toward the side and back of the post, speakers had
been erected around a stage where a local band was set to perform later that
night. Picnic tables painted in bright colors were arranged to the right side, and
a taco stand occupied the opposite corner. A long folding table stood beneath an
awning beside the post's front porch; on it, bricks to be dedicated in the memorial ceremony were laid out in neat rows, each engraved with a name, rank, and
unit of service. A group of Cub Scouts clustered around the table, a small herd
of little boys in uniform.

When the time came for the ceremony to begin, there was an announcement
over the loudspeaker, and I excused myself from Melissa and moved up toward
the front. Folding chairs assembled in rows on the front porch had gradually
filled with men and women who were now introduced as Gold Star families,
those who had lost sons, daughters, parents, and spouses in the war. The master
of ceremonies was holding court at a podium about 20 feet away, facing the Gold
Star families across a short stretch of dusty parking lot that now became center
stage. A line of VFW officers marched around the corner of the building and took
their places near the podium, standing taut at attention in white shirts with the
post's insignia stamped on chest and shoulder. Onlookers formed a crowd scattered across the driveway and in among the picnic tables. Despite the morning's
cool and rain, it was the hottest day of the summer so far, and the smell of frying
onions wafted out from the taco stand on a muggy breeze.

The ceremony opened with the national anthem, and those in uniform
removed their hats respectfully. The anthem was followed by the Pledge of Alle-
giance, the crowd's eyes turned upwards toward the center flagpole, its flag dark

against the bright sky. There was an invocation prayer. Then the emcee gestured the day's speaker, a retired army general, to the podium, where he began the memorial and dedication, slowly reading off the name of each service member who had been killed. He did not describe their connection to San Antonio, whether they had been born or lived or gone to school there. He did not describe how they had died.

As every name was spoken, an engraved brick was carefully lifted off the nearby table by a VFW officer and handed to one of the Cub Scouts, who had come together to form a line beneath the awning. The boys looked to be between the ages of five and eight or nine, and many were so small they had to hold the bricks against their chests with both hands as they carried them. Clutching their burdens, they walked in a staggered line past the podium and past the families on the porch to where another VFW officer stood waiting. The officer took a brick from each boy, solemnly, with a stiff little bow, before stooping to place it in a tight configuration on the ground—laying, piece by piece, a pedestal around the flagpole. Each Cub Scout, relieved of his charge, walked on to be met with a grin and a gentle slap of the hand by another VFW officer, a Native American veteran who stood waiting beyond, with a beaded dreamcatcher around his neck and a walking stick hung with feathers in one hand. Every boy passed him before returning to rejoin the line alongside the canopied table, waiting in turn to carry again. Some of the smaller boys, as they passed the man for the third or fourth time, became visibly excited about getting to slap his hand, running toward him and hopping up with a wild swing toward his outstretched palm. Even in such a solemn atmosphere, the older man had a hard time suppressing a smile at their glee.

As each brick came out and the name written upon it was read by the general at the podium, the service member's family rose to their feet. Some shed tears, but most did not. A blonde woman in a pink blouse sobbed helplessly, supported by the woman beside her. There was a tall Latino man in a yellow polo who, when he stood with his family, carefully wiped his eyes. One or two of the Latino families wore oversized T-shirts bearing a photo of their warrior across the chest—one couple wore the face of a man with a firm look in his eyes, his shoulders proud under his marine uniform.

All fifty-three names were called. The bricks were stacked on one level and formed, in the end, a rectangle about three feet wide and five feet long—smaller than a coffin. Oddly small to represent so much life.

As the general brought the recitation of names to a close, he made a short speech, leaning over the podium to say, 'When you command a young soldier, you feel responsible for him.' He told the families on the porch that those who had died were a highly select bunch because they had been chosen not only to serve in the military on earth but also to be members of the army, navy, air force, and marines in heaven. He said that Americans were living in a semidivided country and that they must not allow these divides to undermine the troops, a statement that earned a hearty round of applause from the crowd.

He then stepped down, and the post chaplain said a closing prayer. A trumpet played taps, and as the mournful notes sounded, hats were again doffed and the people in the crowd lowered their heads—with the exception of one boy of about four who had settled himself in the dirt, and of several red-cheeked clowns who came tramping through the gate just then in full regalia. The emcee announced that there was food available free in the banquet room or for sale from the taco stand and that there would be clowns for the children and plans for music and dancing later in the evening. The line of VFW officers made an about-face and marched back around the building, and the ceremony was over.

There was a moment's hush, and then the audience began to scatter. As I walked up the driveway, I noticed that the picnic tables were full now—the crowd seemed to be growing rather than diminishing—and a group of kids had gathered over by the clowns in the area set up for dancing.

Later that night, several friends and I went out for a drink along the River-walk, San Antonio's busy waterfront tourist area, where the San Antonio River is lined on both sides with shops and restaurants. All the tables along the river were full to capacity, and it took us a while to find a place. Moving slowly through the throng, we passed a family sitting together, a group of three or four adults with a few small children. At the head of the table, facing us, was a good-looking young man who, at first glance, I thought was wearing some kind of funny collar. I looked again and saw that he was badly burned, with thick vertical bands of scar tissue encasing his neck.

We kept moving until we found a garishly lit bar called the Republic of Texas. We sat there and drank sangria and margaritas ("Texas-sized!") for a while, watching the families come and go around us. Our table, as it happened, was situated at the base of a stairway leading to a pedestrian bridge over the river. After a while, I looked up and saw the young man with the burns and his family making their way toward the stairs. At the first step, he stopped and knelt down. Taking one of the smaller kids by the hands, he pulled the giggling boy up onto his back and carried him up the stairs. It was a small gesture, but it seemed to close a circle begun earlier in the day. First the skittish, shy, gleeful Cub Scouts in their uniforms, carrying bricks too heavy for them. The bricks themselves, with their encoded tales of loss and sacrifice. The faces of the Gold Star family members, blank or teary. The VFW veterans with their uniforms and memorials. And now, this young man with his face clear and smooth but his body a testament to what can be survived, hauling another little boy up the stairs on his back.

On the drive home, around midnight, we passed the VFW. The lights hung around the bandstand were still on, although it was too dark to see if anyone was dancing. I thought about the memorial service late into the night. Even in the context of a ceremony honoring the dead, confronted by the grieving families of those who had lost their lives in the line of duty, there were Cub Scouts running around giddy at the pageantry and older veterans proudly reliving the marching of their youth. The tradition of military service hung thick in the humid air, a heavy tapestry of hope and promise and sorrow and sacrifice.

WAR STORIES
Case Studies of Combat Deployment

This chapter introduces four veterans who describe their own experiences of war in Iraq and Afghanistan in the months and years following 9/11.[1] These four veterans—although all male, all American, all combatants—make it clear that that war is a big enough territory to leave room for a wide variety of experiences: combat and quiet, anger and love, peace and boredom. This is not a new observation. Most war movies have their token scenes depicting funny things that happened on the way to the land mine and the camaraderie between brothers-in-arms, bright moments amid the irregular storms of attack and counterattack. The war stories retold here reflect that same complexity. They are as often humorous as they are sad, describing joy and pride as often as they do horror and grief. For many veterans, their time in Iraq or Afghanistan was one of the highlights of their lives, even as it may also have been what one veteran called the "hinging point," the period of time that marked the separation between before and after in their lives.

In approaching these stories, it is important to note that going to war does not mean suddenly stepping outside life as we know it. Wartime may, in many ways, be an aberration in the course of a life—a period of time different from any other—but it is still part of that life course. A soldier's time in Iraq or Afghanistan is as deeply shaped by his own personal history as it is by the gun (or mechanic's wrench or medic's kit) he carries with him into combat. Throughout these stories, I have left in the parts that too often get skimmed over in war movies: how the service member came to be in a conflict zone, key aspects of his life before deployment, and the people he left behind at home. When it comes to combat

PTSD, there is a tendency in casual discourse to talk only about combat, as though entering a war zone is like passing through a portal that suddenly deprives the service member of a past and present aside from war. It is easy to understand why we might think this. For civilians who have never been in conflict war is enough of a mystery that we can easily imagine it as a vortex that erases all else. These stories, however, insist that we think more carefully about this tendency. War may be all-consuming, but it is impossible to understand the experience of combat without understanding the richness of life going on around it.

There is one last thing to point out before beginning, one more commonality among these four male American combatants: each of them came home to find himself struggling after the war, and each ultimately received a diagnosis of PTSD. As a result, in these varied stories we find some of the events these veterans would later came to think of as "traumatic," the memories that would later be blamed for their PTSD. For this is in essence what post-traumatic stress disorder means: an event occurred that led to psychological, physiological, and emotional disorder. Any mental health clinician making a diagnosis of PTSD must first identify what the *Diagnostic and Statistical Manual of Mental Disorders (DSM)*—the manual that psychiatrists and psychologists use to determine a diagnosis—calls "Criterion A," or "the stressor." There can be no PTSD without trauma, just as there can be no war stories without war.

But before any of these events were called traumas, before they were recognized as some distinct kind of experience capable of causing mental illness, they were just things that happened. They were just war stories.

The Medic

I met Brian O'Neil because of an ongoing joke between him and his boss. Brian had given his boss a phone number and told him to call it, saying it was the number to get a free DVD from Best Buy when it was really, as he put it, a "gay love hotline." Texas office humor. A short time afterward, his boss picked up one of the flyers I had posted at a local college advertising for participants in a study about post-deployment challenges for recent veterans and their families. Brian's boss tore off one of the strips listing my contact information and threw it on Brian's desk. "What's this?" asked Brian. "It's a study about PTSD," said his boss. "You should do it."

So Brian called and left a message on my voice mail, thinking it was another joke. By the time he talked to me, he told me later, he had figured out it was for real, but he told me the story anyway, laughing. Brian laughs a lot. He is in his early forties, of medium height and a little husky, with blond hair and ruddy skin. He seems like the guy who got along with everybody in high school—smart, easy-talking, sensitive to what is going on around him. The first few times we met, it was in the same room where I interviewed most of the veterans, an office on the eighth floor of the VA hospital, a stuffy white space dominated by a laminate desk and decorated on the far wall with two framed pictures of Raphaelite cherubs. At the beginning of the study, I was strictly instructed by the clinicians and nursing staff I worked with to sit by the door, where I would be able to make a quick escape if one of the patients became violent. So I sat on one side of the desk, by the door, and any visiting veteran sat across from me, his back to the opposite wall. From my vantage point, the two cherubs invariably hung on either side of the veteran's head like a pair of slightly bored-looking guardian angels.[2]

Brian grew up fascinated by battles in faraway places: "My uncles were both in Vietnam and I can remember my older uncle being in Vietnam and his younger brother was in Guam. And my uncle would send things home like—you know, we all had toy M-16s back then. And he would send TA-50, the web-belt stuff. And he sent my grandfather a bayonet and I can remember that bayonet."

Brian's father was also in the service, and he remembers growing up with the idea that military service was a duty: "your democratic obligation to serve." In the mid-1980s, after years of buying fatigues at the surplus store and debating the merits of army versus navy, he found himself in a recruiter's office, signing up to be a combat medic for the army. He was sent for medical training to San Antonio, where he met his wife, Lisette. For the next eleven years, they lived on military bases in North Carolina, Georgia, New York, and Germany and had two sons and a daughter along the way.

He was sent to Iraq in the first Gulf War, the news of his impending deployment coming out of the blue one day in 1990, when he was serving as a medic attached to an artillery unit in Germany. They were out on the firing range, in the middle of practice, when the battalion commander and the command sergeant major pulled up in their Humvee.

"They sent everybody to the chow hall. So we all get out of our vehicles and walk to the chow hall and they flip on the TV, punch on the VCR and put a video in, and they start showing Kuwait being invaded." The video showed Kuwaiti tanks clustered protectively around the main palace in Kuwait City, under attack by Iraqi forces. "And they're firing and firing and firing, and they move in to cover each other and another one blows up. And the whole time they're defending an empty palace, because the king and his whole family had already been gone. But these Kuwaitis and their army…"—he interrupts himself—"I get chills thinking about it…are defending an empty palace because they want the Iraqis to think [the royal family is] still there so they don't shoot down their plane when it takes off. And you're watching this and thinking, 'My God, you know, the *duty.*' And then you're pissed. Those bastards, they went and attacked Kuwait."

Brian pauses before continuing. "That was August 2, on the day they were invaded. And so November 17 we sent our vehicles, and we left on Christmas Day. And five days later my oldest learned how to walk."

He admits that when he joined up, he had never expected to go to war, much less in a desert. He says, "I used to laugh. I'd spent all my life preparing to fight Russians and the only place we ever fought was in a desert." He still marvels at how long it took for the army to catch up with the new realities of war, pointing out that even though his unit was far forward during Operation Desert Storm, they were among the last of those deployed to replace their forest green uniforms—which didn't provide much camouflage in the beige Iraqi desert—for the "deserts" that quickly became a familiar sight on the American news. "Literally, I got my desert uniform three days before I got on a plane and came back to Germany. It was the dumbest crap I'd ever seen."

All the usual jokes about army incompetence aside, the first Gulf War remains clear in Brian's mind. His voice is steady, matter of fact, as he says, "In Desert Storm, we killed an entire battalion of people in one night, in less than an hour. Two hundred and eighty people died because they shot at us, and three days later I had to go back and help bury every one of them. And the engineers come in and dig a big pit, and you're going through these guys' personal effects and bagging everything up and tagging them. But you're pulling basically their lives out of their pockets, and you got pictures of their wives and kids. Iraq is very cosmopolitan...." He halts for a second, "Well, *was* very cosmopolitan for that region, because even those little towns, they had lights and generators and streetlights and normal things. And you drive in and people are shooting at you, so you blow the town to hell. It was weird seeing those guys and they're dead and they're wearing stuff like Knicks' hats and they're very Americanized. And they were probably conscripted off the street and we went and killed them."

Brian says that he didn't have any problems after coming home from Iraq in 1991, which he attributes to the fact that he was still on active duty then, still surrounded in day-to-day life by the other members of his unit and by all the support services the military had to offer. He left active duty a few years later. He had run into some staffing and management problems in his job at the base hospital. "I came home complaining one day and my wife said, 'You know, when we did this, you said that when it's not fun anymore you were going to quit.' I said, 'Yeah?' She said, 'Well, it doesn't sound like it is very fun anymore.' I said, 'You're right.' And so that's when I quit."

He and his wife moved back to San Antonio with the kids, and Brian transferred over to the army reserves, meanwhile working full-time at a local doctor's office. In 2002 he was deployed as a reservist, this time to Afghanistan for eleven months.

He served as a medic with a reconstruction team in the southern part of the country. He was attached to a civil affairs unit, conducting water and sanitation assessments for local villages. "We did all kinds of hearts-and-minds stuff. We gave 'em all their school supplies. We did a lot of humanitarian aid drops. We filled the back of a truck with soccer balls and went around town and kicked them out on Christmas morning. Those kind of things."

He says that Afghanistan was the best job he ever had, at least in the military. "I could get up in the morning and be on combat patrol in the morning, in the afternoon be on a humanitarian aid drop, and by evening I'm going down to a village to do an assessment of their well, or getting them a well built. It was so varied. You never knew what was going to happen every day. It kind of makes it interesting. It kind of scares the crap out of you too, but you know, you've got a road block and you're checking every vehicle and somebody starts shooting at you, you're like, 'OK, that's what's in store today.'"

His later deployment to Iraq was similarly challenging. As the head of a team of medics stationed in the north, he used to volunteer to go on public relations missions. He liked it because it involved going out to give food and candy to Iraqi children: "It was nice to make a kid smile." Still, he didn't mind getting tapped for combat patrols and kicking down doors when necessary, and he faced his share of horror during this deployment. One day while he was working with his team at an Iraqi army recruitment center, a suicide bomber drove his car into a crowd just outside the door of their building. Forty people were killed, dozens wounded. "We were right there and two guys, our security guys, had pieces of flesh raining down on them. [The bomber] was actually trying to get inside but he didn't make it, so he got to the door and blew himself up there."

That, he says, was one of the bad ones. "Because I was the senior medic in charge there, and they sent reinforcements in, but the families came quick. They were like, 'God, help me, help him.'" Half-living bodies and family members surrounded him, all begging for help. Brian says, "I couldn't waste time and equipment on this person when there's a person over here I can save. Their families are crying, crying and screaming, and you got to…just let 'em die. My junior medic in particular, he worked on two people who both died. Yeah. It was bad."

Of all the stories Brian shared in our conversations, this was for him the most upsetting. The trauma was, in part, the ruptured bodies, the gore of flesh raining down from the sky. Beyond the gore, the trauma lay in the families' outpourings of grief for those he couldn't save despite his skills as a medic. He is torn by remembered empathy for his junior medic, who was deeply affected by the two men who died under his care, insisting he never wanted to work as a medic again. The difference between this story and Brian's many others can be seen in the manner of the telling, his usually hearty voice slowing, the sentences strung together without jokes between, and the fact that afterward he seems relieved to move on to something else. To shake it off, wiping away the sounds and smells that lingered.

The difference can be seen, too, in how he tells another story, one he uses to explain his continued trouble with driving in San Antonio (a common problem for recent veterans). By this time, he is back to his jokey self.

"And if I stop in traffic, oh my God. It just makes me batty. So...my kids laugh at me because I sit and scream in traffic because I can't take it." He chuckles. "Well, that's when people got killed in Afghanistan. We watched when the Canadians who were a couple of vehicles in front of us...a suicide bomber jumped on the front of their car. And blew himself up and of course killed everyone in the vehicle. Now that happened, oh, twenty-five yards in front of us, and all we see is a guy, and boom! And we're out of the vehicles, and we're running over trying to figure out what's going on. We had a crowd—I mean a crowd of Afghans, and these people were pushing towards the vehicles. And we're—that was tough..." He pauses for a moment, thinking, and then chuckles again before diving back in.

"I was telling one of my buddies this story the other night....I pulled a grenade out, and I pulled the pin out and held it up in the air like that, so all of them could see I had a grenade. And we kept telling them 'Za!' which means 'Get back! Get away!' And of course it's a bastardization of the word, we GIs make up our own words, but I was telling them 'Za! Za!' You know, a couple of them were still pushing forward, yelling at us, and I threw the grenade. I threw it right in the middle of them. And when you pull the second one out, they all listen to you."

Brian does not flinch from such stories, nor does he apologize for them. He can speak of death in bursts bracketed by laughter. He is fully aware that these tales take on different qualities at different times, often to intended effect but with sometimes unlooked-for consequences. At the time when I first knew him, his teenage son was looking to join the army. He told the boy, "You need to wait. Because whenever you hear me and [my friends] get together and we're all talking and laughing and drinking beer and giggling about stupid crap that happened while we were at war. You're only hearing the stupid crap. You're not hearing the sad and scary crap." In an effort to fix this imbalance, he took his son out to the truck one Sunday afternoon, out of earshot of the rest of the family, and they sat there for a long time. "I had to let him in on a lot of scary, crappy things. And I said 'You know, I've done things that I don't ever want you to have to do, ever.

And I did them because I didn't want you to have to do them. You know. I don't want you to have to enlist because I needed to enlist.'"

He is rueful as he tells me this, cognizant of the ironies embedded in such a conversation. *He* chose the military—he even thinks the military might be the right choice for his son, who is finishing high school and at loose ends about his future. But he joined the military in peacetime. War was an unexpected corollary for him, not something he planned on. His son was talking about joining in 2007, when the United States was deeply imbedded in two wars, neither of which appeared to have any end in sight. This was a different kind of decision. He admits that years of joking about combat mishaps around the backyard barbecue with his army buddies may not have done much to dissuade his son from service. But he has a hard time telling the other kind of story, the sad and scary kind. It gets too overwhelming, he says, too much. "I can talk about it off-handed. Something like a little short story, I can do that all day. Which is pretty much the way veterans talk to each other about it. You don't ever get in-depth enough about it that it bothers you. Just a real quick, superficial, 'Hey, I remember when this guy did x, y, and z ...' And they're usually funny. Not sad."

As a result, his wife was surprised and aghast to learn, seventeen years into their marriage, that her husband carried grenades while deployed, in the course of his daily work. He says it freaked her out. She said, "You're a medic!" He said, "Yeah." She asked, "Well, why do you have grenades?" He said, "Because Mr. Grenade's your friend sometimes." These are the things that don't get told around the backyard barbecue. Brian says, "I would not burden her with knowing...horror....I wouldn't burden her with the thought of what I'm carrying. Because it's hard enough for me, I wouldn't want to have to put it on her to deal with or think about. She doesn't need to know." Similarly, when his younger son turns away from the Military Channel and his usual eager questions like "Well, what if Australia invaded Hungary?" and asks instead, "Dad, did you ever kill anybody?" then Brian says, voice very firm in the retelling, "You don't need to ask that question. It's not something you need to worry about."

Brian's stories demonstrate the ambivalence with which service members and veterans often describe their military service, mingling pride with full recognition of the sacrifices and moral ambiguities involved in offering up one's life and will to a global superpower in a time of war. Without doubt, Brian is proud of his time in the service, but he also recalls the bodies of the Iraqi men who died in that onslaught of the first Gulf War, who were killed in less than an hour, he says, even though they were "probably conscripted off the street." There are stories so bad he prefers not to tell them, not to remember them at all. I ran into him shortly after his older son finally enlisted and Brian expressed his support for the young man's choice. But his demeanor was uncharacteristically tentative as he spoke of how his son would receive training as a nurse and would have gained valuable skills upon leaving the army. He said that he would rejoin the reserves and try to go with his son while he's deployed, but that they want him to do emergency work and he doesn't think he can anymore. "It's the smell," he said. He looked hesitant for a moment, but then brushed it away, joking about having to smear Vicks VapoRub beneath his nose to kill the smell, miming taking great gobs of ointment out of a jar and spreading it over his nose and upper lip.

I remembered Brian and his description of how veterans tell their stories a few months later, sitting in a room full of soldiers at Fort Sam Houston. I was there visiting an on-base program for "wounded warriors," as they're called, soldiers wounded in the line of duty. At the time, the program was run out of a crowded suite of three open rooms, overflowing with sofas, boxes of donated gifts, computer terminals, and all the miscellaneous paraphernalia of a social work service/lounge/bunkhouse. There were about a dozen soldiers in there, dressed in uniform, mostly standing around in a group and cracking jokes. None of them was obviously wounded. The performer of the bunch was a stocky guy in his physical fitness gear, shirt and shorts, who told a long story about taking his laptop into the repair shop to be cleaned out after three tours in Iraq. 'Where the hell have you been with this thing?' the repairman had asked, taking off the backplate and pouring sand out on the table. 'Iraq,' he said, grinning. Another guy chimed in, 'Yeah, I go there for the summer,' and they all laughed. Somebody else broke in, 'For the fishing!' The guys got a kick out of that.

Funny. Not sad.

The Marine

Tony Sandoval was seven years old the first time he had a gun pulled on him. His father used to take him to a bar down by their house on the south side of San Antonio, and they would hang out there, not arriving home until long after Tony's bedtime. He would sit at the bar and do his homework, watch TV while his father played pool, and swallow the soda and chips his father's friends bought for him. The fights would usually start later in the evening, when the men were drunk and Tony was getting tired, watching the TV over the bar with his head resting on his folded arms. Once in a while somebody would pull a gun, and this time—the time Tony remembers—the guy pulled the gun on Tony. The man was in an argument with his father and his friends, and pointing the gun at them didn't get the reaction he was hoping for. So he swung it around to where Tony was sitting, and held it on him until the bartender talked him into calming down. Tony thinks his father was so drunk that he doesn't even remember.

Home was not a lot better. Tony doesn't talk about his father's beating him, although he is careful to say that his father never hit his sisters, a caveat he doesn't extend to himself. What he describes instead is those moments in the middle of the night when his father would come home and Tony would turn off the TV, run to his room, and wait, hardly breathing, to hear whether his father would wake up his mother in the next room. Sometimes he heard his father bellow for his mother to make him dinner. Sometimes he would hear the slap of his father's belt.

There were times on the weekends when he wouldn't see his parents at all. His mother would be working, since his father wasn't good at keeping a job or at least at bringing home the check, and his father would be out somewhere. He might come in at 3:00 a.m. and wake them up to eat the box of fried chicken or fish he had bought. But in the meantime, Tony was left to look after his two younger sisters. His grandparents lived across the street, so there was backup in emergencies, but Tony remembers washing and peeling the potatoes to make French fries, then walking down the street to get a two-liter bottle of soda so the kids could have a picnic in the living room. He still feels guilty, he says, for having been "mean" to his sisters when they wouldn't obey him. He says that the youngest girl, to whom he is still closest now, shakes her head when he tells her this. "You were ten years old. If CPS [the Texas Department of Child Protective Services] had come by, they would have taken us out of that home."

Twenty years later, now a big-shouldered man with warm brown eyes, Tony still looks after his sisters. He is proud that he has never let them down and that they come to him regularly for help—for money, for help in moving, to babysit his nieces. He is glad, too, that he can say about his siblings, "We're not statistics. We're doing pretty good." He prides himself on being a devoted uncle and a hard worker, on being a different man than his father and escaping the rough streets where he grew up. He and his friends used to joke when things got rough in Iraq, "How can I get killed here? I've been shot at in my own neighborhood. I'm not going to get shot out here." Having survived childhood, they'd laugh, how could war be any worse?

In making the decision to join up, Tony says that choosing to be a marine was a "calling." "Growing up the way I did and being exposed to the things I was exposed to, [joining up] wasn't anything. I mean, it seems like if I can handle growing up the way I did, I can be a marine." He says that his extended family was not universally in favor of his decision, and some people tried to discourage him: "'Like, why do you want to be a marine? You think you're bad, or you think you're all that?'" He says his only response was, "I'm nothing yet. But I will be." He was determined to make something of himself.

He became a grunt, a marine infantryman, and after a few years a sergeant. He could not be more proud of his success in the service. I asked him once, after he had gone on about the Marine Corps for a while, "What does it mean to you to be a marine?"

"It means everything to me," he said. "Literally, I think, it means everything to me."

He went on to say, "Everybody in the service has their characteristics, their personalities. And I think the marines have the strongest. You can be in a room full of soldiers, airmen, and there will be one marine and everyone will be paying attention to the one marine, because they want to know what he knows. They want to know what weapons he is using, what his job is. I guess the characteristics of my own—which is strong characteristics—were attracted to the marines." He grinned. "I love the Marine Corps."

Tony was one of the first marines to make it to Afghanistan after September 11. He and his battalion were training in Australia when the attacks happened; they had just been released for twenty-four hours' leave off the ship and had gone into town to make the most of the evening. It was around midnight over there on the other side of the world, the early morning of September 12, when his commander got word that the Twin Towers had gone down and sounded the ship's sirens, broadcasting that all navy personnel needed to report back to the ship. By 3:00 a.m. Tony and the rest of his company were back on board and standing in formation on deck; his commander announced the news. By 6:00 a.m. the aircraft carrier and two submarines were on their way to the Arabian Sea. It took them two weeks to get there, and then they set up base in Pakistan before moving into Afghanistan, where they spent the next four months.

I ask him what that deployment was like, so early in the post-9/11 world. "A lot of patrols. Freezing cold. Our company got to go up to Kandahar, and all we had to do was surveillance. A lot of civilians killing each other." He shrugs. "It was kind of boring because everything was already done. We went on patrols every day looking for somebody, looking for Osama Bin Laden. We saw [the Taliban] a lot—if we saw their trucks we'd just bomb them. We'd call in orders—'We've got trucks down here, about two thousand meters'—and we'd send bombs down on them. Afghanistan wasn't too bad. Well, for me. I didn't see too much. It wasn't real stressful. We could sleep."

Tony doesn't muster up much energy talking about Afghanistan. It wasn't that big a deal for him. He gets much more worked up talking about what happened right after he got back to Camp Pendleton, when the battalion was gathered together for a final set of workshops before a three-day leave. Someone up the chain of command decided that the best way to bring the battalion together as a unit—all five companies, some 1,500 marines—would be to have them run three miles, separated by company and singing cadence all the way.

"So we're doing this run.…And we have our flag and we take turns carrying it. And [our Sergeant]'s like, 'We're Bravo—and we're the best! I don't care about Alpha and I don't care about Charlie.'" A marine from one of the other companies ran to the man carrying Bravo's flag and tapped him on the shoulder. Tony was watching and saw the flag bearer pass the flag to the new guy. For a minute he thought maybe the new guy was just somebody who had recently transferred in, but then the guy took off running and he realized that their flag had been stolen by someone from another company: "And two guys and me, we're like 'Let's go!'" He and his friends ran down the thief and Tony jumped him and threw him down to the ground. "I got on top of him and I was like, 'Don't *ever* do that!'" Tony's face lights up as he is telling me this; he is leaning so far forward he looks ready to leap out of his chair. The rest of the company saw what happened and quickly hailed him as a hero. "And everybody in my company's going crazy yelling and it was so intense. And they let me sing cadence and I'm like," he starts singing, loud and proud, "'Corporal Sandoval come on out! Let me hear you scream and shout!' And I run out there and we're yelling and the battalion circles around us and everybody's 'Ahhhh!' And it was intense!"

He finishes the story and glances back at me, eyes bright. He looks like a retired football player watching his own highlight reel of touchdowns and impossible interceptions. This one instant seems to crystallize everything he loves about the marines: the camaraderie, the competition, the physical challenge, the chance to be the very best. It's all there.

He tried to leave the marines shortly after this. He had fulfilled his active-duty contract and went ahead and separated from service, planning to move on with his life and spend more time with his family. He took it easy for a while, not working, living off his deployment savings, but it didn't take. He was bored. He says that he walked into the recruiter's office more than once but couldn't make the decision to go active again. His mother was against the idea. So he compromised—he joined the marine reserves. He says, "It was fun. I got to train, to teach other marines. It was cool because I brought active duty with me." He was unpopular with the other reservists because he pushed them to live up to the same standards as those required for an active-duty unit. "They hated it. Because they think you can do it just for that one weekend and that's it. But no! You have do it the whole thirty days, every day of your life. You have to be able to do a PFT [physical fitness test] at a moment's notice."

He got the call to go to Iraq in late summer 2004. The United States had invaded the year before, and Tony, as a post–active-duty reservist, had the option not to go, but it wasn't even a question for him. "I'd been training these reservists for what, a year and a half? I could not NOT go. It's not possible....You train with these marines and you can't abandon them. You're a marine and you're a squadron leader and it's your job." He says, though, that he cried when he had to tell his youngest sister he was leaving. She cried and cried. "I was like, 'Don't worry. I'm going to Iraq with a bunch of marines just like me!' She was like, 'OK.' It was like that made her more comfortable, that there were other guys there just like me, that were taking care of me." He told her, "There are people who don't get to come home, but they're looking over us. They're watching over us like guardian angels."

Once in Iraq, his conflicts with the other reservists settled down. His squadron came to realize that his combat experience meant something, and that his efforts to push them had made them better prepared for the work they had to do. They began to trust him. In return, he says, "My concern the whole time was, first, my marines. Were they getting enough sleep? Were they getting fed? A lot of them were having marital problems. A lot of them. Girlfriends, wives cheating on them. Things you just couldn't do nothing about. I knew that. I already knew that, being in for so long. So I just tried to help them out, tried to get them through." Without pausing, he goes on. "It's scary when you hear mortars landing. Boom. Boom. Everybody stops—how far is it away? Where's it at?" It was interesting how he moved—in the space between one sentence and another—from cheating wives to falling mortars, as though these things were perhaps not so different, both just potential threats to his men.

It wasn't long before knowledge of Tony's experience in Afghanistan got around and he was transferred to a unit closer to Fallujah. He hated being taken away from his unit, although he knew trouble was brewing. The first battle in Fallujah had been the previous spring, after Iraqis captured four American contractors, burned their bodies, and hung them from a bridge. The marines had gone in then and, as Tony describes it, put a cordon around the city. "No coalition troops went in there, nothing. So we knew we were going to have to go in there eventually. It didn't take a rocket scientist to figure that out."

"So...in late October we did what's called a feint, where we went to the south side of the city and just kind of did a probe, you know, a small little quick battle where we just pushed in real quick and fought for a few minutes and backed off. Just to test their defenses and see how well defended it was." There were no casualties then, no wounded. But by early November, momentum was growing for a larger onslaught. "All the ammunition started to come in. I mean piles and piles and piles, just massive amounts. And all the commanding generals were coming by, and they were talking to us, and we all knew it was going to be a big battle. It was going to be big and somewhat historic as far as Iraq went. But the commanders and generals, everybody was building it to be...we were going to live in history books and they were going to mention us in the same breath as Kai San and the Cho-Sun Reservoir and Iwo Jima, and so it really started hitting home to all of us, all of the marines."

On November 9, Tony's new unit moved into position. They began the push through the city, and for the next several weeks the battle was his whole world. He thinks the first time he actually got out of the city was December 15. "So it was thirty-five, forty days, something like that, without a shower, just eating MREs [meals ready to eat] and stuff like that. I got to sleep in a bed, on a bunk, instead of on concrete and stuff. That was nice. I shaved all my hair off because I didn't want to wash it." He laughs. It was a short reprieve, and he went back into the city in the morning.

His battalion, he says, had a reputation for "showing no mercy." "When we would go through houses, we would burn them down. The ones that were stone and stuff like that, we'd bring bulldozers and bulldoze them. You could look at satellite images of Fallujah now and there's a road that runs north and south and everything between that and the river was ours and it is flat. We just flattened it. Because the enemy...we would push south and the enemy would move back and around and would try to rebuild behind us and flank us and do all that. So...we dropped bombs on it, and whatever didn't flatten we bulldozed or did whatever we had to do."

There is a sudden shift in his tone as he says, "Saw lots of dead people, lots of bodies. Enemy and friendly. Saw lots of wounded marines. Marines get killed. So...been there. Seen it all." He falls silent.

I was struck by how he ended his story of Fallujah. He had spent a long time telling me about the buildup to the offensive, the artillery used, summoning the long-winded detail of the expert. And then, in a series of fragmented phrases at the end, he touched so superficially on this other part of the story: the carnage he witnessed, the death, the consequences of all the military muster. His extended narrative drifted apart in a string of words, and I found myself thinking of all that was left unsaid.

He admits that he prefers not to talk about that part of his time in Iraq. The second time we spoke, he told me about a new guy at work who was a former marine; he had cornered Tony during break one day and started asking about Iraq. Tony thought he wanted to test him, to see whether he had really been in combat, as veterans will when sussing each other out. When the new guy found out that Tony had been at Fallujah in 2004, he shook his head in acknowledgment: "Y'all had it rough out there." As Tony looked on uncomfortably, the guy went on, "You lost a lot of dawgs out there. Y'all got into a lot of shit." Tony replied, "Yup, and that's how it was for me the whole time." Then he shut down the conversation and walked away, hiding the tears in his eyes.

Reflecting back on his time in Iraq, he says, "We took it—my guys and I and everyone we were with took it as second nature. It was just our life, we had to survive. Do what we had to do, you know what I'm saying." But the encounter at work opened something in Tony. "He stirred up some emotion, and I was just like, 'I don't want to talk about it.' And then some other guys were like, you know, in shock, because they don't know anything and I've been working with them for three years. And this guy comes up and opens his big mouth and starts spreading the word of what I've been through."

Tony, like Brian, is a talker, chatty and articulate. There are plenty of things he is happy to talk about—boredom in Afghanistan, his love of being a marine, ground offensives in Fallujah, even, although cautiously, growing up with an alcoholic father. But the consequences of war and the bodies of his marines—this was something he wasn't ready to discuss, and in some vague way he resented being pushed into it. When I thought about it later, I realized the problem. He had chosen to keep silent about those experiences, and the new guy didn't show proper respect for that silence. It wasn't the new guy's story to tell.

The Witness

Jesse Caldera looks like a lot of veterans who have been home a few years, with his service-time leanness replaced by some extra weight. Many veterans pick up a few pounds in the early years after they get out of the service, a predictable result of the usual decline in physical activity once PT is no longer mandatory. The change in Jesse's life lingers around his belly and jaw line, softening the lines of his face under his hazel eyes and dark hair. He is an anxious man, shifting constantly in his seat, never quite at ease. Sometimes when he speaks, his eyes seem very far away, taking on the "thousand-yard stare" so commonly described on the faces of combat veterans who have seen too much. Other times—when he becomes a little agitated—he talks a mile a minute, rushing nervously over a river of words. He grew up in San Antonio, the son of a Mexican American father and a German American mother. His father served out his career in the military, and so Jesse followed in his footsteps when he came of age, signing up for the air force at the age of eighteen, in 1999.

He loved the military and the friends he made there. "I loved the fact that I was just—it felt like a family. All these people I didn't even know, but we loved each other. There were a couple of guys—we went through basic together, then school together—it was like watching each other grow up. And then when we went to Iraq it was difficult because we were with different detachments. We would run into each other but then it was like, 'See you when

I see you. See you when we get out of here.' It was hard, it was like a part of me had gone with them."

He was sent to Kuwait in the early stages of the United States' preparation for war. First posted to an air base there, which he said was like "Candyland" because there was no threat of attack, he remembers the start of combat operations in March 2003. He watched the overhead flight of Tomahawk missiles heading north from the air base to rain "shock and awe" down on Baghdad. He got settled into his work loading and unloading aircraft at the base, and it was there that he encountered the first consequences of war.

"We started having bodies coming in. That was the first time I saw *that*. I dealt with HR—human remains—moving the bodies into the plane. I didn't think about it much, but it made me sad." He starts to change the subject, to begin talking about the convoys he began accompanying later on, but returns quickly to the remains, his face becoming more animated as he strings the sentences together. "A lot of bodies. A lot of bodies. And that really made me sick." In the course of his duty at the air base, he ran into soldiers and marines and Special Forces operatives who were on their way north to Iraq. He would have just enough time to learn a new acquaintance's name and face and attitude before the guy would go up across the border, and then, he says, "A few weeks later he'd be in a box. You'd be cussing him out, 'Fuck you, you marine!' Just playing around, and then you'd read in the newspaper that they're dead. And you're carrying the bodies, carrying the boxes. You think about their families, and it was just really sad. And a lot of them at the time were younger than me. Life's just starting off and they're dead. There were so many of them it was hard to comprehend. Then they started coming out in bags, and you could see the perfect outline of their bodies, and that just made it more real."

Jesse stayed on HR duty at the Kuwaiti air base for a while, until a friend working transport told him that they had a shortage of people working out of the Baghdad airport. He talked to his commander and got permission to work on convoys going between the two air bases. He says, "I don't know why I did that, but this guy was the only guy on the whole base that I knew. So I volunteered to go and we went to Baghdad airport when it was still Saddam Hussein Airport. It was weird as shit. I was scared...real scared. But I ended up doing a lot of [convoys] with him." It was a strange experience. "You never knew if somebody was going to try and shoot at you...seeing the little kids...it was awkward. The little kids would try to sell you ice. They'd have soldiers' uniforms on...we used to have candy and we'd throw it away from the truck so they wouldn't come near the trucks and get...It was weird." He seems stymied by how to explain it all—the children he saw while running convoys and his discomfort at being dressed in unfamiliar Kevlar and carrying a borrowed rifle, issued to him only for the duration of the convoy since his day-to-day work didn't require the combat gear. He repeats himself often, eyes wide and distracted, describing these experiences as "weird" or "awkward."

He found himself in ever-odder territory, farther and farther away from the Kuwaiti air base to which he was originally assigned. Six months into his first deployment, he got stranded for a week in an isolated army outpost, having delivered a supply load from Baghdad as part of an air force transport team. There wasn't enough food or water there at the time, so showers were in short supply and tempers were hot. They did have electricity, though, so he holed up with some army guys he met while off duty, watching TV and DVDs and listening to music.

The soldiers described their unit as one that had been functioning well until they arrived at the new camp, which was housed in an old Iraqi prison. They had found the place still filthy with blood and feces, with bodies hanging in an area they figured had served as a torture chamber. They cleaned it up, only to find they were there without a steady supply stream and no clear orders for what to do next. At that point, they told Jesse, "The attitude changed and everybody was like, 'Do it your fucking self.' People just getting to be real aggressive with themselves and everyone else. People were passing out from dehydration and there was a stomach virus going around. You're talking about bad." Jesse woke up one morning and climbed outside the tent to find a cluster of soldiers watching a sergeant use an air compressor to blow sand off an area to the east of camp. There was nothing visible beneath the sand except more sand—no concrete slab to uncover or equipment buried there. It was just an open space of desert, with the sergeant standing there blowing away layer after layer of sand. Jesse laughs, remembering. "It freaked everybody out. We were all looking at him like he's lost his mind. But there he is with rank."

He noticed that there was a lot of conflict between officers and enlisted at the outpost. Regulations were inconsistently enforced, with proper dress and salutes required some days and ignored others. The more disgruntled soldiers were getting into trouble, copping an attitude like, "I'm in Iraq, what the fuck are you going to do? You going to shoot me? Go for it. Send me home!" Stranded in the middle of a desert with daytime temperatures hitting 130 degrees, with short supplies and sergeants standing around blowing sand into nowhere, Jesse began to understand how getting shot might begin to look like a decent alternative.

He was nearing the end of his first deployment himself and didn't need any convincing that it was time to go home. A few weeks after he returned to Kuwait, he was shipped back to the States and spent the next six months back at Lackland Air Force Base in San Antonio. He received orders to deploy again, this time to a base within the hotly contested area known as the Sunni Triangle.

His unit landed first in Kuwait, and he settled in for a few days of waiting for a flight north, drinking beer all night with a rowdy group of coalition forces—Australians, Lithuanians, Latvians, and Estonians. Midway through the party, his sergeant came to find him, announcing that they were taking an early flight out to the next stop. He was still a little drunk when he climbed onto the plane, so it took him a minute to process that everybody else was sitting on their helmets, something he hadn't seen before. He describes the next period of time as leaving him "pretty fucked up." As he describes the flight and the days to come, his story falls apart, becoming scattered and confused.

"So I was sick, and then I saw everybody sitting on their helmets...why is everybody sitting on their helmets? So then everybody's coming out and telling us we're doing a combat landing and I was sick. And we were escorted...couldn't go anywhere in the town without body armor. I was thinking 'What have we gotten ourselves into?'" He begins describing the town where they landed, focusing on the only things that mattered at the time. "A guy had gone into the town the week before and gotten himself blown up—lost all of his appendages except for one arm, but he ended up living. Nobody knew where we were supposed to go, so we were all over the base. We got to see the POWs and the Iraqi prisoners in the orange jumpsuits." He continues without a break, a little breathless, "And they started mortaring us, and I heard these sounds...we were running with this colonel....I'd been on the phone with my mom when they started mortaring us. I had to get off the phone and she was crying...running with this guy and hiding behind this concrete wall. We didn't have our body armor so [the colonel] gave us his, and we were like, 'Who is this guy?' He was one of the commanders, but we were like 'Holy shit!' And they were firing on the runway, and the radio was blaring, and I remember that after one hit I couldn't remember for a few seconds what had happened. I was dazed and confused. They kept mortaring us, and we called it 'Mortaritaville.'"

He stayed at this base for a few days, long enough to begin sleeping with Kevlar slung over his body in case they were bombed at night. Long enough to remember watching a string of football games that were interrupted by mortar attacks. He remembers wondering, "Why the hell are we out here?" and describes feeling caught in a strange helpless recycling of events: mortar, sleep, waking, work, mortar, sleep, waking..."It was like the same old thing, it just kept reoccurring."

Somewhere in the midst of all this—the football games, his mother in tears at the other end of a phone call interrupted by mortars, the flight across base under fire in body armor handed over by an unknown colonel, the postattack jokes about "wasting away in Mortaritaville"—he and his sergeant sat down to write up a transport plan, having found themselves a spare corner near the intelligence office on base. The intelligence section was monitoring the radio at the time, and they overheard a call coming in from a squad on patrol in the city. The squad's gunner had been wounded, and they were calling for a helicopter to come and pick him up. Jesse ticks off the minutes in this overheard tragedy, which went on for more than an hour. He remembers the voice of the squad's communications guy coming over the radio: "Please come. Please come, this guy is bleeding to death." The command back at base answered quickly, reassuringly, telling the squad over and over to stay in place. "A helicopter is on its way."

But as Jesse tells it, "A helicopter is never on its way. So finally about an hour passes and [the squad is] like, 'We can't wait anymore, we have to get to someplace.'" The squad decides to drive to a medical facility about fifteen minutes' drive from where they were hit. They don't make it; the wounded soldier dies along the way. In Jesse's calculation, the soldier would have survived if the squad had just driven for help in the first place without waiting for the helicopter promised by the command. "He probably would have lived. And you hear that whole thing transpire on the radio. And the guys in the command are saying, 'The pilots are on the tarmac right now. They're walking towards the verge. The helicopters are going to leave in just a few minutes.' And that satisfied the guys on the other end, but all it was was a lie. And it's very apparent at the end when the helicopter never shows up."

I ask him why the command lied, but he says he doesn't know. No more than he knows why a sergeant would stand on the edge of a desert blowing sand into the wind or why a colonel would hand over his body armor in the middle of a mortar attack. His whole experience of Iraq seems to be one of wandering across a surreal landscape, passing from one inexplicable event to the next without any sense of order or reason. As a low-ranking airman (first class), Jesse lacked access to the kind of intelligence or operational information that might have given him a broader view of what was happening around him. Since he served as support personnel for the most part, rather than as an officer or technician or active combatant, his version of Iraq lacks the expert's sense of a job well done that often organizes tales like Brian's and Tony's.

After the Sunni Triangle, he returned to Kuwait, where he went back to running the occasional convoy as a break from his loading job at the air base. He shakes his head and concludes about the convoys, "It wasn't part of my job to do that, but I guess I'm glad I did, because it needed to be done." Loading human remains was still part of his job, and at a certain point he was also assigned the transport of wounded soldiers and marines, some with bullet wounds, some with limbs shredded by explosives. "You'd be carrying them and be like, 'Fuck!' You'd look at them and be like, 'I don't know, it looks like he's gonna die.' It was really awkward."

There was something about the way he said this word, "awkward," that struck me. Perhaps it was the at-times panicked look in his eyes as he spoke, but somehow that single word communicated what a more articulate phrase might not have. In contrast to the parts of his deployment that he speaks openly and freely about—laughing with drunk Australians in Kuwait comes to mind—there are other parts where his narrative falls apart entirely, days and events swimming together, and where he seems at a loss to describe his feelings except as weird or awkward. These are general words, usually applied to small events in daily life, small abnormalities in the fabric of the universe: "I had an awkward moment at the meeting today," or "That man we met last night seemed a little weird." They seem odd when applied to the shattered body of a fellow service member or to the act of tossing candy for Iraqi children from the convoy trucks rolling through their villages.

Late in our interview, the weirdness of the children he had described earlier became a little clearer. In response to a question about why he doesn't like to talk about Iraq, he says suddenly, "I think I killed a little kid when I was over there." His next few lines become jumbled, as he veers back and forth between explaining how he doesn't like to talk about it and explaining why it was unavoidable: "They told us not to stop. I think I only told my brother-in-law when I got drunk when I got back. Oh God. He reminded me of my niece and my nephew. He told me, 'What were you going to do? It was either them or you....If you woulda stopped...' Because what they would do—let me tell you this real quick—they'd stop us, then shoot a rocket until we started a sniper attack. They'd have a lot of little kids running around the truck..." And then he veers off again, referring to a movie that reminded him of Iraq and then a dinner he had eaten in the palace of a Kuwaiti millionaire.

Over the intervening months since we last spoke, Jesse's descriptions have stayed with me in a way that other veterans' more elegant phrases have not. This is, I think, partly because his inability to speak more eloquently about what horrified him points once again to the problem of what is left unspoken in war stories—those silences that also reverberate throughout Brian's and Tony's accounts. But there is more to these words than simply the jagged ellipses they glide over. There is also the way in which Jesse comes back to them over and over again, picking away at the wounds they cover because they have not healed. He is not at peace with these memories; they seem to clutch at him. He says he has frequent panic attacks during which he begins hyperventilating, unable to breathe. It is as if the sum total of everything he witnessed in Iraq—the surreal, the wasteful, and the tragic—has somehow caught in his throat.

The Wounded

Derek and Laticia Johnson come into the hospital together to meet with me. He is tall, well above six feet, in his late twenties, and walks in wearing baggy shorts and a titanium prosthesis where his left leg should be. His skin is very light, his features dominated by a pair of sharp green eyes. Laticia, by contrast, is quite dark, her skin and hair highlighted by the gold necklace and bright pink shirt she wears. She has a delicately shaped mouth and a subtly pretty face that becomes more beautiful the longer she speaks. She lets loose with a loud, infectious laugh a few times during our talk but for the most part speaks with a quiet tone, clear-eyed and focused.

Derek grew up in the Deep South, raised by his mother's family after his father, himself a medevac helicopter pilot in Vietnam, disappeared from his life when he was a child. He joined the army in 1998 and thrived there, studying communications and moving steadily up the enlisted ranks. He was introduced to Laticia in 2004 by a mutual friend. They were a long-distance couple from the start. She was working on a bachelor's degree at Texas State University and taking care of her two children from a previous marriage, and he kept getting sent around the country for training. But they spoke every time they could, and they brag proudly that their longest conversation in those early days stretched for nearly ten hours. They say they both knew from the beginning that this was it.

When it came time for Derek to deploy to Iraq in mid-2005, Laticia was there to kiss him and send him off. "We didn't get married because we didn't want to get married just because he was deploying," she explains. "I wanted to finish my degree under my maiden name so my daddy would be proud and my mama would be proud." After they said good-bye, she drove back to San Marcos and threw herself into her coursework and caring for her sons.

Meanwhile, Derek was moved out of the communications unit he had been serving with and was reassigned to a patrol unit in Baghdad, much to his disgust. "Things started blowing up, people started getting hurt, and I was like, 'Anybody can do this.' We were pulling security, going out on trucks, and I was like, 'Send me back to where—I don't know if I can keep these people alive or not, but at least I'll be participating. I'll be helping out in some way.'" After seven years of training as a communications analyst, he was overwhelmed with frustration at being unable to use his skills to protect the men and women around him. Looking back, he thinks that frustration probably fed into a "very very mild depression."

Within a few weeks, however, he was patrolling nonstop. He and his new unit were "constantly busy. Constantly busy. Constantly. When we first started there, we started running night patrols and stuff. Day and night patrols. We were working seventy-two hours straight. Just constant go go go go. And we were able to work, able to do it because we were so pumped with adrenaline because so much was going on."

After living like this for a while, he found it difficult to remember anything else. "We felt like we were these timekeepers. We could control time and space and whatever. But then you're trained to believe that you're like a machine. You're unstoppable. And it was good and bad in a way. It was good because that's what will keep you going—that's what will keep you doing your job as well as you did it. But it was bad because whenever something did go wrong, *you* would be blamed for it, not anyone else but yourself. And that would mess with a lot of people, it messes with a person's head a lot."

Things began to go wrong, as they will in a war zone. Little things, at first, like a mission that didn't go as planned or someone getting injured in a training accident. His unit was posted adjacent to Sadr City, then the most dangerous area in Baghdad, and even minor problems reminded them how high the stakes were. "You wouldn't think so, but being where you're at and knowing what you know, it puts a lot of unnecessary questions—a lot of doubt—in your mind. You start doubting yourself. You start doubting the military—what are we doing here?— after a while. You start doubting your support at home, after a while, like no one cared about us."

He lingers on this sense of uncertainty and isolation. "Being in a third world country like that is just so different—it's like going to a whole new planet." He came to a point where he began to embrace the disconnection, where he found himself making an effort to forget his fiancée and family while on duty. "And that was the only thing that kept me from getting killed, or letting somebody else get hurt or killed. Because if you're constantly thinking about home home home…" He shakes his head. "If you saw somebody and they were down and they mentioned something about home or family or something like that, we wouldn't take them [out on patrol]. It's a simple fact, because that's the person that might get you killed. They'd be like, 'I'm all right, I'm all right.' And we'd be like 'Unh-unh,' and take somebody else."

I look over at Laticia as he says this and see that she is nodding, focused on him. I speak up to ask Derek, "What would you say to them? What would you do?"

He answers, "'Just relax and just take it easy for tonight or today. Tomorrow if you feel better we'll go ahead and take you. We'll try to take you to a phone so you can call back home.' Which is the right thing but at the same time the wrong thing to do. Yeah you want them to call home and let his family—or her—reassure that soldier that everything's okay. But what if it's not and that just makes the situation worse? So being a supervisor was kinda tough because you had to make those decisions….There's a lot of decisions that you're faced with that were not easy at all. None of the actions that we took were easy. Not a single one, the whole time we were there."

Meanwhile, Laticia was back in Texas, taking twenty credit hours a semester in an attempt to rush through the remainder of her degree. "I just wanted to get it finished. I had it planned so if I needed to pack up and go to Tennessee and be an army wife the real way, that part of my business was already taken care of. And he told me," she pauses, swallowing, "that he was safe, in an office, doing communications type stuff, so my mind wasn't thinking, you know, about what he actually was doing. I didn't see him as in danger. I guess in my mind I was thinking he's in this thick underground building, milling away." They kept up their habit of talking often. "None of the e-mails were strange," she reflects. "A couple of the phone calls were strange."

"How so?" I ask.

"They were, 'Oh, I love you. I love you so much.' They'd just be kinda solemn. I'd be like, 'What's wrong? What's wrong?' And he'd be, 'I really just want you to know that I care about you.'" She compares the tone of those calls to talking with a family member who is dying. "You know how they go over how much they love you, how much they're going to miss you? It kinda felt like that—a couple of the e-mails, a couple of the phone calls. But I didn't know what was going on. So I would just be there supportive and back him up." Hearing from a friend at Fort Hood about infidelity among spouses and girlfriends back home, she made sure to let him know, "I'm on the straight and narrow. I'm doing what I need to do. I've got my nose in a book. So just come back! Come back!"

On his end, things were heating up, which explained the solemn calls. They started running into explosives, snipers, and mortars at periodic intervals; Derek counts off a string of holiday attacks. "Halloween we got hit. Thanksgiving we got hit. And then Christmas Eve was probably the first major phone call to her like that. We got hit coming in. We were OK. We got back to base and a little while later we got a phone call that—there was another truck out, in the same city, got hit with an RPG [rocket-propelled grenade]. And it was this weird freak occurrence because somebody shot an RPG, it skipped off the ground, stayed intact, and it hit between the wheels....It went under the truck, bounced off the top of the tire and went straight through this girl, was sticking through her armor and everything. And that one took me a while to deal with and get over because she was twenty or twenty-one. She had just got there a few weeks before. The sweetest girl you could meet, and on Christmas Eve, an RPG comes through her. So that one rattled me a lot. Especially because I was there in the same part of our compound, for our section, and I spent a lot of time with them. So they became my quasi-soldiers. That was like one of my own.

"And that one still hurts. But I realized then, I think, that if a freak accident like that can happen on Christmas Eve to the sweetest person on the entire FOB [forward operating base], then it's anytime. So that was one of the phone calls [Laticia] got. And then my grandfather's birthday was January 18, and one of my best friends [got hit]. We'd been briefed for a week and a half that there's always IEDs in the afternoon at a certain checkpoint. We've known this. Ten days in a row. Find a different way around it." The advice was ignored by the higher-ups. The first team—Derek's team—made it through that checkpoint, only to be hit by the detonation of a dump truck on the other side. No one was wounded, although Derek's truck was torn up by the blast.

"After we had gotten back, we had just taken everything off, parked the trucks, filled them up, taken the guns off, and sat down to play dominoes. And there was just this huge explosion. We could see the smoke from where we were in the town, and it looked like it was from the checkpoint we had just come through." His friend was in the vehicle. "It looked like their truck had been picked up, turned on itself, and the whole truck was just crushed. Killed everyone in the truck. On top of being my grandfather's birthday and he was not in the best of health, I get blown up, and then a good friend of mine who—we had a lot of similarities, he was like a younger version of me—that one hurt the worst. And I know I called her that day." Laticia nods, remembering.

After this, he says he stopped doing "anything." He stopped smiling. He stopped eating and sleeping. He stopped caring about anything. He began counting the days until he made it back home. In the meantime, he stayed in his position, going out into the city every day. They got hit on Valentine's Day, and then the string of bad-luck holidays seemed to break. His birthday passed without incident, and he began to relax. There were good times amid the rest of it, sitting around playing dominoes or drinking tea with Iraqi leaders, chasing donkeys. "You can imagine all six feet of me on one of those donkeys."

One day, working with the Iraqi police, Derek and his team accompanied a group of Kurds going to arrest a Sunni leader, an unpopular arrangement in the increasingly divided nation. "Suddenly all these guys showed up." He says it was like a "Western style standoff." "We were all playing dominoes, sitting in the trucks, waiting for this guy to come out in handcuffs. And then these guys show up, so we all load our weapons. So they load their weapons. We put on our armor, and they started putting their vehicles in little strategic places, so we get in our vehicles and load the big weapons. And then the Kurds are pointing their weapons at the Sunnis, and it was one of those moments where it was real tense at the time and on the way back we laughed the whole way. Because it was comical." Listening to him, I got the sense that certain stories began to seem hilarious just by virtue of having a happy ending.

He made it to April before his luck ran out. He and his team were escorting an Iraqi politician through the city and stopped in front of an all-Iraqi police checkpoint. "Three days earlier the snipers had shot one of the Iraqi policemen because he was putting an IED on the side of the road in police uniform. Same spot. I talked to my vehicle commander and I said, 'Sir, of all of the places to stop in this country? You don't stop for fifteen minutes in front of this checkpoint and then drive through it, because they're going to radio ahead and something bad is going to happen.' And he said, 'I know, I talked to the major. The major says we're stopping here. I'm with you, but there's nothing I can do about it.'" They took the precaution of staggering the American and Iraqi trucks, with an Iraqi vehicle between each two American ones, and they went on through the checkpoint.

He is succinct. "Two explosions. One on the front of my truck, one on the back, and my foot is hot. It's in pain, and it's wet, and that's all I knew at that point. There's gunfire everywhere. And I'm a fifty-cal gunner, so I'm up on my gun, just spraying everywhere, because I don't know what's going on, I can't stand up, I can't see. The medic—and I blacked out, so I didn't know what happened until they told me later—my medic was frantically beating on my window, trying to get me to wake up. Because we have the combat locks on the door so nobody can get in, so he's just frantically beating on his window trying to get in the window. And my first thought, and this is as soon as I wake up, as clear as anything, was 'Why is this crazy medic beating on my window in the middle of a gunfight? What is he doing?' And he's trying to get to me. But I open the door and he comes in and puts a tourniquet on me, checks me from head to toe, checks everybody else in the vehicle, calls in a medevac. We got our vehicle back the four kilometers to base, and then at some point I had had four morphine injections and I was completely stripped naked under some shiny metal blanket on the helicopter, flying through Iraq.

"I remember the helicopter landing—I remember going through some weird place—I remember waking up. And one of the army nurses was like, 'You're going to be okay. They had to amputate.' I was like, 'OK.' Because I had seen—when the shrapnel came through my foot, my foot was hanging this way, and if the boot hadn't been there it would have fallen apart. As soon as they put the tourniquet on, I knew I was losing the foot." He was pumped full of narcotics, and is still not sure how long it was before he realized he had to call Laticia. "I knew they were going to have my unit notified, they'd have my mom notified, but I knew nobody was going to call [Laticia]. I was like—I need to call my fiancée. That's rule 1. I'm not going anywhere, I'm not getting on a helicopter or anything until I talk to her. So they give me a wheelchair…" He inserts a joke: "Try to figure out how to use a wheelchair when you're really really loopy." He grins. "I tried to stand up and every time I tried to stand up I fell over. So I called her."

Laticia remembers the phone call better than he does. "One of my friends—she was staying with me, because she was going through some stuff. We were watching a movie that night, and the movie was *Jarhead*. I was like, 'I can't watch this! My baby's in Iraq. This is too much.' So I went to bed, and that night I get a phone call. He was kinda foggy, disoriented. He said, 'I got some good news and some bad news. I'll give you the good news—I'm coming home early!' I'm like, 'WHY?' All I wanted to know was 'Why?' And all I heard was, 'We got hit.'

"And then I couldn't hear anything. And then I heard 'amputate'—oh my God! What's going on? I heard, 'I'm fine…blah blah blah blah I love you blah blah blah blah blah blah I gotta go, they're wheeling me…Blah blah blah blah blah.' And that's all I heard. And since I'm not married to him, I don't get any information at all. So I was like, I'm going to call his mother. So I called his mother in the middle of the night and told her and she was able to get all the information from the formal side. And I called friends—he'd left me all their numbers—and got all the information on the internal side. And then we just mixed all the information together until he was able to call me back five days later."

Derek reaches for her hand and says, "They shouldn't let people use phones when they're on heavy narcotics."

Laticia shakes her head. "I will never forget that night. Never."

In talking of Iraq, Derek ends by saying, "One of the things we study is weapons and how weapon systems work. Grenades are an area weapon—they detonate and spray shrapnel everywhere in the area. That's what they're designed for. The grenade that came through the truck, all of it came through in one chunk and was embedded in my foot. I had my foot up on the rail like this, so I could move my trigger because my trigger was heavy. Had my foot been an inch here, an inch there, all that shrapnel would have come through, spread out, and because of the way I was sitting—I wouldn't even be sitting here. And then the two guys behind me—it probably would have gotten them right in the neck. So the way I see it, I traded my leg for all three of us in the truck. So that alone really helped me deal with it, and my attitude, and I was home and other than missing a leg, I was pretty much intact."

I noticed a contrast between this last story and the others he had told, whether about his frustrations with the command structure, his grief over the deaths of his friends, or the explosion that claimed his leg. Listening to the recording of our conversation later on, I realized that this last anecdote represented a different kind of war story altogether. This was a story not about describing an experience in an effort to share it with others but about making meaning out of the injury he had suffered. This story offered an equation—one leg for three lives—that added up to Derek's way of justifying the loss.

His injury was the beginning of a long journey for them both, beginning with his flight to Germany and then Walter Reed and later to Brooke Army Medical Center. There were several surgeries, the amputations moving up his calf until the stump was placed just below the knee and healed sufficiently to support a functional prosthesis with a minimum of pain. He and Laticia got married and lived in outpatient quarters at the hospital for a while, until he was given a medical board review and discharged from the army. Now she works full time at a local bank, and he goes to school. He moves so easily on his two legs—flesh and titanium—that it is hard to look at him and think he is in any way handicapped, although there have been, and continue to be, struggles along the way.

Still, when one watches the two of them together, it is impossible to ignore the fact that Derek and Laticia have achieved something difficult: they have created a shared version of their own war story. They have taken the story of his deployment—recognizing all the events of the eight months he was in Iraq without her, the way he tried to keep her out of his mind when on patrol, and all the dangers and losses she did not then know about—and found a way to emphasize the bonds that connected them during that time. I do not know if they had formalized this war story before or whether they created it together the afternoon of our interview, but there was a grace and a beauty in their words that I found deeply moving. As they walked out of my office, Laticia turned to me and said, 'I think we just fell in love all over again.'

In laying out this array of stories—traumatic and not traumatic, alarming and heartbreaking and funny—my aim is to hint at the wide range of what these war stories can look like, of what a service member's time at war can look like. It is not possible in this short space to reveal all the ways that veterans describe their time in Iraq or Afghanistan, and so I have chosen to focus on this group of veterans because their experiences at war and at home are so distinct from one another. Collected together, reflecting on one another, their stories begin to illustrate the individuality of what constitutes a war story, a trauma, or even, as we will see later on, PTSD itself.

Although each account is unique, as a group they provide insight into more than just the variety of experiences lived by veterans who have served in Iraq or Afghanistan. To begin with, not all war stories are stories of combat. Brian says that his time in Afghanistan was the best job he ever had. Tony has an expert's pride in all that his unit accomplished in Fallujah. Derek can laugh about trying to hold up his long legs while riding on a donkey. Much of what goes on in a war zone is affected only peripherally by war.

Going further, even among the tales of combat warfare, stories in which there was danger or horror, there is wide variation in what the veterans themselves find to be haunting or traumatic. The issue is made more confusing by the fact that "trauma" is a word that has drifted into common usage in the United States, describing any number of distressing events that occur in the course of everyday life, even those that are unlikely to be remembered beyond the next few months or years. One VA psychologist I know responds to this slippage of meaning by regularly opening presentations on PTSD with a list of what trauma is *not* (at least in clinical terms): it is not breaking up with a partner, failing an exam, or losing a job.

Even a war story, no matter how severe, cannot become a trauma until someone begins to think of it as one (although it may have been the cause of significant distress long before that). This transformation from war story to trauma usually happens about the time a veteran is diagnosed with PTSD, a process I will discuss in more detail down the line. Most war stories, however, never grow into traumas, either because they were never traumatic to begin with or because there is some quality of the veteran or the story or the way the story is told that allows it to lose its power, to loosen its grip on memory and the senses and remain just a story.

So it was that the events described in the stories above, although some are deeply troubling, were rarely considered traumatic by the veterans themselves. There were exceptions. Brian expressed his feelings of horror and helplessness after the mass casualty in Iraq; Jesse talked about the fear he felt under mortar attack and the powerlessness of hearing a wounded soldier dying on the other end of a radio broadcast. However, I found that when prompted gently with open-ended questions about day-to-day life in Iraq or by a question following up on some phrase that hinted at an unsettling truth beneath,[3] few veterans spontaneously described the more horrific events. There are many possible reasons for this, including the always uncertain etiquette of introducing disturbing images or emotions into a conversation. How does someone bring up, for example, that he has picked up the pieces of his best friend's body? Or that he has witnessed the dismemberment of a child?

On the other hand, this desire to avoid talking about truly traumatic events is also considered emblematic of PTSD; the effort at what mental health professionals call "avoidance" is one of the criteria for diagnosing the disorder. Most of the veterans I spoke with had been through at least some psychotherapy, and were—when we sat together in a small hospital room—predisposed to speak to me in a comparably intimate way no matter how frequently I clarified that I was an anthropologist, not a clinician. Many came prepared to share difficult details about their lives, including dozens of war stories associated with a degree of fear or shame, and yet relatively few offered up descriptions like Brian's or Jesse's. It was more common to hear something like Tony's description of Fallujah, with its emphasis on the detailed work of mounting an offensive suddenly disintegrating into fragments that reference rather than revealing the trauma of the battle. References were frequent; details were not.

This seemed to be because some stories stick in ways that protest retelling—either because they are too hard to tell or because there is no one to whom to tell them. They can be, as Brian said, too overwhelming to remember. There are certain stories one does not want to inflict on the listener, on certain listeners, perhaps particularly on those loved best. Brian was perfectly happy to tell me about responding to a mass casualty after a suicide bomb attack, when so many died so quickly that the sky rained blood and gore, but this was not something he wanted to tell his wife. There can be a protective wistfulness in not sharing such stories, as though the not-teller is putting forth a silent wish for the not-told:

> May your sky never be one from which blood may fall.
> (As mine is; we live, now, beneath separate skies.)

It was in considering the issue of *which* memories veterans found so horrifying, so disturbing, and so unmanageable that they register as traumatic that I first began to appreciate the place of culture and meaning in the acquisition of PTSD. Over the past two decades, anthropologists have assembled an expansive literature describing experiences of trauma occurring around the world, but they have only rarely examined what culture might mean for shaping the impact of the trauma itself.[4]

In approaching this question, it helps to begin by noting that when veterans described their traumas, they typically did so in the context of other memories which—albeit awful—they did not find to be traumatic. Brian described seeing dead Iraqis during the first Gulf War and being saddened but not overwhelmed by it, before describing what was to him far more upsetting: the inability to save Iraqis placed in his care after a suicide bombing. As a medic, it was the deaths of those he had tried to save that were traumatic for him, not just the fact of people dying. That said, certain traumas do seem to run along common lines: many veterans speak of experiences like Jesse's in which children were hurt or killed. Frequently these individuals also describe how these children reminded them of a son or daughter, niece or nephew.

Looking at these veterans' trauma stories as a collective, then, reveals two things. First of all, an event that is pathologically traumatic for one individual may not be so for the next, and as a result, we can conclude that there is a great deal of individual variation in the experience of trauma. This variation, as is the case for most health conditions, appears to be driven by both life history and physiological factors; for example, for veterans traumatized by seeing injury to children, their horror may be exacerbated by having a beloved child in their own lives and/or by having a genetic vulnerability to experiencing events as traumatic. Second, and with the potential to affect both individual and group variation in responses to trauma, there may be a role for meaning—inevitably embedded in cultural signs, systems, and beliefs—in determining which events are experienced as traumatic. Culture, with its capacity for shaping the emotional resonance of events, would seem to play a central role in making this determination.

A certain subgroup of narratives illustrates the place of culture in dialing up the perceived trauma of an event. Many of these veterans were noncommissioned officers (NCOs) during their time in the military. The position of NCOs within the social and power structures of the military is marked by a responsibility to preserve the well-being of soldiers under their command. The importance of this responsibility is matched only by NCOs' duty to complete their mission and obey their commanders, following the orders that come down the command chain. When these obligations come into conflict, the results can be devastating. The classic example of this occurs when another service member, particularly a lower-ranking one, is hurt while following orders to which the NCO personally objects. This was Derek's experience when he lost his best friend because of the orders of his superior officer, orders that Derek protested at the time but had also, along with his friend, felt compelled to obey. His story and others like it reveal that the trauma of these events lies not only in the wounding of a fellow soldier but in the inability to protect a subordinate for whom one feels deeply responsible, and the sense that the damage might have been prevented. Thus the meaning of events creates much of their resonance, and their cultural embeddedness—in this case, in the communal socialization and strict power structures of the military—is partially responsible for the emotional overload that defines trauma.

However, even though culturally embedded meanings can contribute to the traumatic resonance of certain events, research has shown that trauma by itself is rarely enough to result in PTSD. Epidemiologists have demonstrated time and time again that trauma exposure is a necessary but insufficient cause for PTSD. In order to more fully understand what puts veterans at risk, we must continue to follow their trajectory beyond combat to the end of deployment and to those moments when they discover that leaving war may not mean finding peace. This will require examining why so many veterans say that their time in Iraq or Afghanistan was the easy part, and why what turned out to be much harder was the last thing they expected—coming home.

HOME AGAIN

Early Experiences of Post-Deployment Stress

When I ask Brian to describe coming home from Afghanistan, he describes the journey first, starting with the hours spent driving through the Taliban-controlled territory between his unit's firebase and Bagram Airfield. He shrugs and says, "When you're there, you're *always* switched on. You can get up and get dressed without ever having a cognitive thought or doing anything. You're up, your boots are on, your body armor's on and you're walking out the door and you say, 'Well, I'm awake *now*.' But you did it all automatically." Upon reaching Bagram, he and his unit waited fifteen hours for their C-5 plane to arrive and then climbed aboard for the long flight to Germany. Brian remembers that the trip was brutally cold. The men lay down to sleep, huddling up together on the aluminum floor in an effort to stay warm.

They were in Germany just long enough "to drink beer and get into trouble" before they were told they were about to miss their flight home and hopped a bus back to the airfield. When they reached Fort Benning, they spent three days doing what the army calls "out-processing"—filling out paperwork, attending briefings, and returning the gear they'd been issued—before the last flight brought Brian home to San Antonio.

It was not long afterward that he had what he described as the "Afghanistan mind-fuck," that moment sitting in his recliner when he found himself utterly at a loss, unsure of what he was supposed to do next. I ask him how long it took him to get over that feeling, and he says it took a year at least "to get back to some sense of normalcy." He tries to explain and can do so only in comparative terms. "Being deployed is easy. You just have to stay alive."

I heard some version of this statement at least a dozen times from veterans and soldiers and support personnel alike. I spent an afternoon in Killeen, Texas, at a workshop of psychologists and social workers from Fort Hood, many of whom had deployed overseas or had spouses who had deployed, and listened as they talked about how much easier many soldiers find life in Iraq. 'You don't have to go buy milk in the middle of the night,' one of them said offhandedly, and the others laughed harder than seemed reasonable, the way people laugh when a simple statement sums up something both ludicrous and true. I was expecting Brian, with his usual humor, to say something similar, but instead he asked,

"Have you ever seen *Band of Brothers*?"

"No, I haven't."

"There's a line in there where one of the lieutenants is standing there fighting, and he is talking to this guy who's hiding down in his foxhole. And he says, 'You know, Clyde, the thing you have to realize is that you're already dead. Once you realize that, then you can function as a soldier.' And it's very true. Once you grasp the fact that you're already dead, you might as well just do your job and drive on. It makes the job easier over there. It makes it a real bitch coming home. Because you're used to being dead and now you got to be alive again."

For Brian, as for so many veterans, the problem wasn't what happened in Afghanistan or Iraq so much as what happened when they came back to the States. Their experiences at war followed them home, partly in their memories and partly in a profoundly altered set of physical and emotional responses to the world around them. Over time, many of these men would learn to refer to these responses as symptoms of PTSD. There were exceptions. Some of the responses would be called by other names, like "readjustment" or "depression" or "violence." We will explore this labeling, and the cultural and historical legacies at work in it, in later chapters. But in order to understand the responses and experiences that come to be called PTSD, it is necessary to begin with the phenomena themselves, exploring a deceptively simple question: what happened to these veterans when they came back home?

Let's begin with Adam Baldwin, a tall thirty-year-old with short gray-blond hair. He stands out among these veterans in that he grew up on the wealthier side of Houston and joined the marine reserves, not because it was the best among a slim set of options but because his grandfather had been a marine in World War II, and he wanted to follow in his footsteps. When his unit returned home from seven months in Iraq, his plane was met by fire trucks shooting plumes of water in a triumphant arc over the runway. They were given a police escort from the airport to company headquarters, where they received a heroes' welcome from families standing on tarmac lined with TV news cameras. His unit was based in a small town, so in contrast to one of the larger bases—where men and women may come and go from overseas almost constantly—their return was something out of the ordinary and the town wanted to celebrate. He found his parents and his wife among the crowd; everybody cried, and there were hugs and kisses and photos and speeches, and then everybody went home.

Adam had married his new wife a few weeks before his deployment, so in eight months of marriage they had yet to spend more than a few nights in the same place. While he was in Iraq, she had gotten them an apartment and furnished it. He went home to the new apartment with its unfamiliar layout and new furniture, closed the door behind him, and didn't leave for five or six days. That first week there was a steady stream of friends and relatives coming by, but after that things began to settle down.

When I ask him what he expected it to be like when he got home, he laughs a little disbelievingly. "I don't know," he replies. "I was more afraid of coming home, honestly, than I was of going to Iraq. I don't know if you've heard that before, but you just, you lose a sense of what normalcy is like. Does that make sense? You forget what it's like to watch TV and sit on the couch and you just…you lose all that. You lose the sensation of walking in grass, walking on carpet, you don't know what it's like anymore…"

Adam trails off and then speaks again, sounding for a moment very much like Brian. "You're scared when you go to Iraq, I think, your first time. You're nervous, whether you admit it or not. But you get there and you start doing your job and you stay scared, and that's how you stay alive. You're alert. And you get so used to it, that's just life. And so you almost fear coming home, because it's another huge change for you. You're excited, because you haven't seen your wife or you haven't seen your kids, or your parents if you're single, or your girlfriend if you have one. But you're scared. You're scared of how much you've changed, of what they're going to think of you, of how they're going to react. I don't know if that makes any sense but…yeah, I was very nervous coming home."

One of the first things that many veterans noticed about their post-deployment selves was a shift in their perception of the world around them. Adam talks about the intensity of those first weeks home, his attention caught by small things, like a new version of Sprite that had come out while he was away and the color of grass and the fact that the air in Texas didn't smell like sewage, as it had in Iraq. His perception of sights and sounds and smells had been transformed during his time overseas, and it was a while before he became reaccustomed to the sensory inputs he had taken for granted before deployment.

Some of these changes, however, were more significant. Cars backfiring now sounded too much like gunfire. Trash on the side of the road looked an awful lot like the debris that is used to camouflage IEDs in Iraq. Driving itself became a challenge. If another driver came up too suddenly beside Adam on the high-way, it felt like an ambush.[1] Walmart with its long lines of people now seemed dangerously crowded, with too many hiding places for unseen assailants. Being out in public left him feeling "antsy, insecure, unsafe." Adam couldn't seem to get back to his old way of distinguishing between threat and safety in the world around him.

This was partly a result of his military training and the skills he had been taught for moving safely through perilous or unfamiliar spaces. Lessons like keeping his head on a swivel, keeping his eyes scanning the surroundings for a possible threat. Keeping his body poised for a quick reaction, if necessary. Being alert at all times. Never letting his guard down. Never sitting with his back to a door. After seven months in a combat zone, these lessons were so deeply in-grained that they had become automatic, patterns imbedded in his muscles and nerves, etched into his brain. Two years after leaving the military and returning home, Adam says that he still finds himself reaching for the pistol he no longer carries.

He is not alone in this. Three years after getting back from Afghanistan, Chris Monroe can still be caught off guard by colored tiles installed in the hallway of the company where he works. Walking along a white hallway, lost in thought, he will catch a glimpse of a staggered yellow or red blotch on the wall and find himself checking his peripheral vision, his sense of danger switched on by the startle of a visual out of place. There is a two-story atrium in his workplace that for months he found it impossible to walk through. He imagined snipers hiding behind columns on the upper level, targeting him as he walked beneath. Even worse is the echo of other sights still lingering behind his eyes. He remembers too many dead bodies, of friends and strangers, and finds these images superim-posing themselves on the living faces around him. "Whenever I look at people, I know what they're going to look like dead. I know what they look like with their brains blown out or jaws blown off or eyes pulled out. When I look at somebody I see that, to this day."

This transformation of sensory perception helps to explain what those fa-miliar with PTSD call "triggers." A trigger is some sight or smell or event that prompts a memory that can, depending on its content, be associated with a sig-nificant amount of distress.[2] Jesse accidentally burned the hair on his hand during a family barbecue and was so assaulted by a remembered smell of burnt hair and flesh that he threw up on the grass. Sounds that resemble gunfire, trash by the side of the road, the faces of people who look Middle Eastern—all of these represent triggers commonly reported by veterans who served in Iraq or Afghanistan, just as the smell of rice and the sound of Asian languages were reported as triggers by Vietnam veterans a generation ago. These triggers may be specific, bringing to mind a particular incident, but they may also call up a more generalized feeling of anger, sadness, anxiety, or fear. Derek was driving home from his class at the college one afternoon when he saw the silhouette of a man holding what looked like a gun on the overpass just ahead of his vehicle. Thinking it was a sniper, he swerved his car across three lanes of traffic before he realized it was a policeman using a radar detector to check traffic speed. He was thankful that he hadn't hurt anyone but embarrassed and humiliated that his reaction had been so severe, so seemingly irrational.

Most of the veterans I spoke with described first thinking that something about them was different—not necessarily *wrong*, at least at first, but *different*—when they began noticing these changes in their reaction to what was going on around them. Jesse says he was "kinda jumpy," and "always waiting for something to happen." Adam says he was on "sensory overload." Another veteran tells me that "you feel unsafe at the same time you know you're safe" and admits that, while driving, he feels as if "somebody's going to jump out of the car and shoot me up." This is one reason many veterans give for drinking too much after they get back. Military personnel are forbidden to drink in both Iraq and Afghanistan, out of respect for local Islamic law, so alcohol has the rediscovered novelty value of having been (at least mostly) unavailable during deployment. More important for many of these veterans, alcohol also acts as a mild depressant, helping to numb the constant vigilance and "take the edge off."

Although this feeling of living in an environment of perpetual threat is problematic enough for the distress it creates, it also gives rise to other problems, not least of which is the gap it opens between those who see the world as dangerous and those who don't. A veteran who has been through combat knows, in an unshakable way, that life is finite and full of risk. His friends and family, especially if they are civilians, may or may not share this way of seeing. Tony describes going to public events with his friends and making "stupid comments" like "We need to be more aware of our surroundings and our situations, because if anyone wanted to, they could literally take thousands of people out right now." He mimes his friends rolling their eyes and groaning, "Why do you always have to say stuff like that?" "Because it's true," he answers, before adding, "Well, to me it's true."

Tony's friends, on the other hand, have an idea, shared by many who live in a relatively safe society, that war and violence should be left overseas. A veteran should come home and put down his gun and return to normal, where normal means shopping at Walmart and driving on the highway without fearing a sniper at every overpass. Normal is supposed to mean relaxing the wariness that was a survival skill in Iraq. This is a big part of what Brian and Adam mean when they talk about getting back to normal, this ability to feel safe in their home environments. With every month or year spent in a war zone, this sense of safety must seem ever more elusive.

But for veterans whose senses are on constant alert for potential danger, there is plenty of ongoing nastiness back at home to justify their continued wariness. Tony—who, having grown up with so much violence, already had more than a passing acquaintance with brutality when he left for Iraq—was the victim of an unprovoked attack that took place between deployments. He went out drinking with his fellow marines one night and left the bar a few minutes before his friends, planning to surprise them in the parking lot. On his way to the car, he was jumped by three men, one of whom was wielding a baseball bat, and beaten so badly that his skull was broken and his cheekbone caved in. In a similar story, an older veteran who nearly lost his arm after being shot in Baghdad was later assaulted on a city bus in New York.

Events like these only reaffirm veterans' awareness that mayhem can appear suddenly out of a clear blue sky, in the most tranquil of places. Loved ones may tell them that now that they're home, everything is going to be all right. And in truth, a bomb is less likely to go off in San Antonio than Kabul. At the same time, life in the United States is not without its dangers. Eight of the fifty men in the PDS study (16%) had witnessed another person being assaulted or killed since returning from deployment. Another eight had been robbed or had had their homes broken into. One man had been subject to sexual assault, and another six (12% of the sample) had been physically assaulted themselves. It is no wonder that veterans caught between experience on one hand and well-meant reassurances on the other can find it hard to reestablish a sense of caution that others would agree is appropriate.

Hearing all this, one might think that these men walked around in a state of ever-present fear, but this was only very rarely the case. Far more frequently, they described *anger*, anger that came out of nowhere and in response to events that might seem trivial. Anger, they said, that lasted longer and felt sharper than it should. Jesse gives the example of being cut off by another driver on the highway. "A week from then, I'll still be pissed off, like 'That guy who cut me off!' Somebody will be like, 'I can't believe you're still pissed off about that!'" He says he will get "overly mad." He recounts a recent encounter with a rude salesclerk who so infuriated him that he began screaming at the terrified clerk, who took off running. He says this was when "I really scared the shit out of myself. I don't know why I get like that. It's just the way I am now. If I'm not sad now, I'm pissed off." Another veteran mentions accidentally running his car into the side of his parents' garage. His response was to ignite, he says, like "gasoline," jumping out of the car and ripping up a small tree newly planted nearby, then throwing lawn chairs and trying to push over some pillars in the yard. As he is telling me about it, he makes a wan joke about how funny his tantrum would have looked if caught on video, but like Jesse, he is baffled and bothered by the extent of his own rage. He copes, in part, by trying to stay within a few miles of home, carving out a bubble in which he feels less likely to be surprised or caught off guard.

There are, of course, consequences to walking around with so much anger. Tony, who got into a series of barroom brawls after he was attacked, says that his anger began to interfere with the way his friends and family saw him. "I think it makes me out to be more aggressive than I really am. Instead of being laid-back and cool like I am in my own backyard. Everyone's like 'You're totally different at home.' In my world, in my comfort zone. When I'm out of it, I'm like a totally different person." After he had gone out a few nights with friends, only to be thrown out of the bar or restaurant for yelling or fighting, some of those friends stopped calling.

There were yet more devastating changes that these men saw in themselves, changes that often became a source of private grief. For it wasn't just that the world had changed in their perception—had become nastier, more dangerous, more frightening and infuriating. The world had turned out to be a disappointment, true, but too often they had found themselves to be a disappointment as well.

The first time Chris Monroe's unit was shot at, he didn't shoot back. He didn't identify a target. He didn't do any of the things he had been trained to do. He pissed himself. He froze for a few seconds. And then he began shooting wildly. "I went through magazine after magazine after magazine, emptying my gun. I wasn't aiming at anything—I don't even remember what it was. Just blurs in the distance. Much too far away to hit anything." When the firefight was over, he covered up the stain on his pants by low-crawling through some nearby mud and tried to look past the querying looks of his friends. He was utterly humiliated.

This perceived failure hung with him for a long time, particularly after his best friend was killed in a firefight and the potential stakes of every moment in combat became more real. Chris explains how the guilt and shame of these events hung together in his own experience, ultimately creeping into his dreams. "Kind of the underlying thing to the events that affected me was that I had no control over them. And the times that I did have control I messed up. And being completely out of control, completely vulnerable....You feel responsible for the deaths of people."

Listening to him, I remembered Jesse's story about the child he ran over in Iraq, the child who reminded him of his niece and nephew, and his description of listening helplessly over the radio as the wounded soldier bled to death without medical attention. There is a litany of such stories, beginning with Derek's tale of his best friend's death at the checkpoint his command had been warned was so dangerous. Or that of Carlos, an air force security officer who saw an Iraqi girl hit by a mistakenly fired grenade launcher. "They thought she was a terrorist and it was a little girl bouncing a ball in the dark." Although he had nothing to do with the event, Carlos visited the girl repeatedly in the hospital, hiding behind a curtain so she wouldn't know he was there. After he returned home, he began seeing visions in which she was "injured or dead or staring at me or pointing at me."

This haunting, often inexplicable sense of guilt and regret was a central reason that many veterans gave for wanting to deploy again, even with full knowledge of the dangers involved. They worried about their buddies who were still overseas, often now on their third or fourth tours, men and women they had trained or served beside and felt responsible for. Over the months and years that followed, as the wars continued, those who didn't leave the military remained in danger. Tony was miserable when he left the reserves, worried that he wouldn't be there to take care of his unit if they ran into trouble. Many veterans had stories of friends who were killed upon returning to Iraq, and found their grief mingling with the guilt of not having been there to save them. One young soldier described how ruminating over the fate of his friends kept him awake at night. "I'd try to sleep and I'd remember times that my buddies got blown up, that I'd lost friends over there, and I'd have trouble sleeping. I'd end up crying until about six, seven o'clock in the morning. All night. Makes you feel like…maybe I coulda done better."

Guilt was only one reason given for being unable to sleep. Of the fifty male OEF/OIF veterans in the San Antonio study, only one reported that he had no difficulty sleeping, and nearly half reported having a hard time getting to sleep or staying asleep "extremely often." Some veterans were kept awake thinking of their friends, their regrets, their memories; their minds turned relentlessly over and over the same events, unable to change the outcomes. Others found it impossible to relax the vigilance that drove them through the daylight hours.

Still others found themselves seeking an unceasing wave of adrenaline. For just as they had become hyperattuned to potential threat, so too had they become accustomed to the high adrenaline of living under extreme stress. In his poems about World War I, Robert Service wrote of dreading the day when he would have to return home to the "dreary grind" of ordinary life, and of how he would long for "oh, the joy of the danger-thrill, and oh, the roar of the fight!"[3] Nearly a hundred years later, mental-health-care providers speak similarly of veterans' search for a rush that can compare with the life-or-death intensity of deployment. This search provides one explanation for the high-risk behaviors many service members engage in upon returning home: unprotected sex with multiple partners, high-speed motorcycle chases without helmets, drinking and drugging too much. One local counselor attended a week-long training and orientation session with a group of newly returned soldiers. He marveled that even after a full day of exercise and training, the men preferred zip-lining down a mountainside in the dark to going to sleep.

Other veterans spoke of lying down at night and waiting for a few meager hours of sleep, needing the rest and yet dreading the dreams that might accompany it. Eighty percent of veterans interviewed reported having at least occasional nightmares about their military experiences, and more than a third said that they had nightmares moderately or extremely often. Brian told me that he doesn't dream, but said also that he wakes up in the night with his heart racing, his body slick with sweat, sometimes in tears and unable to explain why. Jesse dreams of sleeping in camp in Iraq and waking to find himself covered in snakes and scorpions that crawl over him in the dark. One of the women I interviewed, a career officer in the air force who served as a nurse in Afghanistan, described nightmares of Afghani children torn apart by an IED. She wakes to the vacant silence of her empty house and turns on the TV to blur the images remaining in her mind. An army security officer who worked overseeing a prison in Iraq muses, looking back, that "every second of the day was that prison. It didn't matter what I needed to do—as soon as something would happen I'd have to get up and run back to the prison. So I never got very far from that prison, and even now I'm still not very far from it—in my thoughts, in my dreams."

In hearing these stories of how veterans first began to realize that something in them had gone awry, I found it impossible to avoid thinking that many of them spoke as though they had gotten lost somewhere in the space between Iraq or Afghanistan and San Antonio. It was as if, halted prematurely on the journey home, they had landed on some muddled middle ground of reality and memory from which they embarked on both dreams and waking life. For lack of a better word, I began to think of what they described as a kind of dislocation. The word has a medical meaning, of course, describing the wrenching apart of two bones at a joint.[4] But it also carries other meanings, being "the act of disrupting an established order so it fails to continue,"[5] and perhaps most aptly, "the state of being displaced."[6] What I heard from veterans was a dislocation of experience, rather than one of the body, but the image seemed to capture something of both the injury and the feeling of being thrown out of one's place in the world, the order of things disrupted. Veterans described dislocations from a previous sense of self, from others in the world, and from feeling truly present in their lives back at home.

One of the first occasions on which this dislocation becomes apparent is in the course of a long conversation with Victor, a Mexican American man in his late twenties. He is sad-eyed, and seems subdued and distracted as we talk. At one point, during a quiet moment when he is filling out the survey, he looks up at me and says, "Let me ask you this. Why is it that I wouldn't mind going back?"

"I don't know," I answer. "But I hear it a lot."

"Whenever I've been in Iraq," he goes on, "you have so much time when you're there. You walk the sand and you hear guns going off and tanks firing. And you feel like nothing was there, nothing's there still. Your wife wasn't there to bitch at you. Your kids weren't there to scream at you. I guess it's the fact that you were alone. I miss that. It felt like I was gone anyway, out there. I don't know."

Initially I was confused by Victor's image of having wandered alone through Iraq, of missing that solitude and longing for it. His other stories of Iraq all involved people—other soldiers, leadership figures, Iraqis. In none of his war stories did he appear by himself, and yet here, in this memory of Iraq, he expressed nostalgia for the isolation. Upon further reflection, however, it became clear that this longing was inextricably linked to another internal change that many veterans described, a shift from being someone who enjoyed other people to being someone who just wants to be left alone. Victor says that before he went to Iraq, "I was more outgoing, more social." Now, by contrast, he says he doesn't talk to anyone. "I feel like everything I'm in contact with is just irritable." One of the Vietnam veterans I spoke with said that he sometimes wishes he could just wander off into the woods and disappear like that, off by himself in the wilderness. Adam did just that as often as he could, driving down to his deer lease out in the country, alone or with another friend who is also a veteran, "just to be alone, in solitude. Just alone with your thoughts."

This changed responsiveness to others is often accompanied by an involuntary flattening of emotion more generally. Jesse describes being unable to feel "any kind of emotional attachment to anybody. I *think* I love my girlfriend, but I can't really feel it. I can't feel anything." When one of his uncles died, he says, "I couldn't feel anything. I was sad, but I really wasn't, and I was like, 'What the hell's wrong with me?'" Over time, he has come to realize that it isn't that he can't feel anything at all. He can feel anger, first of all, as when he screamed at the salesclerk or lost his cool in traffic. Sometimes he will cry for no reason he can understand. He compares himself to a pregnant woman, with hormones going wild. "I'd see a movie and I'd cry. I'd be fine and then I'd be crying."

Victor, speaking haltingly, links a similar kind of numbness to the loss of his sex drive. "I don't even care for [sex]. That's what's weird. I honestly feel so emotionally detached. If you don't feel emotionally attached you don't feel for somebody, you don't desire them. That's becoming a problem with me and anybody I'm with. It's kinda weird that like, you wanna be loved but then you can't be. And that's hard to feel—you'll never be loved." He looks up toward the closed office door as he says this, perhaps thinking of the girlfriend who sits waiting for him in the lounge beyond.

This feeling of being cut off from loved ones reverberated throughout the tale of almost every veteran who described himself as struggling post-deployment. This withdrawal was more acute in some cases than in others. Victor, for example, had sustained a severe leg injury while working as a mechanic in Iraq and was facing an upcoming surgery to repair the torn muscle. In the meantime, he was keeping away from his three children, who were living then with his ex-wife while he bounced back and forth between his mother's home and his girlfriend's. At the time we spoke, he hadn't seen his children in nearly two months.

"I don't want to see them look at me and see me hurt," he explains. "I can't pick them up, I can't hold them. I guess that's why. Protect myself from that predicament. I tell myself that I can't give them something I don't have…they live with her, with their mom. So if I don't see them as much, I won't miss them as much."

Most often, however, the withdrawal from loved ones was less direct. Brian describes the change he saw in himself between the time he entered the military and his return from the first Gulf War. "Prior to coming into the Army, I was very…I'm a pretty happy guy, I'm pretty jovial. But I'm only jovial this far with you, because I don't know you, and it would take me months before I would be able to buddy up to you…" He pauses, then admits, "My wife and I will never be as close as we were before I—when we were dating and first married. And it's just because I've constructed enough barriers that if anything happens I'm not going to get hurt by it. If she dies I'll be sad, but I'm going to go on. It's not going to stop my life, whereas beforehand it probably would have stopped me. I would have been so emotionally attached that it probably would have been too painful to comprehend. And part of that, I think, is just a little bit of a disconnect and not being able to have that tight attachment or tight emotional connection."

The double impact of these withdrawals is that they affect Victor's children and Brian's wife as much as they do Victor or Brian. This is, inescapably, the case with all these post-deployment challenges. A veteran who is avoiding crowded places is likely to have a wife who feels deprived of help with the grocery shopping and kids who don't understand why their father doesn't take them to football games anymore. If a veteran's sleep is disrupted too much or too often, he may be short-tempered and impatient. If he has a history of becoming violent while dreaming or on sudden waking, he may be afraid to share a bed with his wife or children. These veterans' changed internal landscapes have an unavoidable impact on the external world they share with their wives, girlfriends, children, parents, friends, and family. These changes signal dislocations from what was normal before the war, but also from the very people who mark the difference between "returning" and "coming home."

Such transformations put additional strain on families already tested by the long separations of extended deployments. By 2007, when I began this study, such separations had become par for the course for much of the American military, although the length of deployments differed by specialization and branch of service. Marines were typically deployed for six to seven months. Soldiers were deployable for as long as fifteen months, up from a year at the time of the Iraq invasion. Air force personnel were generally looking at six to seven months per tour, although there was some variability in all the branches. Combat surgeons, for example, deployed for only three months at a time, since their work was considered so high-stress that they risked burnout with longer periods. By the beginning of 2007, one-third of American troops had served at least two tours in a combat zone, and seventy thousand individuals had deployed at least three times.[7]

This far into the conflicts, the military was recognizing the debilitating effect of such extensive deployments on service members' families, with research documenting increases in divorce rates among enlisted personnel[8] and an increase in child abuse and neglect among the children of those deployed.[9] Twenty-four men and women who had lived through the deployment of a spouse, partner, parent, or child participated in the PDS study. Although sending a service member off to war can be incredibly hard on families under even the best of circumstances, these family members described a wide range of experiences, with some sailing through the deployment fairly smoothly while others found it to be a crisis from which they struggled to recover. Certain factors seemed to make the process more or less difficult to bear. During deployment, the most important determinants seemed to be the number of deployments, the length of the absences,[10] the quantity and quality of communications during deployment, and the state of family relationships prior to the deployment. After deployment, service members often returned home to find that their role in the household had changed during their absence and that they now had to readapt to their families even as their families readapted to them.

Nonetheless, most veterans and family members accepted deployment as a necessary part of military life, and nearly all took steps to manage the challenges it created.[11] Romantic partners, married or not, struggled to maintain a viable relationship across long absences and under the extreme stress of having one partner in a war zone. Those with children found ways to arrange child care during one parent's absence, often retooling the structure of family roles and responsibilities. The logistical difficulties associated with deployment were daunting; the emotional challenges required creativity and commitment to surmount.

Laticia, Derek's wife, dealt with the deployment by taking an intimidating course load so that she could complete her college degree by the time Derek came home. Many of the military wives I spoke with described utilizing similar strategies to "get through"—focusing on work or school or a new job or their children as a way of making the best of the time apart and of distracting themselves from the constant worry of wondering whether their partners were safe. The amount of communication between family members during deployments varied a great deal. Those deployed early in the conflicts often had to make do with sparse e-mail or telephone contact, since communications infrastructure was slow to develop in postinvasion Iraq and Afghanistan. In contrast, service members deployed later on were sometimes able to manage daily or weekly phone calls, although many found that this accessibility did not lessen the sense of distance. For those, like Jesse, whose loved ones were upset by hearing mortar rounds exploding in the background over the phone line, such contacts could do as much to emphasize the separation as to narrow it. Invariably, no matter how frequent the contact, those deployed and those at home were leading very different lives. While Derek was going out on patrol every day, Laticia was watching the kids, studying for tests, and—since Derek hadn't been entirely honest with her—imagining her fiancé safe in a bunker running communications systems. Coming home meant trying to take those different lives and bring them back into alignment.

This was not an easy task for anyone. Victor's marriage was on the rocks when he left for Iraq; his wife never replied to his letters while he was gone. When he came home, he was shocked to learn that his father had had a heart attack and his aunt had died in his absence. Although he and his mother had been in close contact during his deployment, she had left these things out, hoping to keep him from unnecessary worry. Meanwhile, furious that he had been gone so long, his wife was barely speaking to him. He'd missed a full year of his children's lives. He felt left out of the family circle and abandoned by his wife, who he believes felt equally abandoned by him. He tried, he says, but they weren't able to close the distance between them. He moved out a few months later.

After that, Victor felt he didn't have anywhere to go. He began looking for a reason to stay in the army, the closest thing to a home he had left. His leg injury, however, was severe enough that it led to a medical evaluation and early retirement from the army. In the end, he didn't have a choice.

Most of these veterans had separated from the military since their deployments, although a handful were still on active duty or in the National Guard or reserves. Some, like Victor, faced "early retirement," meaning they were forced out of the military because they were no longer thought able to perform their duties as a result of physical or psychological injury or illness. A few were discharged for drug use, for inability to meet weight requirements, or as punishment for other offenses. Most, however, made their own choice to leave the military. Some men had completed their service contract (which came in installments of three, four, or six years, depending on the branch of service and the length of their career to that point) and were tired of military life and frequent deployments. Others, like Tony, said that they were ready for a "new chapter" in their lives, usually driven by a desire to spend more time with their families, begin a new job, or go back to school. Even those who left the military voluntarily, however, often found it to be a difficult transition. Separating from the military can be as stressful as any other major life change—starting a new job, moving, getting a divorce, etc.—and in fact can involve taking on several of these at once.

One reason that leaving military service can pose such a challenge is that the military has its own way of doing things, its own ranking structures, priorities, expectations, and identity (identit*ies,* really, given the different branches of service and their many internal specializations). Attending a workshop for civilian health-care providers, I heard a psychologist, herself a former army officer, try to explain that people in the military really "live in a second culture." She pointed out that military training is intended to rebuild individuals into a "group-based culture." Service members don't think about themselves first, she explained. They have to be willing to put their lives on the line to serve a military objective or to save the lives of their buddies. She read off a list of the army's seven Core Values: Loyalty. Duty. Respect. Selfless Service. Honesty. Integrity. Personal Courage.[12] She insisted that it is essential to respect those values when dealing with current or former members of the military; they make up an ethical code, and one that is not taken lightly.[13]

Veterans reentering the civilian world face the additional challenge of creating a new identity there as a student, employee, or citizen. Some of this difficulty lies in getting used to a civilian attitude and way of approaching daily tasks that differ from the military's. Some of the disparities veterans pointed out were small enough. Brian says wryly that after a career in the army, he is on a different schedule than most civilians. "Five minutes [early] is on time. On time is late." Josh irritably describes trying to work with civilians on a shared project, griping, "In the military, if you don't understand, you don't ask questions about it. You just do it. Do it. You've got a problem, go solve it!"

But veterans who have recently served in a war zone may also have a difficult time appreciating how some civilians establish their priorities. Jesse talks about going, in a relatively short period of time, from deployment to a college environment. At the age of twenty-six he finds himself struggling to relate to the younger students who make up the majority of his classmates. "I go from [Iraq] to all these little kids who think they have it so fucking hard and…oh my God!" Carlos admits, "Adapting to the civilian world has been rough, too. Seeing war and children murdered and raped and beat up and mutilated, I don't understand how people who live here…" He cuts off and mimics a high-pitched voice: "'Oh my daughter's cell phone broke! I have to get my four-year-old daughter's cell phone fixed!'" He says, "It's just idiotic to me. It just upsets me how people have these priorities that are like this," forming a tiny space between two fingers, "and to them it's just huge!"

Many veterans are like Carlos in this. They find it difficult to readjust to a world where the stakes are rarely life and death. Others may find that the skills they took such pride in learning in the military are not valued in the civilian world, making it difficult to find satisfying work. One officer's wife told me that even with a distinguished army career in health care and management and an MBA earned during his time in the service, her husband still found it hard to get work after his separation. He was not alone. A full half of the veterans in the San Antonio study reported having been unemployed for at least three months since separating from the service.

Many of those who did find work discovered that the same problems that were causing trouble at home—irritability and anger, withdrawal and difficulty communicating, the desire to avoid crowds and other perceived dangers—proved equally challenging at work. Some 74 percent of the sample also reported having difficulty concentrating for more than ten minutes at a time, a problem that made studying for school or completing tasks at work unexpectedly difficult. Facing these combined difficulties, a third of the sample had lost at least one job since separation.

Even among those who appeared to be outwardly successful at forging a new postmilitary life, a surprising number found work to be a challenge. Because Brian was a reservist, he returned home from Iraq and went back to his old job at a doctor's office. This didn't spare him a transition, however. "My coworkers—when I got back I think they were all afraid of how to treat me. They're afraid to say the wrong thing or do the wrong thing. When you go to work and everybody's looking at you like you're a freak…" No wonder Tony says of the "politics" of work that "I tell people I should have just stayed [in Iraq]. Sometimes it's better over there than it is here."

And even Tony, who has a girlfriend, a close relationship with his family, and a well-paying job, shrugs and says, "I'm still trying to change. To become a civilian. I mean, I am a civilian, but in my mind, I'm still—once a marine, always a marine. I haven't been able to convert into being a normal civilian. To becoming part of society." He still wears his hair in a marine high-and-tight and swears he is going to keep it that way.

Like a lot of veterans, he struggles to say why he has found it so hard to re-imagine himself as a civilian. He reminisces about practicing close combat skills with his friends in the service and adds, "I miss the camaraderie. There's no ca-maraderie out here." He wonders aloud whether he would be happier working in law enforcement, which many veterans go on to do, because it would allow him to draw on the skills he worked so hard to acquire in the marines. "What I do is just so stagnant. It's the same thing every day. Man, I'm wasting away. That's what I feel like. I feel like I'm wasting away."

In focusing so extensively on the aspects of postwar life that these men found difficult, I don't want to obscure the fact that many service members come home from Iraq and Afghanistan having gained something positive from the experi-ence and without what they consider lingering negative effects. I interviewed one young couple—the husband was an officer out of West Point and the wife had her master's degree in counseling—and she threw her hands in the air when I asked whether he had experienced any post-deployment stress. With her back-ground in mental health, she said she had obsessed over everything he said or did for months after he came home, convinced he must have PTSD. But he's fine, she said, sounding relieved. Moving throughout the community, I regularly encountered veterans and family members who all asserted the same thing. Per-haps the veteran had some hypervigilance when he came home. Maybe it took a little while to get used to going out without a gun and holster. Maybe he even had a little trouble driving. But these feelings were manageable and eventually passed.

Veterans like these, who report a temporary period of readjusting to the con-ditions of life at home but otherwise experience no extraordinary difficulty, might be said to be "resilient"; that is, they demonstrate the ability to remain healthy and functioning after a potentially traumatic experience.[14] Even among those veterans who went on to develop PTSD, there was generally an acknowl-edgment that their deployment had left them with new skills and strengths. Many felt more confident, more assertive, and more appreciative. They placed a higher value on their home country, their freedom as citizens, their health and safety, and their families. They might be said to have undergone what psycholo-gists call "post-traumatic growth," in which a difficult experience leads one to positive psychological change. This might take the form of a greater appreciation of personal strengths or a reassessment of priorities, both of which were com-monly described by veterans.[15] Nonetheless, the problems they encountered on coming home were also real and raise the question, what is it that causes some individuals to struggle with PTSD while others do not? How do we understand this variation?

According to the current edition of the *DSM*, an event can be considered sufficiently stressful to prompt a post-traumatic reaction if the following two criteria are both met:

(1) the person experienced, witnessed, or was confronted with an event or events that involved actual or threatened death or serious injury, or a threat to the physical integrity of self or others

(2) the person's response involved intense fear, helplessness, or horror[16]

Trauma, at least in its clinical meaning, describes an event that involved a direct threat to self or others and that provoked a response of profound stress and anxiety.

That said, most people experience one or more traumas in the course of their lives without ever developing the sort of long-term emotional disruption associated with PTSD. In 1996 a team of researchers conducted a randomized survey of more than two thousand individuals living in the Detroit area; they found that 89.6 percent of those surveyed had experienced at least one trauma, with nearly 40 percent having survived a violent assault of one type or another.[17] What is remarkable, however, is that only about 10 percent of these individuals went on to develop PTSD. The likelihood of developing PTSD was far greater among those who had experienced sexual assault or a violent attack; still, even among those who survived these kinds of violence, the probability of later developing PTSD rose to only 20.9 percent overall. Other studies report widely varying rates of trauma exposure and PTSD in the general population, largely depending on the population investigated and the definitions of trauma or PTSD used in the study. Even so, these studies invariably come to similar conclusions, reporting a wide gap between the number of people exposed to trauma and those who go on to experience PTSD.[18]

This gap holds true for veterans as well. A recent army study of combat exposure among some eighty-eight thousand military personnel returning from Iraq and Afghanistan found that 66 percent reported firing their weapon, witnessing death or injury, or feeling in danger of being killed. At the same time, only 12 percent of individuals in this same group were found to be showing signs of possible PTSD.[19]

Thus although PTSD is an understandable outcome of living through some of the events described above, it is not an inevitable one. One man's horror is another man's difficult-but-not-devastating-just-another-day-in-Iraq. In chapter 2 Tony admitted that mortar attacks were frightening but ultimately shrugged them off as part of ordinary life, whereas Jesse was so afraid in "Mortaritaville" that he slept under his body armor as if it were a security blanket, knowing full well it was unlikely to save him if he were hit. Mental health clinicians and researchers have spent decades trying to understand why two individuals may live through the same event and have dramatically different reactions, why one soldier may develop PTSD and another may not. One of the key findings of the work in this area has been the recognition that the *accumulation* of stressful events over the course of a lifetime increases an individual's risk of developing PTSD.[20] For example, Tony was put at greater risk for developing PTSD related to combat because he had been exposed to family and street violence as a child. As his story makes very clear, trauma is not only a characteristic of combat zones. It is also abundantly available in the abuses, accidents, disasters, rapes, and other violences of life at "peace" as well.

In an effort to learn whether any such accumulation of violence had an impact on Iraq and Afghanistan veterans in the San Antonio study, I included measures of both predeployment stressful events and combat exposure as part of the interview itself. Veterans completed a written survey in which they filled out a checklist of stressful life experiences. What emerged from these data was the crucial recognition that stressful experiences were part of life for many of the fifty men in this group even prior to deployment to Iraq or Afghanistan. Twenty percent had already engaged in combat or been exposed to a war zone prior to landing in Baghdad or Kabul. Twenty-two percent had witnessed physical violence between their parents or other caregivers. Another 22 percent had grown up with a parent who had a drug or alcohol problem. Some 30 percent reported having been emotionally mistreated—being "shamed, embarrassed, ignored, or told I was no good"[21]—while 52 percent reported having been physically injured by another person in childhood. Four percent had been sexually abused or assaulted as children. This is not inconsistent with what one might expect from a predeployment military population. A study of more than fifteen thousand active-duty military personnel conducted in the late 1990s (i.e., before the beginning of the current wars) found that 65 percent of military men and women had experienced at least one trauma in their lives.[22]

The San Antonio veterans who participated in the PDS study, however, did report levels of combat exposure that were considerably higher than those documented among a general sample of soldiers serving in Iraq and Afghanistan.[23] Among this group, 84 percent reported going on combat patrols or other missions, and 98 percent reported being on the receiving end of incoming fire.[24] Another 78 percent reported having witnessed a fellow service member being injured or killed, and almost half, 48 percent, believed they had killed someone in the line of duty.[25] During the survey, veterans also completed the

Post-Traumatic Stress Disorder Checklist—Military Version (PCL-M), which collects information on the severity of PTSD symptoms within the preceding month.[26] When veterans' self-reported PTSD symptoms were analyzed alongside levels of combat exposure, past combat exposure and current PTSD symptoms were significantly correlated. In other words, those veterans who reported witnessing and engaging in more combat in Iraq or Afghanistan were also likely to report more severe PTSD symptoms.[27]

And, as we discussed above, these men faced yet another set of stressors when they returned home. Those who left the service embarked on the process of creating a postmilitary life for themselves. More than a third of these veterans (38%) were also injured in combat, with wounds ranging from scrapes and bruises to severe burns and amputations. Those—like Derek—who faced injuries requiring long-term care were forced to put military, school, or career ambitions on hold, at least for a time, while they shifted onto a trajectory of recovery and rehabilitation.

Among the myriad experiences of homecoming, one of the greatest sources of variation was the social world to which the veteran returned. Most veterans returned home to wives or girlfriends, but veterans and support personnel often suggested that single service members might be at particular risk for becoming isolated after deployment. One veteran whose marriage had fallen apart prior to his tour in Iraq said that when he returned home, "I didn't want to be home. I wanted to be back over there [in Iraq]. I got nobody back here. I see everybody else has wives, kids, fiancées, girlfriends, and they're all happy, and I'm just getting off the bus, just trying not to cry." He moved into an apartment equipped only with a mattress and a TV and took refuge in his work and his friends.

Even for those service members who return to wives or girlfriends there is no guarantee that all will be well. Suicide among military personnel has been on the increase in the years since the wars started. Two thousand eight was another record year for army suicides (since record keeping began in 1980), with 128 confirmed suicides. This puts the army suicide rate at 20.2 per 100,000, surpassing the 19.5 per 100,000 rate in the nation as a whole, which is remarkable given that the military has traditionally had *lower* suicide rates than the general population.[28] In May of 2007 the press reported that army officials were, as one article put it, "reluctant to draw a link between combat exposure and suicide" and instead pointed to failed personal relationships stressed by long and repeated deployments.[29] Colonel Elspeth Ritchie, chief psychiatrist for the army, said during a conference call with reporters that "multiple deployments and long deployments put a real strain on relationships." She also noted that "there's also normal girlfriend-boyfriend breaking up, marital difficulties that arise in both civilians and soldiers."

My initial response to hearing these statements was, I must admit, some frustration at what seemed to be a blatant minimization of the role of combat exposure in soldier suicides. The epidemiological data, however, bear out the influence of personal relationships on service members' health and well-being, both during and after deployment. Among soldiers who committed suicide in 2007, 50 percent had had a "recently failed intimate relationship."[30] In addition to shaping suicide risk, relationships also play a role in mental health more generally. Research conducted since the 1980s has consistently shown that social support is an important piece of understanding warriors' vulnerability to PTSD. Higher levels of social support—that nebulous term that describes having people to turn to for practical and emotional help and encouragement—have been found to mediate the effects of combat exposure and to predict lower susceptibility to PTSD and greater resilience to stress.[31] In one 1994 study, Alan Fontana and Robert Rosenheck found that two factors made the greatest contribution to PTSD risk among Vietnam veterans: combat exposure and a lack of perceived support from friends and family at the time of homecoming.[32] A variety of other studies have come to similar conclusions,[33] which makes sense. Social support is regularly found to help protect against most mental health problems, so why not PTSD?

The challenge with PTSD, however, is that although social support can be protective, there is evidence to suggest that veterans with PTSD symptoms are likely to receive *less* social support over time. Because PTSD can have a detrimental effect on social relationships, those who develop it may find they have fewer social ties to draw on as the years go by. This pattern was first identified in a retrospective study of Vietnam veterans in 1985 and more recently replicated in a longitudinal study among veterans of the first Gulf War.[34] It points to a vicious cycle in which struggling veterans may find themselves with dwindling access to the social resources necessary for a sense of well-being.

Given the experiences that these veterans have described upon coming home, it becomes clear that both deployment and PTSD have the potential to wreak havoc on family life. A host of studies emerged in the years after Vietnam that spoke to how the families of veterans with PTSD were hard hit by divorce, substance abuse, and family violence.[35] More recently, research among OEF/OIF veterans and spouses has found that both partners express lower relationship satisfaction if the veteran is experiencing trauma symptoms.[36] Studies have found that spouses of veterans with PTSD have more emotional distress, more somatic and sleeping problems, less social support, and less marital satisfaction than do the partners of veterans without PTSD.[37] Among the mental health clinicians I interviewed, it was a common observation that many older veterans with PTSD had gone through three or four marriages over the course of their lives. PTSD is hard on veterans, hard on spouses, and hard on marriages.

These findings are mirrored by the experiences of the San Antonio veterans. Of the fifty I interviewed, nineteen (38%) reported having been divorced or left by a partner since their return home from deployment.[38] Moreover, there was a significant inverse correlation between current PTSD symptoms and lower reported social support since the return home. In other words, veterans who were receiving less social support were likely to have more severe PTSD, and vice versa.[39] Veterans who had been through a recent divorce or breakup *also* reported significantly lower levels of perceived social support, suggesting that the loss of a romantic partner could be a heavy blow to veterans' sense of having adequate social ties.

It seems reasonable that we would see heightened distress related to the failure of relationships after deployment, because these breakups come as a sort of double whammy during what is already a vulnerable period. The veteran may be losing a key source of social support (the departing loved one) at the very same time he is experiencing an additional stressful event (the breakup itself). Linda King and her colleagues have found that such postwar stressful life events, perhaps no less than the beating Tony suffered in the nightclub parking lot, can influence the severity of a veteran's PTSD symptoms.[40] Certainly, men who had been through a recent divorce or breakup described feeling loneliness and isolation, distress at the loss of daily contact with their children, and a sense of failure and betrayal.

What these data suggest is a downward spiral that can begin in the months after homecoming, with a cyclical effect on veterans and their families. Veterans experiencing the problems of early PTSD—anger, withdrawal, disconnection, emotional numbing—are more likely to have trouble holding together their personal relationships. The loss of personal relationships in turn can increase the likelihood that they will experience more severe distress, more anger, and more disconnection. Tony described how this sort of cycle had played out in his own life: "A lot of friends don't call anymore, because when I would go out [after returning home], I would be more aggressive. I would be more alert. Picking fights—not picking fights, but always on the defense. Getting in trouble. Getting thrown out of bars." His friends would tell him, "You're making trouble. People don't want to go out with you." After a while they stopped calling. "Then," he said, "you start getting lonely. Then you start getting depressed." For someone who had always been proud of his close network of friends, the loss was a very real one.

In Tony's depiction of these events, it is striking that none of his friends said to him (at least as he retells it), "Gee, Tony, you've been off at war, and you seem to be having some trouble calming down now that you're back home." No one said, "Tony, have you been checked out for PTSD?" This story illustrates something important about what happened when these veterans came home, which is that the events and experiences described in this chapter mean very little without an understanding of *how they were interpreted* by those involved. In 1973, using what has become a classic example, the anthropologist Clifford Geertz described how culturally specific interpretations can change the meaning of an event.[41] He cited the case of two small boys contracting their right eyelids, one in an involuntary twitch and the other in a purposeful wink. Although both boys make exactly the same movement, one is experiencing a random muscle spasm while the other is conveying a complex message, a "conspiratorial signal." This, says Geertz, is the essence of culture, that the second boy could know there is a public code in which winking conveys a certain message and could communicate via that code simply by twitching his eye at a friend. As Geertz writes, "That's all there is to it: a speck of behavior, a fleck of culture, and—*voila!*—a gesture."[42]

Something similar occurs when a phenomenon like Tony's quickness to anger is interpreted as an act of aggression or, alternatively, as a symptom of PTSD. There is an action or event, which is locally understood to have a particular cause. That cause is understood to prompt one of a range of culturally appropriate responses. The schoolboy's twitch, understood to be a wink, might merit a wink in return, or a giggle or a prank. Witnessing Tony's anger, his friends saw only unacceptable aggression. In response, they just stopped calling.

OF MEN AND MESSAGES

How Everyday Cultural Influences Affect Living with PTSD

Certain kinds of crises make it easy to know what to do next. For air force veteran Chris Monroe, a long period of steadily worsening family conflict, drinking, and hopelessness came to a head when he got drunk one night and, although he blacked out and does not remember, tried to commit suicide. When he came to, he says sheepishly, "I was being wrestled down by half a dozen San Antonio cops. They threw me in the back of the car and took me to the hospital. Fortunately they didn't arrest me. My wife told them I was a veteran, and actually, considering that I hit them and stuff—I physically assaulted an officer—they did me a good one. They didn't arrest me, they took me to the hospital, and I stayed at [a local substance abuse treatment facility] for a few days." He says now, "I just basically knew I had to do something, somehow, somewhere." He went to the local VA hospital and asked for help.

Any number of crises may drive veterans to seek professional mental health care, but four stood out among those I interviewed: persistent thoughts of suicide, domestic violence, alcohol or drug use, and panic attacks. Of these, suicidality is perhaps the most extreme, and is alarmingly common. A recent VA study found that OEF/OIF veterans with PTSD were four times more likely to describe thoughts of suicide than were those with no PTSD (rates are even higher among those with PTSD and other mental illness, such as depression or alcohol or drug abuse).[1] But violence directed against the self was not the only problem. An episode of violence against a family member or a rising rage that seemed to threaten future violence was another crisis that could prompt an immediate response. Carlos remembers that "I started having nightmares.

I'd been having them before that, but I figured it was just the environment. It wasn't until I woke up one day choking my wife that I realized I had a serious problem, and I went to see the mental health people that day." Heavy use of alcohol or drugs, growing worse over time, was another catalyst, particularly when family members became involved and urged the veteran to get help.

For Jesse the crisis was a panic attack, which, although not itself a symptom of PTSD, was ultimately what brought him to the psychiatrist who gave him a PTSD diagnosis. "For four days I had to really concentrate on breathing," he says. "It was like if I stopped concentrating on my breath I would stop breathing. I thought I was having a heart attack. I thought I was dying. I was really scared." It happened again a month later. He went to the emergency service on base and passed out in the clinic "in front of my supervisor and two of my friends. And it was like, 'I came back for *this*?'" One of the friends who had witnessed his attack, and who had served with him on convoys in Iraq, told him that he should go over to the mental health service. Jesse was concerned about losing his security clearance if he sought psychiatric care, but his friend, who also had a security clearance and who had also sought help for PTSD-related problems after he got back, reassured him. Jesse went to the clinic and got help.

But though many veterans seek mental health care because they reach a tipping point, most of the time the challenges that spur veterans to seek help are not so dramatic. In fact, most symptoms and other problems related to PTSD lack this black-and-white immediacy, and thus the task of figuring out how to deal with them is left open to a certain amount of interpretation. In this chapter we will hear how veterans and family members describe responding to PTSD symptoms, particularly in the early period of their emergence. I will also explore how a variety of cultural influences, including American understandings of PTSD and appropriate male behavior, affect these responses, with important implications for practical matters such as how much support family members provide, how veterans perceive and manage their own PTSD, and when and how they may decide to seek care. Finally, we'll also examine how other cultural factors—in this case, Latino ethnicity—may be widely *expected* to shape veterans' responses to PTSD, although the evidence for their actually doing so remains inconclusive, for reasons we will discuss later on.

Derek and Laticia first started to think that Derek might have a problem after he was released from the hospital with his new prosthesis. Memory of the IED that had taken his leg remained fresh in his mind. He says, "[I]t took me a while to get down from that. Especially driving on the road, anything that looked like trash or debris on the side…I had nightmares."

Laticia chimes in, "For the record, we were watching TV with my cousin and they flipped it on a channel and there was two guys joking and laughing in the desert, riding in a Humvee…"

Derek nods, remembering the incident. "Mmm-hmm…"

She continues. "And the next second it blew up. And I turned and looked at my cousin and she turned [the TV] off and I turn and look at Derek. 'You OK?' He says, 'I'm OK.'" Later that night they were driving home, Derek behind the wheel, and, Laticia says, "[H]e's driving like a maniac down the highway." She stopped him: "'You're going to kill us—pull over.' And he was shaking, clearly disturbed." She drove the rest of the way home.

There were other signs. His fear of crowds was so bad that he couldn't go to the grocery store, to the mall, to Six Flags with their kids. I ask how they dealt with that and Derek answers, shrugging toward Laticia, "She busted me a lot."

"Did I?" Laticia asks.

"You busted me a lot."

She nods, accepting this, then adds, "I think I would cry a lot. It was a mix of things—frustration, you don't understand. You don't really understand." Back then, she says, she tried to hear him out but found it difficult to be patient when she couldn't make sense of his problems. They fought on New Year's Eve when she wanted to go spend the holiday with her family and he wanted to stay home, dreading the party crush. Derek remembers that he was still angry when she came home. She defends herself. "You know—it was going from one lifestyle to another, and then dealing with something I couldn't even comprehend. To me it was like, my family's calling, we gotta go to my family. It's my *family!*"

By spring, however, they had fallen into a pattern and things seemed better. That summer they took the boys to Six Flags, and Derek was able to stay for several hours before he began shaking, unnerved by all the people. Another night that summer they tried going out to a club with some friends. Derek says, "I was not having that. Too loud. Too many people. Cannot see everything at once. There was smoke everywhere. And I felt really bad, because we don't get to go out much, with two kids. She was having a really good time, joking. She wants to dance and I'm trying to look everywhere at once. I had the racing heartbeat and I couldn't breathe, and we had to leave."

When fall came, he started college. He purposely chose one of the smaller schools in the area, thinking it would be less crowded and less likely to unnerve him. But over time, he found that he increasingly needed to get to campus a half hour early. "I would walk the perimeter of the buildings and I would walk around inside the building, just looking at everybody and making sure everybody fit and there wasn't a problem before I went to class. And that started becoming a problem, because—if I was out of one class a little late and I couldn't make it to one class without walking around?—I had a really difficult time focusing in class." One day he saw a man standing on the roof and nearly dived to the ground, thinking he was a sniper. "I knew it was crazy. I was thinking, he's either a sniper or he's going to radio ahead. And then I thought, this is San Antonio. There's not snipers on the roof, nobody's going to blow me up here. But I still had to walk around so I wouldn't be nervous in class."

Wives and family members play a key role in helping to shape veterans' experiences of illness, both through offering their own opinions about the source of the problem and in suggesting an appropriate response. Wives in particular are often the prime movers in getting veterans into treatment, and Laticia was trying. She had been telling Derek for months that he needed to go get some help. But the final straw came one day during a class on international terrorism. The professor finished the lecture early and put on a video for the class to watch. Derek says, "And it starts with the Islamic call to prayer, there's one of the jihadist group's flags with the AK-47s, and then this mosque just blew up." He was so upset by the unexpected explosion and the triggers of Iraqi sound and symbol that he fled. And that was it. As he saw it, his problems were now interfering with his ability to pursue a college degree and move ahead with his career plans, and that was unacceptable. He spoke with his vocational rehabilitation counselor about getting some help, and within a few days he had an appointment at the VA for a PTSD evaluation.

In Derek's story, there was no crisis, no single event that forced him into treatment, no immediate danger to himself or his family. Instead, there was a long, slow series of events that made it clear he had a problem, one that was not going away and one that could get in the way of fulfilling his plans for himself and his obligations to his family. This necessitated action.

Both Derek's and Chris's stories have the same sort of narrative sequence. A veteran comes home, faces a series of escalating problems, and ultimately seeks professional care for a possible mental health concern. He may be urged along the way to get help, whether by friends or family members or his military command. This is an easy story to get one's head around because it fits an understood trajectory for what happens in a time of illness. Something goes wrong; we consider the possibility of illness and seek out help of one form or another.

What was striking among veterans, however, was that so many put off seeking care of any kind for the problems they were having. Given the many problems that veterans have described thus far—irritability, nightmares, disconnection from family and friends, difficulty feeling at home in the civilian world—it seems reasonable to ask, why would they hesitate, sometimes for years, before seeking some kind of psychological help?

It turns out there are a variety of answers to this question. Derek and Laticia, for example, first responded to Derek's problems by simply recognizing how they interfered with family life (going to Six Flags, attending family events). It was only when Derek found that his reactions were making it difficult to pursue his educational and career goals that he sought professional mental health care. Derek and Laticia, however, were fairly well informed about PTSD. Derek had spent months in inpatient and outpatient care at Brooke Army Medical Center for the injury to his leg and had received education about PTSD symptoms as part of his regular care.

For those veterans who were not knowledgeable about PTSD, the situation was often less clear. One army veteran named Miguel had no idea what was going on until he went in for a physical at the VA, filled out some questionnaires, and was told he had PTSD. "I'd never heard of it," he recalls. "I was oblivious as to what was actually wrong with me until I was told, 'this is what you're going through.'"

Others had very different ideas about what was happening to them. Chris, for example, never thought of his suicidal urges or his drinking as PTSD-related; he thought it was all explained by depression. Jesse was told at the emergency service that he was having panic attacks, and for a long time he took that to mean that panic attacks were the central problem. Both Chris and Jesse understood their problems as falling under the broad rubric of mental illness and sought out mental health care as a result. But for a surprising number of veterans, particularly those who went off to war in 2002 or 2003, PTSD was simply not on the radar. It had not yet been the focus of the intense media attention that came later, nor was it something—yet—that the military was actively taking steps to educate service and family members about.

As a result, veterans and family members who were unaware of PTSD didn't always understand the phenomena they were experiencing as symptoms that were part of a larger illness. Brian, who had been educated about PTSD during his training as a medic, says he first began to seek out information leading to treatment when he began having memory trouble and started missing important meetings at work. He also says, "[O]ne of the things that tipped me off was my wife said, 'You know what? You're an asshole.' I said, 'Why?' She said, 'You're *mean*. Why are you so mean?' I said, 'You think I'm *mean*?!'"

His wife wasn't saying to him, 'Gee, Honey, I think you have PTSD. I'm worried about you and I think you should go get help.' Instead she told him that he was an asshole. In other words, she was responding not to something she perceived to be a symptom but to what she perceived to be a behavior—or worse, a character flaw. Brian is a medic, and PTSD was something he was already concerned about, and so he understood her comment as a tip-off about the possibility of PTSD. But she wasn't talking about PTSD (in fact, she remained skeptical even after he was formally diagnosed). She was talking about how he was acting, and she wasn't happy about it. Where he saw symptoms, she saw meanness. Where he saw illness, she saw asshole.

Even those families who accepted that a PTSD diagnosis could explain veterans' post-deployment struggles marshaled a wide variety of responses. Some wives, like Laticia, viewed PTSD as one of many things that could happen to service members in wartime, and as something she and Derek needed to face together. Some family members researched PTSD online or in the medical literature, seeking to better understand the diagnosis. Others seemed to mourn their veterans' suffering. I asked a young veteran named Eric about his parents' reaction when he was diagnosed with PTSD; he answered that "they're sad that I had to go through it" and then dived so quickly into another topic that I was unable to find out whether he meant the war or the illness that followed it. Tony told his sister about his run-in with the marine at work, about how it had conjured up memories of Iraq and left him feeling off-kilter and emotional. She cried for him, although once again it was not clear what piece of her brother's story upset her. Perhaps it was the sheer, overwhelming whole of it. These family members saw PTSD, or even war-related suffering more generally, as an experience that called for understanding, the search for more information, and sometimes grief.

But this was not always the case. In some families there was very real stigma. Mariana, the wife of a Vietnam veteran, describes with horror listening to friends and neighbors talk about Iraq veterans who returned home with troubled minds. She recounts conversations overheard at weddings or family gatherings. One mother spoke of her son, who had been diagnosed with PTSD: "I got the idiot here in the house now. He's afraid to come out." A young wife, asked about her husband, responded, "Oh yeah, that dude's a no-good mama's boy—won't come out, just stays in his house." At such moments, Mariana says, "I want to grab the woman by the neck and say, 'Don't ever say those words again. This boy, this *man*, went and fought a war for his country…and you're going to put him down?'"[2]

Such attitudes toward the expression of postwar grief and suffering may make it more challenging for some veterans to settle back into civilian life. They may also make it more difficult for veterans to justify seeking care for what those around them may dismiss as problems of weakness or failed character rather than signs of an illness of great suffering.

There were other, darker notions of PTSD circulating as well, many of which were influenced by wider cultural perceptions of veterans as dangerous men, which also played a role in shaping how veterans and family members viewed and responded to PTSD. In January of 2008, the *New York Times* featured an investigative article claiming to have "found 121 cases in which veterans of Iraq and

Afghanistan committed a killing in this country, or were charged with one, after their return from war." The authors wrote that "[i]n many of those cases, combat trauma and the stress of deployment—along with alcohol abuse, family discord, and other attendant problems—appear to have set the stage for a tragedy that was part destruction, part self-destruction." The authors' language was dramatic; they called such killings "gut-wrenching postscripts to the war for the military men, their victims, and the communities."

The article incited considerable ire from veterans' advocates for its portrait of veterans bringing disaster to the nation they once had served. One blogger for Iraq Veterans against the War responded in a long diatribe entitled, "Does the *New York Times* Hate Veterans?"[3] But the image of veterans as damaged and dangerous was hardly new. It bore the familiar stamp of the post-Vietnam "wacko vet," the subject of films like *Born on the Fourth of July, The Deer Hunter,* or even *Rambo: First Blood.*[4] Nor was the *New York Times*'s viewpoint unique. Other media coverage also linked PTSD with incidents of violence committed by OEF/OIF veterans. The *Economist* published an article in which it was claimed—without citing a source, as though this was knowledge that could be taken for granted—that the effects of PTSD "can range from temporary readjustment problems to suicide and murder, both of which have reached alarming levels among soldiers returning from duty."[5] Beyond their controversy, these media representations resonated with a wider social concern about the unpredictable nature of men who have been taught to kill and then sent off to do it, often unspoken concerns that began coming to light in stories heard around San Antonio.

On October 20, 2009, a group of teenagers were walking down a street in the northeast part of the city when they encountered a twenty-eight-year-old army veteran, Michael Greenstone, standing outside his home. Although the details remain sketchy, it is clear that words were exchanged and threats were made. The teenagers moved on. Greenstone went inside and got his gun. The boys came back by the house a little while later, and Greenstone opened fire, wounding a fifteen-year-old boy. In the police report, the victim and his friends said that Greenstone told them he had just gotten back from Iraq.

In a report of the incident that appeared on a local news station's website, the boy was said to be in good condition. Greenstone was charged with aggravated assault but released on bond shortly after his arrest. Several people weighed in on the shooting in the online story's comments section, offering their own opinions about the event: the kids' parents were to blame for not supervising them; the kids were young punks who should have known better than to tangle with a stranger. One respondent asked, "Anybody know this Michael Greenstone and what kind of character he is? Might have had a roadside bomb blow up too close to him and he's now wacky."

In reply, a respondent calling himself disabled_vet_71903 wrote in: "I know Michael Greenstone, he lived with me for a while when I first got to San Antonio. He is a very nice guy most of the time....He has post-traumatic stress disorder (PTSD) from being in Iraq and literally killing many people during the war. I have seen the pictures first hand, and I know that he was just doing his duty over there, but now that he was thrown into the 'real' world, he can't function. This kid, no matter how old, just pushed the wrong button on a soldier who was trained to do nothing but defend himself when he feels threatened." Disabled vet 71903, in other words, immediately placed Greenstone's act of violence in the context of his personal background as a combat veteran with PTSD. In this account, as in so many, PTSD emerges as associated inevitably with violence: the result of it, the reason for it.[6]

Many of the veterans I interviewed had heard such stories or had their own versions, which they put forward as cautionary tales of what trouble can come to troubled veterans. Manny tells me one day, "I know we had one guy heard a car backfire and he jumps on the median and takes off. And the cops are like, 'What's this guy doing on the median?' I think he gets out of the car and sees their guns, pulls his gun out of the car and, thinking he's in Iraq, he gets into a shoot-out until his wife tackles him or something." Manny says that he doesn't like to tell people he has PTSD because "people will think I'm going to go crazy and shoot everything up." These images of veterans with PTSD as dangerous could permeate home life as well. "She thinks I'm going to get scared and try to kill her or something," Jesse says of his girlfriend and then adds, "A lot of people have that idea, honestly." Carlos felt the need to tell his wife, "I'm not going to be that person who climbs up on a tower and starts shooting."

Sadly, violence among veterans—as attested by the Greenstone shooting—is not only a matter of media-fueled suspicions. Although rates of partner violence among most active-duty military personnel are comparable to those in civilian populations,[7] veterans with PTSD have consistently been found to commit partner violence at rates as high as two or three times the national average.[8] The National Vietnam Veterans Readjustment study found that 33 percent of veterans with PTSD reported having been violent with a spouse or partner in the previous year, while only 13.5 percent of veterans without PTSD made such a report.[9] PTSD has also been found to predict violent behavior among World War II veterans who were prisoners of war, as well as among more recent veterans with other severe mental illness.[10]

Regardless of these numbers, individual veterans may or may not have PTSD and may or may not have violent tendencies. It is easy to understand why PTSD may be associated with increased aggression, given symptoms of elevated irritability and arousal, but violence is not an inherent—or necessary—part of

PTSD.[11] Nonetheless, post-combat veterans remain linked with danger in the public imagination. For some, this fear-tinged, quasiexpectation of violence can become yet another obstacle in their struggle to perform as civilians after years of military life. Even veterans who report no experience with postwar violence may be aware of their own potential for aggression and concerned about it. "I can control myself and I'm fine," Tony says, "But I don't think I've been pushed, and I don't want to be pushed. I know what I can do. One of my jobs in the Marine Corps was to be a close-combat instructor." His girlfriend, he says, "doesn't understand that. I just want people to leave me alone sometimes. When I say leave me alone, please leave me alone. She won't leave me alone, she just gets in my face. So yeah, it worries me. Like, wow."

Though many of the post-deployment phenomena we have discussed may be thought of as PTSD symptoms, they also map onto a series of American cultural ideas about appropriate male behavior. For veterans and family members alike, this overlap can make the task of choosing how to respond to these problems all the more difficult. When Chris first began having trouble, right after he got back from Afghanistan and long before he ended up in treatment, his wife didn't respond by suggesting that he go for medical evaluation. She left him. Tony's friends didn't suggest he get help; they just stopped calling. How do we understand this?

In answering this question, it helps to take a step back and consider normative expectations for men in contemporary American life. In every society, there are cultural expectations that men and women will act within a range of specified behaviors, and these expectations are passed on to children through messages both subtle and direct. Boys may be shamed when they cry ('Don't be such a girl!'), and praised when they demonstrate independence or risk-taking behaviors.[12] Masculine norms that have been identified among American men (which usually means young white men in college, the most frequent sampling pool in psychology research) include an emphasis on competitiveness and winning, desire for dominance, self-reliance, control over emotion, and so on.[13]

In 2006 Matthew Jakupcak and his colleagues, clinicians working out of a VA clinic in Seattle, published an article in which they pointed out that some PTSD symptoms seem to overlap with these traditional American expectations for masculine behavior, citing in particular the tendency toward social withdrawal and restricted emotionality.[14] I also saw this overlap in my conversations with veterans and their wives. Perhaps as a result, veterans' post-deployment symptoms were often interpreted by family members as examples of male behavior rather than as signs of trauma-related illness. Taking it a step further, these symptoms were frequently interpreted in terms of *negative* aspects of traditional masculinity, not just as male behaviors but as unacceptable male behaviors. So, at least from their partners' perspectives, many of these men were viewed not as being ill but as being, to quote Brian's wife, assholes.

In the realm of everyday life, these disjointed viewpoints can create conflict. A veteran experiencing anger and irritability might be told by a clinician that his symptoms indicate PTSD-related hyperarousal. His girlfriend may see it very differently—as testosterone-fueled aggression or an unpleasant tendency to be overly controlling. A clinician might take a veteran's flattened emotional register and desire to isolate as evidence of numbing and withdrawal, but his wife may just wonder why he is being so distant or why he isn't romantic anymore. (She may also personalize the change, believing that he is unhappy with their relationship or doesn't love her anymore.) An inability to hold down steady work may be viewed as a PTSD-related functional impairment, but it may also be seen as a failure to live up to cultural expectations that a husband and father will provide for his wife and children. One of the clinicians I interviewed pointed out this disjuncture, noting that men in particular may display irritability as an alternative to showing anxiety, and so veterans' avoidance may look very much like what she called "macho withdrawal."[15] Another clinician pointed out that although she tries to make educating family members a part of the care she provides to veterans with PTSD, very few spouses will agree to visit the clinic because they don't give much credence to PTSD as the source of their husbands' problems. As she said, 'They just think they're plain angry mean people.'

Among the nine Iraq-era couples I interviewed, nearly all had mismatches between the veteran's post-deployment experiences and his partner's gendered expectations. Laurie described how Josh would yell at her "like one of his marines" after he returned from his first deployment, which she found infuriating because "usually the woman's the boss of the house." One couple who was clearly still very affectionate (she kept her feet up in his lap throughout their interview) was struggling because he had become distant with her, short-tempered with their kids, and uninterested in their previously active sex life. He was failing to live up to her expectations of him as a husband, father, and lover. Thus it was ideas both about illness and about male gender roles that were important in shaping family members' responses to veterans' post-deployment struggles.

Struggling with symptoms they may not always comprehend, and surrounded by the intensely personal words, actions, and judgments of families and friends, individual veterans must find a way to get the support they need while retaining an identity they can live with. In this way, male veterans' own understandings of masculinity also play a role in shaping their experience of PTSD and care seeking.[16]

In the United States it has been widely recognized that many of the messages men receive—about self-reliance, for example—can run into direct conflict with the need to reach out for help when injured or unwell, a finding that may help to explain why many men express reluctance to seek out health care or social support.[17] Ximena Mejia has described the essential features of American manhood as "toughness, fearlessness, and the denial of vulnerability" and suggests that these expectations may create unique challenges for men who have been exposed to trauma.[18] Men may find it difficult to identify with the idea of being traumatized (which can carry with it some implication of being a victim), or may, when they experience uncontrollable emotion, see it as a threat to their sense of themselves as invulnerable and tough.[19] When at last they do seek help, men may also receive less empathy from those to whom they turn for solace and treatment. Edward Thompson and Joseph Pleck offer the example of men who are turned away from rape crisis centers after surviving sexual assault.[20]

When I set out to conduct this research, therefore, I was interested in finding out more about how male OEF/OIF veterans understood their own masculinity and whether this had any impact on their experiences of and responses to PTSD.[21] I have already described how PTSD may be stigmatized or seen as a weakness of character. In addition, many of the post-deployment life impairments we've been discussing, such as failing relationships, the inability to hold a job, etc., may be viewed as not living up to one's role as an adult American male.

Of course, because San Antonio is a majority Latino city, and because 50 percent of the veterans in this study identified themselves as Hispanic or Latino, I found it impossible to ignore the question of whether Latino and non-Latino veterans might describe *different* images of masculinity, with potentially different implications for how they viewed their own PTSD. There was another good reason to ask this question. Researchers in the United States have found that Latino populations exposed to traumatic events are significantly more likely to develop PTSD than are non-Hispanic whites or African Americans with similar trauma exposure.[22] One study among Vietnam veterans found that whereas only 13.7 percent of white veterans met the criteria for current PTSD, rates among Latinos climbed to 27.9 percent, even after controlling for risk factors known to be the strongest predictors of PTSD, such as cumulative exposure to life stressors.[23] These findings stand out, it should be noted, because they go against the observation that Latinos in the United States generally have *better* mental health than do their non-Latino white counterparts.[24]

This, however, is where it's a good idea to come clean about a few problems with clinical and epidemiological research, particularly when it comes to race and/or ethnicity.[25] Epidemiology, which provides the science behind much of public health policy and decision making, tries to make sense of patterns of health and illness as they occur among people with different characteristics—for example, where they live, whether they may have been exposed to an epidemic, whether they engage in risk behaviors like smoking, etc. For this very practical reason—as well as the fact that attempting to explain anything having to do with human beings gets very complicated very fast—most epidemiological research is better at lumping people into analytic categories than it is at reflecting individual differences. As a result, when studies set out to measure "ethnicity," they may actually be measuring a number of different things, not all of which are comparable. In my study, I assessed ethnicity by asking people to tell me what their ethnicity was. This is generally considered a good way to go about it—better, anyway, than using last names or other proxy measures—but even so, it often fails to account for a wide variety of very real differences among people: whether a person was born in the United States or Honduras (immigration status, personal history); whether a man's father is of Mexican but his mother of German descent (heritage); whether a woman identifies as Cuban American but has spent her life living among whites in a wealthy suburb where there were few minorities, much less a strong Cuban presence (socioeconomic status, ethnic composition of community). Ethnicity is a fuzzy thing to measure in research because it is equally fuzzy in real life.

One of the most important consequences of this fuzziness is a tendency to conflate ethnicity with *culture*.[26] As an illustration, a number of hypotheses have been put forward to explain findings that Latinos are more likely to develop PTSD than their white or African American peers. One recent study, which identified elevated PTSD symptom severity among Latino police officers, suggested this might be explained by cultural factors such as coping through self-blame, perceived racism, and dissociation at the time of trauma (a factor identified elsewhere as increasing risk for combat-related PTSD).[27] Other physicians and epidemiologists have attempted to explain ethnic differences in PTSD risk in terms of common Latin American idioms of distress such as *ataque de nervios* or *susto*. Although these illnesses are characterized by slightly different symptoms (listlessness and general malaise in the case of susto, and nervousness and irritability in ataque de nervios), both are thought to occur when acute stress or fright results in a dislocation between body, soul, and the social world—a set of culturally local phenomena that bear strong resemblance to biomedical definitions of dissociation.[28] Though both of these suggested explanations draw on cultural norms among (some) Latinos, they run the risk of assuming that ethnicity and culture are one and the same, when in fact both are heterogeneous and may or may not overlap as expected.

This messiness gets even worse when we begin to consider where discussions of ethnicity and masculinity intersect. When Mexican American or Latino men are the focus of scholarly discussion, their identity as men is often described in terms of *machismo,* a complex of masculine behaviors and attitudes widely held to be common across Latin America.[29] The literature on machismo often casts it in fairly negative terms, emphasizing hypermasculine traits such as physical and emotional toughness, sexual jealousy, a stiff-necked and unbending aggressiveness, and the exercise of control over women (particularly over women's sexuality).[30] As Latinos have come to represent a larger and more influential percentage of the U.S. population, the word "macho" has slipped into common American usage, and machismo has become something of an American folk model for how Latin men behave.[31] Alfredo Mirandé has argued that since this development, "macho" has come to have dual meanings.[32] When used to describe athletes and entertainers and other high-status individuals (of all ethnicities), it denotes strength, sex appeal, and a virile masculinity; in contrast, when used to describe the average Latino, it remains linked to stereotypes of male dominance, family violence, and patriarchy. Machismo is an idea that, although problematic, retains a powerful hold over the way that many Americans think about Latino men.

Given the increased risk of PTSD among Latino veterans, I was curious when I began the PDS study to see whether Latinos and non-Latinos would have different views of their own masculinity and whether this might have any implications for shaping vulnerability after trauma. Four of the clinicians I spoke with—three of whom were Latina—were enthusiastic about this idea, endorsing the role of a macho identity in shaping the responses of Latino men to experiences of suffering and illness. One Latina clinician told me, 'There's a macho image in our Hispanic patients and Mexican patients,' before elaborating on what this meant to her: 'They're very resistant to showing they're vulnerable. They're tough, they're soldiers, they're not going to cry.'

For all the discussion of macho and machismo, however, I often found it difficult to reconcile the common view of Latino men with my own experience of living and working among men in San Antonio. I encountered dozens of Latino men whose behavior belied the stereotypical macho image: men who spoke proudly about their role as primary caregiver for their children, laughed their way out of potential confrontations, and publicly and privately nurtured their wives. This is an inconsistency that has been noted by other anthropologists as well. In the mid-1960s Arthur Rubel wrote of his surprise upon visiting the homes of his young South Texas informants—who had complained at length about the gruff authoritarianism of their Mexican American fathers—to find these fathers cradling infants and playing with small children, their suggestions and commands largely ignored by other family members.[33] By contrast, I found that the idea of machismo often seemed quite applicable to some of the white men I encountered. Certain Texas Anglos (a local term for whites) reflect what

I have come to think of as "cowboy macho," demonstrating a marked hesitation to show emotion and bragging about incidents in which they have refused to back down from a confrontation. One (white male) clinician I talked to about this described the phenomenon as "the Bubba Syndrome" and acknowledged that both Latinos and whites can have difficulty accepting a diagnosis of PTSD because it doesn't "fit with the masculine stereotype."

This close resemblance between local Latino and non-Latino masculinities came through in the PDS study as well, although the participation of only a handful of African American, Native American, and Asian American veterans made it difficult to tease out what may be finer distinctions among non-Latino white and minority veterans (hence my use of the broad-brush term "non-Latino," which is admittedly as hazy a category as any critiqued in the above discussion of epidemiology). Study data showed no differences in symptom severity for PTSD, depression, or anxiety between Latino and non-Latino groups.

In another part of the interview, veterans were asked to rank their expectations for themselves as adult men in order of priority, drawing on a list of items that were volunteered by a pilot group of veterans and included things like holding a job, making a romantic partner happy, caring for children, and so on. When these rankings were compared between Latino and non-Latino groups, there were only two variables on which there were significant differences by ethnicity. For one, men in the non-Latino group were significantly more likely to rate the importance of the item "maintaining my pride in myself" as of a higher priority than were men in the Latino group. The second difference was that individuals in the Latino group were significantly more likely to rate the importance of "caring for my parents" higher than were non-Latinos. In other words, Latinos appeared to be more likely than non-Latinos to prioritize other items on the list above personal pride, particularly caring for their parents and being a spiritual person, although the latter did not achieve statistical significance.[34]

Looking at the data more closely, however, reveals that individuals within the groups varied quite a bit on their responses—some ranked "being able to hold a job" as of primary importance, while others put this item in last place. There was nearly this great a range on every item. When the data were lumped together into ethnic groups, these differences disappeared almost entirely, a finding that reinforces one of the great and too rarely asserted facts of any research around race or ethnicity in the United States: the differences between individuals are often far greater than the differences between groups.

Thus, rather than supporting my initial hypothesis that differences in masculinity norms might help to explain supposed differences in PTSD risk among Latino veterans, the San Antonio data do something very different. They point to key *individual* differences in how Latino and non-Latino men have absorbed the messages and influences of their own social and cultural milieus, and in how these influences have shaped the expectations against which they measure themselves. An individual's ethnicity may, in some circumstances, provide a clue as to what cultural influences are most salient for him or her, but no stronger statement can be made, particularly for those living amid the kind of rich cultural mix that characterizes both San Antonio and the United States more broadly.

Nevertheless, norms for masculinity do turn out to be important, as shown in another study conducted out of the San Antonio VA clinic.[35] Examining masculine behavioral norms and PTSD symptoms among OEF/OIF veterans receiving VA treatment for PTSD, several VA colleagues and I found no significant difference in the masculine norms reported by Latino, white, and African American veterans. However, we did find evidence to suggest that men who identify with different kinds of masculine norms are likely to have different patterns of PTSD symptoms. Men who reported being very self-reliant and concerned with maintaining control were more likely to have higher PTSD scores overall and showed markedly higher symptoms of hyperarousal and hypervigilance. This makes sense. Men who are uncomfortable feeling out of control are likely to feel doubly threatened by the extreme feelings associated with PTSD; not only are the feelings themselves overwhelming, but the very fact of *feeling* them may seem like an unbearable failure to maintain self-control.

But what was really striking in these findings was something unexpected: men who reported having a greater dedication to achieving success—another important aspect of American masculinity—were *less* likely to experience symptoms of avoidance. In other words, this facet of masculine norms appeared to have some protective or adaptive function for these men. We can only speculate as to the reasons for this. It may be that men with a stronger dedication to success are more likely to push through feelings of avoidance in pursuit of their goals or to seek treatment when they encounter problems.[36] Derek, for example, put off seeking care until his symptoms began to interfere with his ability to attend class, thereby threatening to interfere with his long-term plan for education and career.

I should reiterate that these are new findings, from a relatively small study, and only time will tell whether other studies bear them out. But they return us to the central point here, which is that cultural influences can have an important impact on how veterans and those around them respond to PTSD, whether in terms of experiencing symptoms, seeking out professional care, or providing social support. How veterans and family members understand early symptoms—as illness, moral failing, or bad behavior—influences what they do about them, whether demanding behavioral change, seeking treatment, or falling into negative cycles of conflict, self-blame, or substance abuse.

Even after his diagnosis, Chris's wife remained noncommittal about his illness. She thought he used it as an excuse for letting her down in other ways. He in turn acknowledged that he had not always lived up to either of their ideas of a good husband—had not always been present, either emotionally or physically, when she needed him. He seemed to be drawing on something like a model of relational exchange as he spoke, as though, because he had not lived up to her expectations, he should not be surprised to find that she was impatient with his PTSD.

Even so, not all cultural influences are necessarily relevant, or at least not in the ways we might expect them to be. The question of whether Latino ethnicity influences risk for developing PTSD remains complex. An important study released in 2008 found that ethnic differences in PTSD rates among Vietnam veterans could be better explained by a variety of other factors: Latino veterans tended to have been younger when they went to war, to have seen more combat, and to have received less education than white veterans, all factors known to increase risk of PTSD.[37] But the results of such studies have not been consistent. A 2009 study looked at civilians who developed PTSD after traumatic injury and found that Latinos typically developed more severe PTSD, and displayed a different pattern of symptoms, than did whites or African Americans.[38] It is possible that some of this inconsistency can be explained by the difference between veteran and civilian populations. William Lorber and Hector Garcia, two VA psychologists, have suggested that the military is itself a powerful cultural influence, with very real implications for veterans' views on masculinity and PTSD care seeking.[39] We may find in future research that this shared experience of military culture is as powerful as ethnicity in shaping veterans' experiences of PTSD. If so, that in turn might help to explain some of the inconsistency of findings from veteran and civilian populations.

In the meantime, the data on Latinos and PTSD remain too contradictory and too troubled by the existence of potential confounding factors to allow us to draw any confident conclusions. Latinos in America are an incredibly varied population, representing the full spectrum of differences in class, education, and cultural background (from Puerto Rico to Paraguay), and it is difficult to account for this kind of heterogeneity in epidemiological studies. Nor can we ignore the role of history in framing experience, as I am reminded every time I encounter Mexican American, African American, or Native American veterans who have stood up proudly to fight for their country, regardless of how this nation may have treated them or their forebears. The lesson to remember is that though it is vital to recognize the profound impact such cultural influences may have on the experience of PTSD, there is no way to predict what they will mean for any given veteran living with that inner turmoil or wondering what to do next.

CLINICAL HISTORIES
From Soldier's Heart to PTSD

As far back as the Civil War, American military physicians have recognized and classified combat stress casualties into such categories as "insanity," "nostalgia," and what was called "soldier's heart," or "irritable heart."[1] Individuals found to be insane were prevented from engaging in military service and dealt with as individual commanders saw fit, often treated as cowards or malingerers. Once the fighting stopped, Civil War veterans appear to have struggled with many of the functional and behavioral problems we continue to see among PTSD-diagnosed veterans today. The historian Eric Dean has uncovered accounts of physically sound veterans who after the war became unable to work, violent against family and friends, suicidal, or addicted to alcohol.[2] Certain individuals, moreover, were even able to secure government pensions for war-related psychological disability, although such claims were denied more often than not.

The American military community, then, has recognized that engaging in combat could have profound psychological consequences since at least the Civil War. Nonetheless, the understanding of combat stress has transformed dramatically in the intervening years, culminating in the American Psychiatric Association's (APA's) pivotal decision in 1980 to formally recognize post-traumatic stress disorder as a diagnosis. Reviewing how expert opinion on combat stress has changed over time reveals significant developments in the scientific observation of trauma and its aftermath, in the evolution of psychiatry as a medical profession, and in the way distressed soldiers and veterans are treated. My aim here is to lay a foundation for understanding these developments, for they will prove to be important when we turn in the next few chapters to a discussion of how the military and VA are responding to the needs of contemporary veterans.

Combat stress acquired one of its most evocative names—"shell shock"—nearly a century ago. Early in World War I, at the end of 1914, British physicians in France first began seeing patients who displayed odd symptoms. Some showed no injury or organic illness but were unable to see, smell, taste, or remember.[3] This form of hysterical paralysis—usually inhibiting the use of a limb or sensory function—was considered a common symptom of combat stress at the time. Its emergence in World War I seems to have marked the tail end of an epidemic of hysteria that swept the United States and much of western Europe during the nineteenth century, for these symptoms virtually disappear from later descriptions.[4] Other stress casualties vomited excessively or were possessed by continual tremors. In 1915 the psychologist Charles S. Myers published an article attributing these symptoms to a sudden shock to the nervous system caused by the explosion of artillery shells within close range.[5] Myers called the phenomenon shell shock, and although he later discarded the idea of physiological shock as the cause of the syndrome, the name lingered on in use for years.

Despite Myers's rapidly developed theory, there was a wider sense that World War I had caught the medical profession by surprise, and without the necessary tools to treat the phenomena they were seeing. Psychiatry as a medical discipline did not begin to take on its modern form until the 1800s, and as of World War I it remained a relatively new field. W. H. R. Rivers, a prominent British psychiatrist and anthropologist, wrote in 1920 that military psychiatrists had been "wholly unprepared for the vast extent and varied forms in which modern warfare is able to upset the *higher functions of the nervous system* and the *mental activity* of those called upon to take part in it."[6] He bemoaned the fact that military psychiatrists lacked a "common body of principles and measures" with which to deal with combat stress. In the absence of such consensus, considerable controversy arose over what conditions were the result of physiological or neurological causes, as shell shock was thought to be, and what conditions were the result of psychological causes, like hysteria or the neuroses. The disagreement took shape as part of a larger debate over the centrality of the physical brain as opposed to the psychological mind in determining human behavior and experience.

This debate—in many ways, one that is still ongoing today—offers one example of how the continuing development of psychiatry as a field would be reflected in the evolution of ideas about combat stress across the twentieth century. During certain periods, particularly in times of war, such evolution could be rapid. By the end of the war, shell shock was no longer thought to require an actual concussion of the nervous system by artillery but was believed to be caused by emotional rather than physical shock. The diagnosis of shell shock was increasingly being replaced by that of "war neurosis" or "traumatic neurosis."[7] Thus the understanding of what combat trauma actually meant—what processes it revealed within the person—changed dramatically within a few short years.[8]

During this same period, clinicians were also engaged in negotiating with military unit commanders over how to distinguish between soldiers whose symptoms reflected true psychological strain and those who were malingering in the face of a grueling war. Ben Shepherd has written that the British army in World War I had a "rough and ready model of human psychology, and its own clear-cut labels. Men were either sick, well, wounded, or mad; anyone neither sick, wounded, nor mad but nonetheless unwilling to or incapable of fighting was necessarily a coward, to be shot if necessary."[9] World War I was, at least for the Europeans, characterized by long battles conducted from death- and disease-ridden trenches, a miserable and exhausting form of warfare.[10] At certain points in the fighting, as when the Germans launched a gas offensive in March of 1918, cases of hysterical paralysis and other psychiatric problems outnumbered the wounded, sometimes by as much as two to one.[11] There was no standard policy for dealing with these cases, and Shepherd has described the resulting chaos: "Depending on the circumstances, a shell-shocked soldier might earn a wound stripe and a pension (provided his condition was caused by enemy action), be shot for cowardice, or simply be told to pull himself together by his medical officer and sent back to duty."[12] Between 1914 and 1918, the British army executed 307 men for cowardice, many of whom, judging by case descriptions, may have been suffering from shell shock.[13] (A group pardon was issued for these men by the British Ministry of Defense in August of 2006.)[14]

The increasingly desperate situation necessitated the creation of a systematic policy for dealing with war neurosis. The system developed by the British and French, and adopted later with minor modifications by the Americans, was designed in part as an attempt to keep fighting men as close to the front as possible. As an added benefit, it provided the opportunity to sort cases of mental and physical exhaustion, which were seen as short-term problems, from cases of severe war neurosis.[15] The model was the result of trial and error in the early part of the war, when it was recognized that soldiers returned to combat seemed to recover more quickly and more fully than those who were sent home.[16]

Briefly, the system relied upon three echelons of care with responsibility for providing triage, treatment, and, as promptly as possible, the soldier's return to duty. The first echelon involved assigning a psychiatrist to each army division, with mobile care units available close to the front. Combat stress cases were given psychiatric evaluation, and the majority returned to duty after a brief rest.[17] Second-echelon care was provided by neurological hospitals behind the lines. These hospitals offered longer periods of rehabilitation to more severe cases; still, some 55 percent of these were returned to duty within a few weeks.[18] Third-echelon care occurred in a rear-located base hospital, where cases received further treatment and, depending on the treatment's success, could ultimately be returned to the front, reassigned to other duty, or evacuated home.[19] This rough system of triage seemed to work, allowing clinicians to sort through psychiatric casualties and channel soldiers into care as needed, and it was ultimately the system that got the British, French, and Americans through the war.

Following World War I, changes in civilian psychiatry prompted a reevaluation of the echelon system's reliance on treatment rather than prevention. Adolph Meyer was the dominant voice in psychiatry between the wars, and his school of thought emphasized the importance of individual characteristics, including past life experiences, in shaping a person's response to stressful situations like combat.[20] World War I had revealed that individuals react in a wide variety of ways to wartime experiences, and this was taken as evidence that it was individual predisposition that resulted in neuropsychiatric disorder, rather than the innate challenges of battle itself.[21]

Impetus to test this new theory was provided by the astonishing amount of money, approaching $1 billion, the U.S. government spent on veterans' psychiatric illness between the wars.[22] In 1940 a shifting and not-well-standardized process of interviewing, records review, and personality testing was implemented as part of a radical new plan to prevent combat neurosis by screening out unsuitable candidates.[23] Though vigorously applied, the new selection process was largely a failure. Some 1.3 million American service members—all of whom had passed without trouble through screening—experienced a psychiatric illness during the course of World War II, and in July of 1943, the three-echelon prevention and treatment system developed during World War I was reimplemented.[24] The old system was updated with new technologies, adding group therapy and sedative drugs to the treatment repertoire of military clinicians.

By the end of World War II, military psychiatrists saw some important gains in their knowledge about combat stress. First, they came to recognize that any individual, under the right circumstances, could be susceptible to combat stress, because intensive screening had done little to reduce the psychiatric casualty rate (the rate at which men had to be released from duty for mental health reasons).[25] Second, they came to appreciate that the greatest source of strength for soldiers was cohesion within the combat unit. Service members who were kept close to their units were more likely to recover and return to duty. Third, they found that normalizing soldiers' experiences seemed to help in preventing an escalation of symptoms, and that treatment was more effective when it included communicating the expectation of a full recovery. It was this realization that led to another change in the way combat stress was named and understood: the term "war neu-rosis" began to be replaced with the less-stigmatizing "combat fatigue."[26] There was also renewed recognition that combat fatigue came in several forms, ranging from a temporary and nondisabling form of fatigue that was seen almost uni-versally across combat units—including symptoms of exaggerated startle, sleep disturbance, and mild somatic complaints—to what came to be known as "old sergeant's syndrome," a condition of exhaustion and burnout in which the most combat-hardened soldiers showed signs of decreased movement, depression, increased aggression, tremors, and fatalism.[27] Last, an effective system of triage and care had been developed, leaving military psychiatrists with an agreed-upon way of handling combat stress while in theater.

But World War II had an important effect on combat stress beyond efforts to develop appropriate diagnoses and treatments. The demobilization of some 10 million men after the war helped to destigmatize mental illness in the postwar period, for the lingering idea that World War II–era service members suffered no ill effects upon returning home does not bear up under scrutiny.[28] The 1946 film *The Best Years of Our Lives* made an Oscar-winning attempt to document veter-ans' turbulent homecomings, telling the story of three veterans who variously fall back upon alcohol, isolation, and the solace of other veterans in their efforts to reenter civilian life. By 1947, the VA was providing pensions for neuropsychiatric disabilities to nearly half a million veterans.[29] There were significant changes in national policy during this period, including the National Mental Health Act of 1946, which provided for the establishment of community-level mental health clinics, allotted funding to support research into the causes and treatment of neuropsychiatric disorders, and created the National Institute for Mental Health (NIMH).[30] Meanwhile, cases of traumatic neurosis that developed long *after* ini-tial combat exposure began to be documented in the clinical literature, and new drugs such as Valium became available for the treatment of anxiety.[31]

When the Korean War began in 1950, the triage system was reintroduced and held up, with few revisions, through the Korean, Vietnam, and first Gulf Wars. Indeed, the U.S. Army's current system of Combat and Operational Stress Con-trol (COSC) is based around the same three-tiered program developed by the British in World War I. A typology of combat stress distinguishes critical incident stress (a reaction to a specific incident), battle fatigue, and other categories—all of which diverge from PTSD because they focus on the stresses of recent or ongo-ing events, whereas PTSD can by definition be considered only when thirty days have elapsed since the trauma.[32] It is significant, too, that whereas PTSD is gener-ally accepted to be a *mental illness,* combat stress is identified in many military materials as representing a *normal reaction to challenging events.*[33] It is officially defined as the "expected and predictable emotional, intellectual, physical, and/ or behavioral reactions of service members who have been exposed to stressful events in war or military operations other than war."[34] The military has retained its emphasis on normalizing the experience of combat stress.

Though it has evolved somewhat, the basic COSC system is still intended to provide a multipronged strategy for the prevention and treatment of combat stress reactions. This strategy ideally includes a variety of activities, including predeployment and post-deployment mental health screenings, a system of mental health surveillance, and multilevel management of stress by individual service members, other unit members and buddies, and leadership.[35] Combat stress control units, composed of army psychiatrists, clinical psychologists, and other mental health professionals, are intended to remain mobile throughout the combat zone and to provide combat stress support to soldiers and leadership wherever necessary, available on demand.[36] In recent decades the ongoing development of second-generation antidepressants and other psychotropic medications with relatively few side effects has revolutionized the pharmaceutical arsenal of clinicians providing care in the field.[37]

In other respects the official protocol for managing stress casualties during the current conflicts remains surprisingly consistent with that of previous wars. Individuals displaying symptoms are supposed to be examined by combat stress control (CSC) units or other available mental health personnel and provided with twenty-four- to seventy-two-hour "restoration" treatment (usually in Iraq or Afghanistan). "Slow-to-improve" cases may be held for four to twenty-eight days and given additional treatment (usually in Iraq or Kuwait). The most severe cases may be evaluated for additional treatment and/or evacuation to Europe or the United States.[38]

In fact, when one glances back over the historical treatments for combat stress, it is the lessons that have survived over time that are perhaps the most striking: keep soldiers as well cared for as possible during their daily engagements; keep stress casualties near the unit and return them to their unit as soon as possible; provide casualties an opportunity to catch up on food, sleep, hydration, and hygiene; and where appropriate, offer simple reassurance, thoughtful listening, the opportunity to talk over events as they happen, and the expectation of full recovery. The guiding philosophy here is in line with the army's stated position that combat stress is a normal reaction to severe conditions and can largely be prevented or treated with basic care. The goal is always the same: get soldiers back on duty as quickly and as safely as possible.

Although stress reactions during combat were the focus of significant attention throughout the early and mid-twentieth century, it wasn't until the early 1970s, in the aftermath of the Vietnam War, that discussions of postwar stress began to take on a new ardor. Many authors have attempted to explain how Vietnam became the conflict that redefined war trauma for the psychiatric community despite the fact that combat stress casualties in the first years of the conflict were at an all-time low. Psychiatric casualty rates were as high as 101 per 1,000 troops in World War II, dropping to 37 per 1,000 in Korea and 12 per 1,000 in the early years of Vietnam.[39] The conflict in Korea, moreover, had provided an opportunity for military psychiatrists to perfect their system for responding to soldier distress, treating psychiatric casualties close to the front, as quickly as possible, and with the expectation that recovery would be swift and men would return to the front.[40]

Nonetheless, by 1973, Robert Jay Lifton had published the influential book *Home from the War,* which described the postwar suffering of Vietnam veterans succumbing to mental illness, substance abuse, and suicide. He began one chapter with the provocative statement, "Everyone who has contact with them seems to agree that they are different from veterans of other wars."[41] The source of this difference was unclear. Some said it was the lingering disappointment of losing a highly unpopular war. Some blamed the draft, others the ugliness of the guerrilla conflict in theater. Others laid responsibility on the widespread rejection of Vietnam veterans upon the return home or on those who blamed veterans for atrocities committed at My Lai and elsewhere.[42] In the wake of this controversy, a number of clinicians and veterans' advocates joined forces to promote formal recognition of what was originally called "post-Vietnam syndrome," a cluster of symptoms including guilt, rage, numbness, and alienation, as a hitherto undiagnosed and untreated mental illness.

These advocacy efforts from veterans' groups and allied mental health professionals might have been ignored had they not coincided with a radical shift then rocking the foundations of modern psychiatry.[43] Up until the 1970s, many would argue, psychiatric diagnosis was considered something of an interpretive art.[44] The American Psychiatric Association's manual of the field, the *Diagnostic and Statistical Manual of Mental Disorders,* provided lengthy descriptions of each recognized diagnosis, with a heavy emphasis on those, like the neuroses, that had come down through the Freudian psychoanalytic tradition. In the late 1970s, however, a committee was formed to prepare revisions of the *DSM* for its third edition (*DSM-III*). Its members oversaw what was to be a sweeping reconstruction. They took it as their goal to provide a list of key symptoms for each diagnosis so that psychiatrists around the country could identify a diagnosis in terms of whether it met specific criteria—going down a checklist of sorts—rather than based on their own interpretation of the patient's experience. Deceptively simple-sounding, this was a revolutionary attempt to standardize psychiatric diagnosis in an entirely new way.

As this profession-changing *DSM* was being readied for publication, several clinicians approached the *DSM-III* committee to request that post-Vietnam syndrome be considered for inclusion in the new volume. As the anthropologist Allan Young has described it, the committee's chair, Robert Spitzer, was initially reluctant but decided to put together a working committee to investigate the disorder, swayed by the political sensitivity of veterans' issues in those early postwar years.[45] Once assembled and presented with the evidence for a unique post-Vietnam syndrome, the working committee remained reluctant to adopt the disorder, for several reasons. There was little epidemiological research to support the idea that post-Vietnam syndrome was distinct from other mental illnesses, and a number of psychiatrists argued that the disorder's symptoms could be accounted for by preexisting diagnoses, such as depression and anxiety. The only thing that was unique about the syndrome, argued these psychiatrists, was the idea that it could be caused by a particular event—a trauma.

Young has illuminated several of the arguments that ultimately convinced the *DSM-III* committee to adopt the diagnosis, renamed "post-traumatic stress disorder," or PTSD. First of all, there was clinical evidence stretching back a hundred years that seemed to identify a consistent neurosis or stress condition arising after experiences of trauma (including rape or child abuse as well as combat). In addition, no federal research funds had been available for the study of PTSD prior to that time, as the diagnosis was not yet recognized by the APA, and so it seemed unreasonable to expect there would be epidemiological evidence to either support or refute the existence of PTSD as a distinct phenomenon. And finally, there were moral reasons for creating a formal PTSD diagnosis. Since many of those who had fought in Vietnam had gone unwillingly, recruited by the draft and sent off to wage an unsuccessful war, there was a sense that their suffering was the more grave for having been involuntary and perhaps futile. In his account of these events, Young has suggested that the "failure to make a place for PTSD would be equivalent to blaming the victim for his misfortunes—would mean denying medical care and compensation to men who, in contrast to their more privileged coevals, had been obliged or induced to sacrifice their youths in a dirty and meaningless war."[46] Thus Young argues that PTSD as a formally recognized psychiatric disorder came about in large part as the result of political processes rather than scientific ones. The diagnosis was officially adopted because it was thought that the suffering of Vietnam veterans should be recognized, not because any evidence existed at that time to suggest that PTSD represented a wholly new disorder.

Nevertheless, PTSD was included in the 1980 publication of *DSM-III* and in that same year was approved by the U.S. Congress as a disorder for which veterans could receive compensation through the Veterans Administration (now the

Department of Veterans Affairs).[47] Within a year, PTSD had moved from a non-existent diagnosis to an accepted disability for which lifelong compensation was available to qualifying veterans. PTSD was unique in being the first environmentally determined mental disorder ever accepted by the psychiatric community, with a causal model presuming that symptoms were the result of a "traumatic event" that "would evoke significant symptoms of distress in almost anyone."[48]

Though the criteria for diagnosing PTSD have been revised in more recent *DSM* editions, the psychological symptom set has remained largely consistent with those described since the Civil War: restlessness, sleep disturbance, recurrent memories and nightmares, aggression, hypervigilance, exaggerated startle response, etc. Many of the somatic symptoms that were so frequently observed in the Civil and First World wars—such as gastrointestinal distress, pain, and heart palpitations—seem to have fallen off this list. This may be due to the fact that the veterans on whose experience the PTSD symptom list was based were no longer undergoing the same terror and physical exhaustion typically experienced by soldiers during acute stress events; it may also reflect a tendency in American psychiatry to separate out physical symptoms as "somatization" of a mental problem rather than an essential piece of the problem itself.

By the late 1980s, PTSD had been internationally embraced. The diagnosis was increasingly given to survivors of noncombat traumatic experiences—including childhood abuse, rape, motor vehicle accidents, natural disasters, and so forth—having morphed in the process from a war neurosis to a phenomenon of the general population.[49] In 1995, Ronald Kessler and his colleagues screened 8,098 randomly sampled participants in the United States and found that 7.8 percent of them (far higher than the psychiatric casualty rates cited from Korea or the early years of Vietnam) appeared to have PTSD as a result of child abuse or involvement in a life-threatening event.[50] It has been argued that this broadened understanding of traumatic stress reflected one of the great successes of the feminist movement because it acknowledged that women's psychological distress following rape and family violence was equal to the suffering of (until recently almost exclusively male) combat veterans.[51] The broadening was also in many ways a product of the Holocaust; survivors of Nazi concentration camps were found to be suffering distress similar to that of combat veterans, even decades later.[52]

The maturation of ideas about combat stress and PTSD reveals how fluid the understanding of human illness may be, reflecting shifts in notions of cause (artillery explosion, underlying neurosis), symptom (hysterical paralysis, hypervigilance), and—as we will see in chapter 7—treatment. Looking back over the past hundred years provides an opportunity to examine how scientific views on war trauma have altered in accordance with changing paradigms and priorities within psychiatry and the military. At the same time it speaks to the complexity of battlefield events and their effects on physical and psychological health. The heavy reliance on improvised explosive devices in Iraq and Afghanistan, for example, is teaching us a growing amount about the effects of explosive impact on the human brain. Traumatic brain injury (TBI) is, alongside PTSD, one of the signature injuries of these wars, and its signs are at times difficult to distinguish from those of combat stress.[53] The old idea of shell shock has therefore taken on renewed significance as we face a growing epidemic of TBI among OEF/OIF veterans.

This short detour through history provides a critical reminder that although debates over combat stress have often been influenced by outside factors such as politics and the ongoing modernization of psychiatry, they are grounded in more than a century of observation and deal with issues of sincere suffering. They also have very real implications for the strategies used to manage combat stress during and after deployment, which have varied dramatically over time, evolving from execution for cowardice to a multistage system for evaluation and treatment. This evolution set the stage for rapid-fire changes that were to come in the years after September 11, 2001, as the United States embarked on what would become the longest period of war in its history.

UNDER PRESSURE

Military Socialization and Stigma

"When I got back [from Afghanistan]," Chris says, "there was not even so much as a briefing that said, 'Let us know if you're having problems.' There wasn't so much as a [phone] number. There was literally nothing." It was early in the post-9/11 era, the spring of 2002, and the American military machine was far from having mustered the full might it would in the coming years. This may be part of why Chris's transfer received so little attention. And then there were the circumstances of his redeployment. "I was pretty much sent out of country because I—I injured a prisoner, pretty severely. And broke his arm."

He explains that he was not equipped to handle the routine prisoner transfer he was overseeing that day and lost control when the prisoner resisted. He does not remember the event itself, although he is clear on the response by his chain of command. "It was pretty much, 'Maybe you need to go home, and we'll send you to Korea.' That's kind of the humorous part about it, and I look back and kinda laugh because I remember this major looking at me and saying, 'You're too fucked up for this war.' I was like, 'What do you want? Do you want killers? Do you want—and if I'm too fucked up for this place, why are you sending me *home*?'"

What began as a violent outburst deteriorated in a by-now-familiar pattern: family problems, violence, substance abuse, suicidal thoughts. "Obviously, because of the way I went home, they don't want anybody knowing about that stuff. So it's not like anybody pinned a note to the back of my shirt and said, 'Hey, this guy's pretty messed up. He just messed up a prisoner pretty bad. Maybe you should take a look at him.' Their answer was just to get me out of an area where there was loaded guns." Chris and another friend got orders to Korea almost immediately. "We were shipped off to a place where it's really easy to get alcohol and we got into a lot of trouble there. And it was just a downward spiral from there, for the next year."

He was arrested six times in Korea. When I asked if he would get in trouble, he scoffed, "Not only would I not get in trouble, I was the only one who would not get in trouble. They said, 'Ah, he's a combat vet. He's got all these medals— we don't mess with him. It's just Chris.' And those were the times I got arrested, and by the Korean police, not the base police. These were international incidents. And for a year I was like that, and nobody ever stepped in."

The question is, of course, why—within the closely monitored social world of the military—Chris's downward spiral was allowed to continue unchecked for so long. And not only Chris's but that of others in his unit as well. "A good friend of mine killed his wife and then himself," he said. "And then another one killed himself and one other person, I think it was his wife's lover. And just recently another friend of mine killed himself, and the war's been long over for him. He was medically retired for emotional imbalance, too, like myself, about the same time. Probably half of that group is either out of the military or dead. It's like the wheels fell off that group."

Chris acknowledges that when he finally became suicidal, it was his military leadership who stepped in and made the intervention that probably saved his life. But that was in 2005, some three years after he had been sent home from Afghanistan, years in which his life had continued to escalate out of control, in which he was less of a husband to his wife and less of a father to his children, and in which he slowly knocked himself out of the running for the military career he had always wanted. Why did it take so long for the military to recognize that Chris was falling apart?

A closer look at this question reveals a deep ambiguity at the heart of how service members experience combat stress while still in the military. This ambiguity stems both from the scenario itself, in which those who are supposed to be the toughest of the tough find themselves beginning to show signs of strain, and from individual efforts to navigate amid a maelstrom of confused messages about illness, gender, and the covenants of military life. In order to understand this ambiguity, it helps to first consider the social and structural pressures placed on the American military as a contemporary institution, exploring how these pressures have encouraged certain cultural and organizational responses to combat stress over time. Let's begin with the early years of the Global War on Terror and the role of the American media in bringing combat stress and its consequences to the forefront of national attention.

The first American military scandal of the post-9/11 world occurred in the summer of 2002, when four Fort Bragg military wives were killed by their husbands in the space of six weeks. Three of the four men implicated in the killings had recently returned from Afghanistan, and the media coverage immediately homed in on the question of whether these killings were related to their deployments. Within days after the story broke, CNN.com posted an article suggesting that the killings "have led commanders to take a new look at whether combat deployments may be causing undue stress."[1]

The summer of 2002 marked the first increase in the media coverage about combat PTSD in the American military since the 1991 Gulf War. After this spike, there was another during the early invasion into Iraq in 2003, and then the amount of media attention paid to PTSD seemed to lessen slightly, although the topic reemerged periodically amid coverage of the war.[2] In November 2006, another story hit the news, this time centering around Army Sergeant Georg-Andreas Pogany, who was formally charged with "cowardly conduct as a result of fear" after he sought help from his leadership in Iraq for what he described as a panic attack.[3] The military—and the army in particular, since it is the largest branch of service and has deployed the greatest number of service members—found itself under increasing pressure to mount a visible response to the perceived threat of PTSD among combat-deployed personnel.

Then, on February 18, 2007, the *Washington Post* headlined the first in a series of articles exposing "neglect" and "frustration" among wounded OEF/OIF soldiers receiving care at the nation's most prominent army hospital, Walter Reed Army Medical Center in Washington, D.C.[4] The initial article in the series described the decrepit condition of outpatient housing, complete with pictures of injured soldiers standing in front of walls crumbling and black with mold, and characterized the institution's outpatient facilities as having become nothing more than "a holding ground for physically and psychologically damaged outpatients." Dana Priest and Anne Hull, the story's authors, also wrote that, in contrast to the inpatient hospital's spotless reputation, "the outpatients in the Other Walter Reed encounter a messy bureaucratic battlefield nearly as chaotic as the real battlefields they faced overseas." They charged that servicemen and women were being denied both psychological treatment and help in maneuvering through the labyrinthine bureaucracy of the military disability and healthcare systems.

Fallout from the story was immediate. By March 1, Secretary of Defense Robert Gates had endorsed the army's decision to relieve Major General George Weightman from his post as the commander in charge of Walter Reed, saying in a press release, "The care and welfare of our wounded men and women in uniform demand the highest standard of excellence and commitment that we can muster as a government. When this standard is not met, I will insist on swift and direct corrective action and, where appropriate, accountability up the chain of command."[5] The secretary of the army, Francis Harvey, resigned the next day. The scandal reverberated across a public landscape in which support for American troops serving abroad remained high. The situation at Walter Reed was widely cited, in the popular press and at the level of everyday conversation, as evidence of how the government was failing America's service members. By the end of March, President George W. Bush had toured Walter Reed, made a formal apology, and established a special panel to investigate medical care for wounded warriors.

But the matter was not yet closed. What had begun as an outrage centered primarily on the army's failure to provide adequate care for solders' physical injuries spilled over into concern about their psychological well-being as well.[6] A few months later, in June of 2007, Priest and Hull again made front-page news with a continuation of their "Walter Reed and Beyond" series. The headline of their story trumpeted, "Troops Are Returning from the Battlefield with Psychological Wounds, but the Mental Health System That Serves Them Makes Healing Difficult."[7] Priest and Hull faulted both the Department of Defense and the VA for failing to make mental health treatment and disability services more accessible to returning service members. Their reporting was met with gratitude by military families and veterans' advocates outraged at gaps in care, particularly for those veterans and service members living in rural areas, and at the dizzying paperwork and long delays associated with filing compensation claims for service-related disabilities. Again the coverage struck a chord, and the head of the VA resigned quietly a month later.[8] In acknowledgment of the Walter Reed series' impact, the *Washington Post* received the 2008 Pulitzer Prize for Service Reporting. The awarding officials praised the paper's coverage for "evoking a national outcry and producing reforms by federal officials."[9]

The 2007 Walter Reed scandal brought the public's attention to the aftereffects of war on service members and clarified two things about the U.S. military and the challenges it was facing after five and a half years of the Global War on Terror. First of all, the military was feeling overstretched by the demands of conducting a ground war on two fronts. Service members were under growing strain, plagued by long and repeated deployments, stop-loss measures that prohibited soldiers from leaving the military when their contracts were up,[10] and the increasing frequency with which previously nondeploying service members were being asked to deploy as support staff for combat troops.[11]

The Walter Reed scandal also made it clear that the American public was not willing to accept substandard care for service members. The very idea ignited public opinion against military leadership. In the wave of firings and resignations that followed, the scandal also demonstrated that the military as an institution was responsive to public pressure and could be made to act quickly and dramatically if subject to the appropriate leverage.

Nonetheless, although it was the Walter Reed scandal that turned military (and VA) responses to physical and mental health problems into front-page news, the military had been on the defensive against charges of negligent mental health services since at least 2003. In July of that year, only a few months after the initial invasion into Baghdad, five soldiers then serving in Iraq committed suicide in the space of a few weeks. The army responded by creating the Mental Health Advisory Team (MHAT)—charging it to go to Iraq and investigate the suicides.[12]

The team's report, known as MHAT–I, revealed that service members experiencing combat stress were faced with both social and structural barriers to care. The report noted how few mental health clinicians were available to provide treatment services in theater. Service members described feeling uncertain about where to go for help and being unable to get time off from work to seek medical care. But the most striking obstacles were related to stigma: 59 percent of soldiers surveyed worried that seeking mental health care would result in their being seen as weak, 49 percent expressed concern that their unit would have less confidence in them, and 46 percent feared their leaders would blame them for having a problem.[13] For their part, mental health providers expressed frustration at the lack of antidepressants and other pharmaceutical medications available for prescription and the inconsistent care accessible to units posted in remote parts of Iraq.[14]

What the MHAT report did not discuss was the change in military life wrought by the 1973 move away from the draft and toward an all-volunteer force.[15] One career army officer I interviewed pointed out that there is now far greater incentive to take care of soldiers than there has been in the past. Because pre-1973 service members were subject to a draft, he suggested, there was less need to provide persuasive evidence that the army was an institution that took care of its own. Or, as he put it, the Vietnam-era army could 'use 'em up and spit 'em out' without fear of draining the available pool of potential recruits. After 1973, the military was subject to a constant need for new people, with the corresponding need to hold on to service members, as it is cheaper and more efficient over the long run to maintain good personnel than to replace them. As a result, the contemporary military finds itself needing to keep its publicity positive lest negative perceptions interfere with its ability to continually bring in new recruits.[16]

Meanwhile, by the middle of 2006 the media was voicing concern about the ability of the U.S. Armed Forces to keep up with the logistical requirements of a ground war on two fronts.[17] Studies conducted during the early part of the Iraq and Afghanistan wars suggested that 11–19 percent of U.S. troops were already showing signs of combat PTSD, and evidence of service members' poor mental health seemed only to increase the sense of urgency.[18] Faced with such challenges, clinicians and some leaders within the military recognized that PTSD and other combat-related mental health problems had the potential to seriously undermine a force already stretched too thin. There was much talk of keeping up "force readiness" or "mission readiness," that level of preparation that allows a military unit to go out and do what it needs to do at any given moment.

So it was that, responding to both external public pressure and a recognition of the need to maintain force readiness, top leadership within the Department of Defense and each of the armed forces set in motion a series of efforts aimed at providing improved combat stress prevention and treatment resources for service members.

Understanding the history and complexity of the army's COSC system (discussed in chapter 5) makes it clear that the U.S. military has long been aware of the potential impact of combat stress on service members. Indeed, the *Leader's Manual for Combat Stress Control* includes a list of dire warnings about how mission goals can be compromised if soldiers begin functioning at less than full capacity (e.g., "vigilance deteriorates" and "decisions become slow and inaccurate").[19]

And yet, reacting to mounting public pressure at mid-decade, military leadership began harnessing the massive resources of the armed forces to push for top-down efforts aimed at improving prevention and treatment of acute and post-deployment stress reactions. Although there was some variation by branch of service, these efforts can be roughly grouped into three broad categories.[20]

The first of these focused on improving access to professional mental health services overseas and on military posts across the United States. Faced with a growing shortage of mental health care providers as military clinicians migrated back into civilian life in an attempt to avoid long deployments, the army announced in the spring of 2007 that it was hiring an additional 200 mental health care providers to help close the gap, a number that had increased to 330 by the following year.[21] In response to critiques that the mental health care on offer was of poor quality, the idea for a new training consortium, the Center for Deployment Psychology (CDP), was developed and funding provided by Congress. The CDP's mission was to train mental health care providers "to provide high quality deployment-related behavioral health services to military personnel and their families."[22] In addition, air force psychologists were called upon to deploy with greater frequency in support of army units, learning to run COSC teams in accordance with army protocol.

Meanwhile, a mandatory post-deployment screening process, which required service members to complete what was called the Post-Deployment Health Assessment (PDHA) within thirty days of returning home from overseas, had been in place for some time. The PDHA was intended to provide surveillance data on the health and well-being of every deployed service member, as well as to ensure that those experiencing physical or psychological symptoms were referred for further evaluation. It included questions about PTSD symptoms, medications taken during deployment, and combat exposure while in theater.

Although the PDHA was a well-considered effort to keep an eye on service members returning home, it quickly became clear that it was inadequate to the task. Among the military clinicians I spoke with, it was generally accepted that the PDHA was largely useless because so many soldiers were hesitant to report symptoms. Word went around among service members that if you reported negative symptoms, you would be held back from returning home for a week or two while you underwent evaluation by the mental health people. In one deployment health workshop I attended, the presenting clinician admitted flat out, 'I lied on mine' because 'if you mark anything you can't go on leave!'

The DOD eventually realized the PDHA was not working as intended and an additional measure was introduced in 2005. This was the Post-Deployment Health Reassessment (PDHRA), a form that was to be completed 90–180 days after the return home. The PDHRA requested further information on psychosocial issues and family problems that might have become evident in the early months after deployment, and according to what I heard from clinicians and at conference presentations I attended during 2007 and 2008, it was thought to be more effective in identifying those in need of professional evaluation.[23]

The second category of changes pushed by military leadership fell under the broad rubric of working to decrease stigma and improve service members' ability to spot signs of trouble. One initiative developed by the Walter Reed Army Institute for Research attempted to educate soldiers about the challenges of transitioning to and from the combat zone using a program called "Battlemind." The goal of Battlemind, which was typically taught by chaplains in a workshop format, was to help soldiers know what to expect as they departed for a combat tour and as they embarked upon the return home to family life. The program was organized around the idea that service members need to develop certain skills— i.e., the battle mind-set—in order to function successfully in the combat environment; these include maintaining close relationships with buddies, practicing targeted aggression, focusing on accountability and responsibility, and taking control of any given situation. Although these attitudes and behaviors can be lifesavers in the combat zone, they can also create problems if retained outside the deployment setting. As one army brochure put it, "Battlemind can be hazardous to your social and behavioral health in the home-zone."[24] Early evaluation of the program found that soldiers who received Battlemind training prior to deployment reported fewer mental health problems after they returned home.[25]

This attempt to normalize post-deployment challenges was only one means by which military leadership has tried to decrease the stigma around combat and readjustment stress among troops. Along the same lines, military mental health services now go by the name of Behavioral Health, a change intended to summon up fewer frightening connotations of shrinks and straitjackets. Concerns about confidentiality led to the creation of anonymous support and referral services available via telephone and the Internet as part of the Military One Source program.[26] And in a practical effort to reassure service members who might be afraid of losing their security clearance—a common outcome of seeking mental health care in the past and one that may have implications for long-term employment prospects—regulations were changed to exempt service members from losing security clearance over a psychological problem related to their military experience.[27]

The third category of top-down efforts lay in the growing emphasis on providing information and services to service members' families. During 2007–8, many of the chaplains I spoke with were offering marital counseling and workshops to reunited families. I attended several local seminars aimed at educating civilian mental health providers about the needs of military families, during which it was usually noted that the newfound emphasis on family life signaled a major change from the old days of 'If we wanted you to have a wife we would have issued you one!' Even the army's Battlemind program included a specific unit for spouses, which provided much of the same information as for service members but with a focus on how spouses could help in easing the transition home.[28]

One can argue whether any of these changes, or the COSC system already in place, represent enough of an attempt by the American military to protect and provide for service members. What is clear, however, is that the military as an institution, much like a veteran's family, is responsive to perceived crisis, acting out of concern that disaster may result if service members' post-combat and post-deployment struggles are left without appropriate attention. Certainly the crises faced by families and by the military are different. The family may be concerned that a service member will become more troubled over time (with potentially tragic results, as cautionary tales of veterans' suicide, substance abuse, and homelessness suggest) or that he will be unable to live up to his expected role as parent, partner, or provider. Within the military, concern arises out of worry over service members' well-being and from the recognition that those struggling with mental health problems are less able to contribute to force readiness. It seems clear, however, that both veterans' families and the U.S. military face pressure to work toward the best possible well-being of current and former service members.

And yet we already know that it does not always work out this way. Family members sometimes lash out at veterans rather than supporting them. Military leadership sometimes directly contribute to mental (and physical) health problems for their troops, continually sending men and women into conflict on the ground in Iraq and Afghanistan and ignoring signs of combat stress among those like Chris. There is top-down pressure to improve access to mental health care and to decrease stigma, yes, but there are also other pressures, from other directions. It is the conflict created by these opposing forces that helps explain why problems around stigma and care seeking remain despite considerable efforts to the contrary, efforts forged from nearly a century of working with combat stress. What, then, are these pressures?

One force working to perpetuate the stigma around combat stress is the socialization that service members are given upon their entry into the military. Until recently, there has been relatively little study of state militaries by anthropologists, an absence that results from a long history of mutual suspicion between anthropologists and members of the armed services, whose priorities have at times been in conflict.[29] Nonetheless, anthropological research among active-duty military personnel in the United States,[30] Bolivia,[31] Israel,[32] and Australia,[33] to name but a few, has found that state militaries make use of a variety of socialization practices to foster a sense of shared culture among soldiers.[34] This socialization usually takes place during some form of basic training and is intended to serve several purposes. First, it supports the group cohesion and bonding that are considered essential for maintaining trust and efficiency in combat settings.[35] Second, it supports the internalization of a disciplinary hierarchy in which orders will be followed without question, even under conditions of crisis and threat.[36] Third, socialization instills service members with the values of a total institution—the sociologist Erving Goffman's phrase for an institution in which individuals live, work, and play, conducting their entire lives within its bureaucratic confines[37]—and is thus intended to overcome previous socialization, particularly that which might impede the use of lethal violence.[38] Given the long history of militaries as exclusively male institutions, it comes as no surprise that anthropologists have observed a self-conscious embrace of aggressive masculinity within these shared group cultures.[39] Some have even suggested that joining the military may serve as a male rite of passage, a culturally authorized way of "becoming a man."[40]

In volunteer militaries like ours, individuals who sign up for military service may already relate to a certain kind of hypermasculine identity.[41] Even when this is not the case, military socialization intentionally fosters values and behaviors emphasizing toughness, emotional control, and self-reliance, those same values we have already discussed as central to American notions of manhood.[42] As we observed in chapter 4, military socialization for San Antonio veterans seemed to translate into the process by which attitudes about masculinity and personhood that came with them into the military, attitudes acquired during childhood and adolescence, were compounded with an additional set of standards for comportment and behavior. This is not to say that the personal and cultural baggage they brought with them was *replaced* (who can wholly set aside the lessons of their early years?) but only that another layer was added to the mix. For example, one soldier's mother bragged about her son's wonderful way with his kids during his premilitary years as a stay-at-home father. He had enlisted in the army planning to become a medic and 'wanting to save lives,' but after basic training his mother overheard him characterize himself as a 'lean mean killing machine,' something she had never heard from him before. He did not suddenly stop being a wonderful husband and father, but he did acquire a whole new way of talking about himself.[43]

As it happens, these are the kinds of no-holds-barred messages we are used to hearing about in books and movies, in stories that focus on how men may push themselves and in doing so accomplish great feats and heroic victories. But it is also essential to remember how important are the bonds between these men, seen in the lasting resonance of phrases like "comrades in arms" and "band of brothers." In other words, to understand the power of military socialization, it is not enough to focus on boot camp and its messages about strength, toughness, and masculinity.[44] Rather it is necessary to understand military socialization as an ongoing process, continually re-created in the often highly valued relationships between service members and those closest to them in the rank hierarchy: their immediate peers, subordinates, and leaders.[45] Military socialization is a set of values and experiences shared by service members, itself an important part of the relationships these individuals have with one another. Military socialization, therefore, continues as the relationships themselves continue, reemerging in the interactions between service members and those they love, respect, emulate, and train.

Since thirty-one of the fifty OEF/OIF veterans in the San Antonio study were officers or NCOs, the men in this group spoke as often about communicating the military's expectations as they did about receiving them. Carlos describes teaching his men to be impervious to pain. "I've been hurt so many times that it's like, 'It's just a couple of ribs, you'll get over it.' I've told that to so many people. 'Just ignore it.' Sprains, whatever. 'It'll go away.'" Chris says roughly the same thing, only adding that he was much harder on his men after returning from Afghanistan. "Whenever I'd see someone limping, I'd be like, 'Pick your ass up and move. You better be bleeding or your bone better be sticking out before you quit on me.'" Physical evidence was necessary—blood or visible bone. Pain was insufficient. "'Oh, my leg hurts!' 'No it doesn't—it doesn't hurt *enough!*'"

But Chris wasn't just passing on lessons he had learned in his time with the army unit. While in Afghanistan, he had watched the soldier he admired most die from wounds sustained in combat. "I knew what the consequences were if you're unprepared," he says. This knowledge only made him push his men that much harder. He was trying to ensure they would survive.

Many veterans had internalized similarly powerful messages from peers or supervisors they admired and wanted to live up to, particularly those who had been injured or killed in the line of duty. One former army sergeant, Jose, describes a friend who died in combat as "just like the perfect soldier you would assume you'd copy. He knew his job, he knew other ways to get the job done. He couldn't be pushed around. He was in his thirties and he ran faster than just about anyone, did more push-ups, never showed that he was sore." He was physically and emotionally tough and unbending. Several years after his friend's death, Jose says that he still judges his own worth in relation to this "perfect soldier" and tries to live up to his example.[46]

It is difficult to overstate the closeness that can arise between service members, particularly between those who have been through combat together. People who are not familiar with the military have sometimes told me they find it strange that men taught to kill should be so loyal and should look out for and look up to one another so intensely. Certainly, there are no individuals more deeply aware of the complex morality of wartime actions than veterans, who often express ambivalent feelings about their own violence and its intended and unintended consequences. But the reality of this violence should not be taken to somehow lessen the intimacy of their relationships or the value they place on their obligations to others—if anything, the opposite is true. Having seen how high the stakes may be, these men trusted and valued their buddies with an intensity they may find difficult to match in civilian life.

Thus forged within the context of military relationships, the shared emphasis on toughness and loyalty fostered an uneasy double standard when troops encountered physical and mental health problems. I heard over and over from veterans about the times that they had urged their buddies to seek mental health care while rejecting the idea themselves. One of Adam's former marines told him, after they had both separated from service, "'Look, I'm in a bad way.'" Adam responded without hesitation: "You're a veteran, go to the VA and get help.'" But even so, he says, "I still couldn't do it myself, couldn't bring myself to do it. I think it was still that macho attitude."

Later on, when I was talking with Adam about the best way to help veterans struggling with PTSD, he said that the best thing to do was to have another veteran or another member of their unit talk to them. The only catch was finding someone "who can, you know, say something other than 'Hey man, quit being a woman and suck it up. Quit being a sissy and move on about your business.'"

One army officer I spoke with, Jordan, remains on active duty despite struggling with PTSD, depression, and a neurological disorder he links to the anthrax vaccine he received early in the Iraq war. He says that he goes through the day feeling as if he is high all the time, distant from his body, from his emotions, from the events going on around him. His despair was palpable when we spoke, although he told me, with a vague fierce fire, that receiving a formal PTSD diagnosis and putting together a plan for treatment had given him a lot of hope.

Nonetheless, Jordan was very careful in selecting whom among his colleagues to tell about his problems. He likened his unit to a "bunch of wolves" who could "smell any weakness." He related this to what he called the "boots-on-the-ground" attitude—the idea that nothing matters except how many service members can be called upon to support the mission at a given time. This was a lesson he had already learned the hard way, having dealt with this attitude at a prior post. When he first developed neurological symptoms, his former chief told him that he didn't want Jordan posted to him if he wasn't in full working order because he wouldn't be of any use. Jordan was flabbergasted. His wife, who witnessed the conversation, was furious. Even so, Jordan acknowledged that he understood where the chief was coming from; it was wholly in line with a boots-on-the-ground perspective. Amid a constant wartime effort to accomplish seemingly impossible goals with too few people and too little time, Jordan felt this attitude was sometimes necessary. At the same time, he was incensed by the army's extension of deployments from twelve to fifteen months, seeing the increase as undercutting long-term troop well-being to serve short-term goals. He was upset with himself for not speaking out more vehemently against the policy.

In this way, Jordan found himself caught between the destigmatizing efforts of official military policy on PTSD, which made evaluation and treatment more accessible to him, and the culture of military life, which places the importance of completing the larger mission above the well-being of any one individual. This was, among the veterans and active-duty personnel I spoke with, not an unusual position to be in. A straight-shooting army chaplain told me that he saw soldiers getting dual messages. He said that they hear 'We can help!' from mental health providers, while at the same time being told, 'If you're broke, we'll kick you to the curb,' from the rest of the military community.

Service members themselves were fully aware of these tensions. Eric, a marine who served in Iraq in 2006, was diagnosed with PTSD while still overseas, shortly after his best friend was killed. It was his leaders who noticed he was falling apart, crying intermittently and having a hard time putting sentences together when he spoke. But, he says, "we were so short on people that I didn't want them to pull me out. So I just sucked it up and kinda did what I needed to do to get through. And just kind of exploded when I got back." Another soldier, Martin, began having panic attacks while in Iraq and sought help from the chaplain. "I tried my best to keep it low-key, so I told him like, 'I wanna see somebody but I don't want the unit to know.' And I thought that was it, I was just going to see the chaplain. I remember that one of the commanders came down to talk to me and I was like, 'I don't want to talk to *you* about it.' And I felt bad, almost like I was doing something wrong. So I stopped going."

For NCOs, it was not uncommon to have been in charge of a soldier who experienced combat stress while deployed, and they, too, recognized the opposing forces of individual and unit needs. "A soldier will usually break down on their first deployment at least once," Carlos tells me. "It's very common. I had two or three who were a suicide concern, and you just send them back for a few days, give them a little break if you can. It's about all you can do, because we're short-handed. Everybody kinda thinks it's not fair, but they kinda understand it too." Carlos shrugs. There were too many needs requiring attention. The unit's mission schedule competed for priority with the well-being of a soldier on suicide risk, which competed with the frustration of other soldiers at losing a member of the team. These concerns in turn competed with the understanding of supervisors who knew that combat stress was a pretty common thing but who also knew that a short-handed team is a more vulnerable team.

In such a scenario, individual service members are left tuning in to messages that urge them both to seek help and to suck it up, to take care of themselves and to sacrifice their own well-being for that of the group. So they diligently fill out the PDHA screening form, which diligently aims to find out whether they are in need of additional evaluation. And they lie.

Amid such a flurry of conflicting pressures, the attitudes taken by those closest to a service member in trouble, often his buddies or direct leaders, seem to take on an added importance. Fellow service members can help tip a struggling colleague in either direction, toward help-seeking or away from it. Chris points out that it was his immediate superiors who kept him from committing suicide. "[T]hey took turns, at my house, in the chair next to my bed, making sure I didn't kill myself before they could get me on a plane. And my first sergeant flew with me halfway across the world and finally dropped me off in San Antonio three weeks later. He took three weeks out of his life, his family's life, to get me here."

In contrast, one army clinician raised his hand in a workshop on PTSD treatment to say that he had had a difficult time even accessing troops while working in Iraq because he kept running into irate commanders who told him that 'every time my people see you they come back wimpy and cry!' An air force clinician at the same workshop reported that he had been summoned to speak with the unit commander the very day he landed in Iraq and had been told that he and his team would have full access to airmen because they were considered vital support.[47] He said that he even saw cases in which a guy's buddies accompanied him to the clinic. When thanked for supporting their friend, they would say, 'Well, this is what you guys do to help us complete our mission, right?' The attitude toward care provided and received in the field varied widely, and had the potential to make a significant difference in who sought what care when and how.

These communicated ideas about illness, loyalty, and strength obviously impact how service members go about seeking help in times of trouble, but they linger on to influence how veterans seek care after leaving the military as well. It was fairly typical to hear a veteran say of care seeking, as Carlos did, "I waited a long time—well, to me it seemed like a long time. I knew I needed to do it and I fought it and fought it and fought it." He gives a dry smile. "'Course I had this military attitude, you know. Suck it up. Get the job done. Be the example. And you know I went through a lot of pain that was unnecessary because of that. I notice that's a problem for a lot of people. Letting go of that tough guy." Carlos did not suddenly stop being responsive to the lessons he had learned in the military when he began the transition into civilian life. Those lessons were hard-won, and hard-lost.

EMBATTLED
The Politics of PTSD in VA Mental Health Care

I was sitting by the entrance of the local VA trauma clinic one morning when a middle-aged man came walking up the main stairway from the lobby, looking a little lost. He wore glasses and an oversized black T-shirt with flames and the name of an auto parts store on the back. I asked if I could help, and he told me he was 'looking for mental health.' I gestured toward the clinic door, then smiled and pointed to where the sign was hidden behind an event poster. He grinned and thanked me, and as he walked over to the door, he said, his smile fumbling sideways a little, 'I hope they can help me before I go completely crazy.'

Helping those in distress is the mission of VA mental health clinics all over the country. Under the sprawling jurisdiction of the Veterans Health Administration (VHA), local VA hospitals and clinics across the United States provide mental and physical health services to veterans of all ages. Determining who is eligible for such care can be tricky, but the criteria can be briefly summarized as follows: most veterans who meet low-income requirements will receive free care at the VA for any condition, and most veterans who have one or more service-connected illnesses or injuries will receive free care for those conditions. Eligibility is based on period of service, length of service, military discharge status (for example, individuals who were dishonorably discharged may not be eligible), income, level of disability and/or unemployability, etc. (For a full breakdown, the VA's online eligibility and enrollment website carries the most up-to-date information: http://www.va.gov/healtheligibility/eligibility/DetermineEligibility.asp). Health care is only one of the services that the VA provides; other rights and resources include disability compensation, rehabilitation services, home loans, education assistance, and burial in a national cemetery.

All these services are of a piece with the larger objective of the VA. Just inside the main entrance of San Antonio's VA hospital, an expansive brick building located to the northwest of the downtown area, the institution's motto is written on the wall in black script: "To care for him who shall have borne the battle and for his widow and his orphan."[1] This is the ethos the VA self-consciously sponsors in its treatment of veterans. Many of the clinicians wear ID badges on lanyards that read, "How May I Serve You?" and "Now It's Our Turn." There is a clear notion of honorable exchange, of services rendered; veterans have served their country, and the VA exists to serve veterans. At the same time, the lanyard is designed to break, allowing the clinician to escape if grabbed too roughly by an angry or out-of-control patient. It is an apt symbol of the relationship between veterans and the VA: a great deal of mutual respect and appreciation and just enough distrust to keep everyone on their toes.

It is in this setting, with the cultural politics of PTSD at a fever pitch, that the future of a new generation of veterans is being redefined. To understand why, we turn now to a small but influential trauma clinic within the San Antonio VA health-care system, located on the second floor of an outpatient facility a mile from the main VA hospital. This clinic, which in 2008 was one of 117 similar clinics around the nation, has as its mission the provision of comprehensive mental health care for PTSD-diagnosed veterans.[2] Its roughly a dozen clinicians provide care for combat veterans of all ages and conflicts—World War II, Korea, Vietnam, the first Gulf War, Iraq, and Afghanistan—as well as for those whose trauma, such as military sexual trauma, may not have occurred in combat at all.

Though the job of the clinic is primarily to provide quality care to veterans with trauma-related mental illness, its clinicians may find themselves doing far more than simply acting in accordance with their professional training. Because they are federal employees and staff of the United States' largest health-care system, their actions are often viewed in relation to national debates around policy and practice. Two issues in particular frequently implicate VA mental health providers: first, whether veterans receive adequate care and compensation from the VA, and second, what kinds of care and compensation are most appropriate for PTSD.

In order to get a sense of these debates—and of the tensions they create for both veterans and VA clinicians—let me begin by revisiting a congressional veterans' forum that was held in San Antonio. In the shouting and speechifying that took place at that event, we find much of the explosive rhetoric that can turn treatment at the VA into a minefield.

In August of 2007, four U.S. congressmen held a hearing, organized by the office of local representative Ciro Rodriguez, to address the needs and concerns of local veterans. I learned about the meeting from Steve, a Vietnam veteran, and his wife, Ellen, whom I had interviewed twice in the preceding weeks. Steve served in Vietnam prior to their marriage and has suffered from increasingly debilitating mental health and neurological problems ever since. He and his wife had spent years wrangling with the VA's Compensation and Pension Service (C&P) in an attempt to get the VA to recognize their claim. More recently, two of their children had served in Iraq and returned home with difficulties.

During our first interview, Ellen wrote me a long note on a scrap of paper while I spoke with her husband. It began:

> PTSD—not recognized with
> my husband/Vietnam
> made to feel he had
> to handle it on his own
> our lives suffered immensely from this

She went on to pour forth the multigenerational suffering that war had brought her family: her husband's drinking and violence, then later her children's repeated military deployments and the problems these absences had created for her grandchildren. She linked this suffering with what the VA did not do: diagnose Steve with PTSD across all the decades of their struggle.

Fueled by this history, Steve and Ellen have become eager advocates for veterans' rights, and insisted I attend the forum. When I arrived at the event, held in a large auditorium at a local university, I made my way past a handful of official-looking young staffers to find the pair perched in one of the upper rows of the packed theater, crowded in among several hundred other veterans and family members. Steve was in his motorized chair that day, looking handsome but diminished by illness. Ellen sat beside him on her own walker, an energy drink clutched tightly in one thin and freckled hand.

I said hello to Steve, and Ellen and I chatted as the forum began. Each of the congressmen was introduced, and then three local representatives each took the podium and gave brief comments, leading up to what was clearly intended to be a keynote presentation by Rep. Bob Filner, chairman of the House Committee on Veterans' Affairs. The local representatives pointed out a series of problems with VA services that were prominent in the national media at the time, including gaps in VA health care related to the influx of OEF/OIF veterans and the need to develop appropriate care systems for dealing with PTSD and traumatic brain injury (TBI). Each congressman made a case for his own track record in standing up for veterans. Ellen cackled irreverently next to me, cynical and unimpressed.

When his turn came, Chairman Filner got up and was greeted with a standing ovation. He said his thanks and then pointed out that getting four congressmen in the same room for an event like this was a rarity, calling the occasion evidence of their 'unity on behalf of all veterans.' This prompted another round of applause; the crowd began to seem primed and responsive. He spoke about Walter Reed, saying that the scandal, while focused on military health care rather than the VA, had helped Congress to 'figure out that we aren't doing enough,' a statement greeted by a chorus of 'Yeah!'s from the audience. Congress had since been taking a much more aggressive stance on veterans' issues, he continued, demanding 'the money we need to take care of our veterans!' As evidence of these efforts, he cited a 30 percent increase in the VA budget for the 2008 fiscal year. Even so, he acknowledged that the VA had too often stood for "Veterans Adversary" rather than "Veterans' Advocate," a salvo greeted with exuberant applause.

Hesitating for a moment, Chairman Filner then asked the audience, 'How many of you are Vietnam veterans?' The majority raised their hands, and he looked at them for a minute, held a perfect pause, and said, 'I have two things to say to you: Thank you. And I'm sorry.' A mingled groan rose from the crowd in response—agreement and relief and fury. He went on, lambasting the moral disgrace of a nation in which there are homeless veterans. It was 'shameful,' he said, that there have been as many suicides among Vietnam veterans after the war as there were deaths in combat during the war itself,[3] at which the audience again gave voice, sending up murmurs of shock, disgust, and anger. 'Never again!' he promised, and cries of 'Never again!' went up amidst the clapping. He said that there are some veterans who are sick, who are fighting cancers, and who are made *more sick* because they are constantly fighting an unresponsive bureaucracy. There was huge applause at this, and Ellen stuck her skinny fist in the air and shouted, 'Yes!'

Chairman Filner then went on to say that there are 'ten to twenty thousand people in the VA whose job it is to say you're a liar'—speaking of the VA employees who evaluate veterans' applications for disability compensation. This process requires the veteran to provide evidence that (1) he or she has a disabling injury or illness and (2) this is a condition resulting from military service. He offered a rebuttal to the status quo: 'You don't *have* to prove it! You served us!' He spoke about Vietnam veterans as 'canaries in the coal mine' for the problems of the VA system and apologized that 'we have not served you!' But then he turned to the problems faced by 'these young folks coming back,' describing the mental and physical health problems of Iraq and Afghanistan veterans and comparing their needs with those that went unsatisfied after Vietnam. He said seriously, 'We're going to try not to make the same mistake.'

His speech was succinct and well-delivered, although he said nothing that was dramatically new. When he was finished, the moderator tried to initiate a question-and-answer period, but it rapidly devolved into a shouting match featuring a handful of self-identified Vietnam veterans with PTSD, enraged at the treatment they had (not) received. There were several attempts to calm the assembled crowd and reorganize a more peaceable discussion, but this became possible only after the handful had said their piece. The forum was brought to a close shortly thereafter, as one local reporter described it, "long before the audience was ready."[4]

Chairman Filner's speech was very much in line with a broader American discourse around the benefits and services due to veterans in exchange for their service. It pointed to a widely shared sense of guilt over those Vietnam veterans who came home and were treated carelessly and without honor by a nation then torn in two over the conflict itself.[5] This sense of past wrongs came up frequently during my fieldwork, in vehement phrases like 'Shame on us if we ever let Vietnam happen again.'

But although such sentiments were commonly expressed during this time period, the urge to repeat them seemed driven by a sense that veterans might become invisible if the wars in Iraq and Afghanistan lingered on too long, if the emerging stories of distress and despair became too familiar. This was 2007, the same year that the online PTSD advocate Ilona Meagher authored a book entitled *Moving a Nation to Care*. The implication seemed to be that the nation did not.

And so the VA at the beginning of the twenty-first century was faced with two challenges for which it was unprepared. First, there was the sheer magnitude of the task of providing services to a new generation of veterans returning from foreign wars in large numbers and with conditions that the VA, after decades of focusing on the chronic illnesses of aging World War II, Korea, and Vietnam veterans, was not prepared to handle, including traumatic brain injury, PTSD, and severe wounds such as burns and amputations. Due to impressive advances in battlefield medicine, mortality rates among those injured have dropped from 30 percent in World War II and 24 percent in Vietnam to around 10 percent in the current wars.[6] This unprecedented survival rate has left the VA struggling with the necessity of caring for catastrophically injured service members at an extraordinary cost of funding and manpower. VA clinicians, at least, were fully aware of how big the challenge was and how much bigger it was likely to get. At a national VA conference I attended in April 2007, one of the speakers looked out over a room packed with several hundred clinicians and joked, 'This looks to me like our waiting rooms are going to look.' The VA was not planning for a flood of new veterans when September 11 suddenly changed the stakes, and in the years since then the VA has been struggling to keep up.

But beyond playing logistical catch-up, the VA has also been faced with the symbolic task of trying to right wrongs done in the years after Vietnam. Caring for the troops is more than an institutional mission. It is a contractual obligation of the U.S. government—a right given in exchange for military service. It is also a promise that, in the current era, falls always under the shadow of what looks to many like the betrayal of a past generation of veterans. 'Shame on us if we ever let Vietnam happen again.'

This, then, is the VA and its obligations writ large. For the individual veteran, however, the institution of the VA is generally embodied in the individual staff members he or she encounters (as well as in decisions handed down from disability claim adjudication boards whose members he may never meet). For mental-health-care providers at the trauma clinic, who already serve as the face of their various professions as psychiatrists, psychologists, and social workers, this adds a level of complexity to their daily clinical practice. They must be both clinicians *and* representatives of the VA, and at times this means their practice may be as political as it is professional. When they fail, as when VA clinicians in Minnesota turned away twenty-five-year-old Jonathan Schulze only days before he committed suicide, those failures become national news. The 2007 *Newsweek* article describing Schulze's death was titled, "How the U.S. Is Failing Its War Veterans."[7]

Jonathan Schulze's death is not the first, and certainly won't be the last, symptom of the crisis the VA has had to cope with. Phillip Longman's fascinating book on VA health care—not irrelevantly titled *Best Care Anywhere: Why VA Health Care Is Better Than Yours*—starts with this passage:

> Quick. When you read "veterans hospital," what comes to mind? Maybe you recall the headlines about the three decomposed bodies found near a veterans medical center in Salem, Virginia, in the early 1990s. Two turned out to be the remains of patients who had wandered off months before. The other patient had been resting in place for more than fifteen years. The Veterans Administration admitted that its search for the missing patients had been "cursory."
>
> Or maybe you recall images from movies like *Born on the 4th of July*, in which Tom Cruise plays an injured Vietnam vet who becomes radicalized by his shabby treatment in a crumbling, rat-infested veterans hospital in the Bronx. Sample dialogue: "This place is a fuckin' slum!"[8]

From such an inauspicious beginning, Longman goes on to describe the series of crises that led the VA to develop its abysmal reputation. Established in 1921, in the wake of World War I, what was then called the Veterans Bureau faced its first scandal only four years later.[9] Its head, Colonel Charles R. Forbes, was found to have wasted or stolen $200 million in taxpayer funds (some $2.1 billion in current money). Stunned by the sheer size of Forbes's graft, VA leadership attempted to prevent future pillage by building a daunting structure for financial oversight, with the result that by 1945 journalists were accusing the new director of tying the bureaucracy up in "needless red tape."[10] After World War II, things became better for a while. The VA was newly empowered by the GI Bill to provide generous housing and education benefits, and changes in its organization allowed veterans access to some of the finest clinicians and researchers in the country.[11]

But what Longman calls the VA's "golden moment of high public esteem" did not last.[12] The VA faced significant budget cuts in the 1950s. Facilities became understaffed as clinicians were laid off in droves, and new legislation left fewer veterans eligible for care. A series of exposés involving the careless treatment of research subjects gave rise to suspicions that veterans were being used as guinea pigs. When the Vietnam conflict began in the 1960s and veterans later began returning from service, many of them encountered woefully underfunded hospitals and doctors and staff who, like so many Americans, were opposed to America's role in Vietnam. Declining conditions at the VA became a target of fury among veterans enraged by a government that they felt had used them and then left them to rot.

Even as the VA was increasingly dismissed as an antiquated and failing health-care system, however, its clinicians and staff were laying the foundation for efforts that would thirty years later earn the VA recognition as a system of innovative and high-level care, with some of the best patient outcomes of any private or public health-care provider in the U.S.[13] Employees within the VA, for example, developed open-source hospital information software called VistA that gave VA staff access to unprecedented electronic health records. The patient-tracking power of VistA made it possible for VA researchers to investigate the health outcomes of patients treated using particular drugs or procedures and therefore to determine the effectiveness of these treatments on a grand scale. (Longman points out that many Americans fail to realize how much of medical practice is based on anecdotal and experiential knowledge passed down through clinical training rather than on the accumulation of scientific evidence.) And because the VA has patients for life, unlike other insurance and managed care programs in the United States, the institution benefits from providing quality preventive care over the long term rather than focusing on acute-care solutions, as do employer insurance plans with a high turnover rate. Although by the 1990s the VA was vastly overbuilt to support a dwindling population of older veterans, these preexisting strengths made it possible for a new undersecretary for health in the VA, Kenneth Kizer, to come in and refocus VA efforts on measuring patient outcomes and emphasizing health-care quality. The cumulative effect of these efforts was so dramatic that by 2003 the VA was the highest ranked of *any* health-care system in the United States, according to the National Committee for Quality Assurance.[14]

Unfortunately for the VA, by 2003 national attention was not on celebrating it as a model for high quality health care. In that year the nation was going off to war in Iraq, and when the VA began to make the news again, it would be for very different reasons. There were a series of highly public problems at the VA after OEF/OIF veterans began returning home, many resulting in litigation. A twenty-three-year-old marine, Jeffrey Lucey, committed suicide after getting back from Iraq in 2004. His family blamed the VA for their son's death, which came only three weeks after clinicians at the Northampton VA Medical Center refused to assess him for PTSD until he got his drinking under control; the family later sued for negligence.[15] In 2006 a class-action lawsuit was filed against the VA after an employee's laptop was stolen, giving the thieves access to personal information, including Social Security numbers, for more than 26 million active-duty military personnel and veterans.[16] Then the Walter Reed scandal struck in 2007, beginning with an excoriation of health care within the Department of Defense but taking the VA secretary down with it before it was over.

The message was clear: the VA, like the military, was going to have to make good on its promise to take care of this new generation of veterans. And in the public imagination, the department was starting from behind.

When I began fieldwork in early 2007, about the same time as the Walter Reed scandal was breaking, the trauma clinic was in the middle of a revolution in both its organization and its treatment plan for PTSD—changes based on a fundamental shift in the way that clinicians were seeing and responding to PTSD. This was a transition several years in the making. New leadership had taken over the clinic in the early 2000s, and with it came a new perspective on how the clinic should view its responsibilities as a care provider. It is not an exaggeration to say that this new perspective may come to redefine what PTSD means for veterans across the foreseeable future. It has the potential to prompt a profound change in the way that veterans live with (or without) PTSD. On the other hand, it also faces significant challenges, risks, and political ramifications. Understanding just how much is at stake requires some discussion of therapeutic technologies for PTSD.

Prior to the change in leadership, PTSD patients—generally veterans from World War II, Korea, and Vietnam—came into the clinic, became part of its long-term care program, and, for the most part, never left. PTSD is one of those contemporary psychiatric disorders for which a variety of pharmaceuticals can be effective in helping to control symptoms (reducing suicidality, aiding in sleep, reducing the frequency of nightmares, etc.) but for which drugs have proven to be less effective over the long term than certain psychological therapies.[17] The clinic's psychologists and social workers focused on providing supportive care through psychodynamic talk therapy, offered individually or in groups, while psychiatrists were primarily responsible for overseeing the prescription of appropriate psychotropic medications. This was the standard of care for the clinic, as it was for clinics all over the country.

The therapy provided during this period, which extended from the founding of the clinic in 1989 to roughly 2006 or 2007, was diverse enough that it is difficult to characterize, although it is fair to say that overall it was more psychodynamically inclined than would later be the case. In other words, psychodynamic clinicians active in the clinic offered individual and group therapy sessions aimed at helping the veteran to develop better skills for functioning in the world. The therapy itself was eclectic, often drawing on a combination of theories and therapeutic styles based on the clinician's own training and preferences. For example, one clinician described a strong reliance on Jungian analysis, while another was extensively trained in the use of hypnosis. There were commonalities, however. In our interviews, psychodynamic clinicians often used metaphors of loss in speaking of PTSD: loss of trust in the self, loss of trust in the world, loss of innocence. They relied upon a language for describing PTSD that drew heavily on concepts like the ego and the self, on listening and empathy, on guilt and shame. Perhaps most important, therapy was understood to require time. One clinician described a handful of cases with positive treatment outcomes, all of which had taken several years to come to fruition. Even in the best scenario, PTSD was considered a lifelong disorder, to be managed rather than cured.

But a revolution was brewing. As this older generation of clinicians—most of whom had been trained when PTSD was a fledgling diagnosis and who could speak at length of the VA's earliest efforts to provide PTSD treatment in the 1980s—grew closer to retirement, a newer generation began coming in and gaining control. The new clinicians noticed problems with the way the clinic was being run. There was a one- to two-year backlog for getting new patients into treatment. The number of patients had steadily grown over time, while the number of clinicians was roughly static. There were no time limits on any of the treatments the clinic provided, and there was no agreed-upon way of evaluating when it was time for a patient to move on. As one clinician described it, there was a 'culture of chronic support and treatment.' This clinician was quick to point out that there are benefits to such an approach—ongoing care for those who need it being one of them—but acknowledged that this plan proved unsustainable over the long run in the absence of a continually expanding staff.

As OEF/OIF veterans began to come into the clinic seeking help, political pressure mounted to ensure that the new veterans received prompt and effective care, and the backlog itself became unsustainable. In an effort to address the problem, the clinic's new administrators hired several fee-based social workers and psychologists to do nothing but intake interviews for a while, routing new patients into services at the trauma clinic or, if PTSD was not the main concern, into the adjacent mental health outpatient treatment center. A team composed of one psychologist and one social worker was put together in August of 2006 to provide dedicated care for veterans of Iraq and Afghanistan. Other providers in the clinic could also see OEF/OIF clients, but the creation of a specialized OEF/OIF team was intended to offer services tailored to the needs of the most recent veterans.

These and other organizational moves were only the beginning. The second and larger shift was one that cut to the heart of how clinicians understand psychological trauma itself. As I spoke with trauma clinic staff in early 2007,[18] clear boundaries had already coalesced around this issue, largely along generational lines. As the older clinicians neared retirement or made the decision to move on (some prompted by the changing ethos in the clinic, if the comments of two departing clinicians are any indication), an effort was made to hire clinicians trained in clinical psychology and cognitive behavioral therapy (CBT), focusing on those conversant with the relatively new and comparatively short-term *evidence-supported treatments (ESTs)*. (The size and influence of this new generation of clinicians should not be underestimated, and not just for their role locally. One clinician described attending a national VA conference on PTSD where the several hundred people in the audience were asked to raise their hands if they had worked at the VA for five years or less. About half of those present raised their hands.)

It is important to note that both psychiatrists and psychologists within the trauma clinic expressed support for the shift toward ESTs, perhaps because it arose out of an effort within clinical psychology that has emerged alongside the move toward evidence-based medicine. Both are founded on the central assumption that treatment modalities should be judged on scientific evidence—i.e., on their ability to consistently produce positive health outcomes in clinical trials—rather than on the accumulated experience of individual providers or the theoretical orientation of professional schools of thought. Psychiatrists at the clinic openly acknowledged that though certain medications can be helpful in minimizing PTSD symptoms, no pharmaceutical treatment has yet emerged that is as successful in reducing PTSD severity over time as the

CBT-based therapies. So while there were differences in viewpoint among providers at the trauma clinic, these did not fall along neat disciplinary lines. Because it is primarily psychologists who are responsible for directing group and individual therapies at the clinic—whether psychodynamic or cognitive behavioral—I found they were typically the most direct in stating their feelings about ESTs. However, psychiatrists and social workers, who often work alongside their psychology colleagues in providing or supporting such care, also remained vocal and influential participants in the ongoing shift.

The area of most active debate was related to the question of whether prolonged exposure therapy (commonly known as PE or simply exposure therapy) is an appropriate treatment for combat PTSD. PE is a form of cognitive behavioral therapy developed by the psychologist Edna Foa and her colleagues for the treatment of PTSD. It has been the focus of a significant amount of research over the past twenty years and is one of only a few therapies determined in a 2007 Institute of Medicine report to have demonstrated clear effectiveness in reducing symptoms of PTSD.[19] For her role in developing this therapy, Foa was recognized in 2010 as one of *Time* magazine's hundred most influential people.[20] Briefly, the model of PTSD underlying exposure therapy goes like this. PTSD comes about as the result of an individual's learning to avoid danger out in the world. When a trauma occurs, the circumstances surrounding that trauma are imprinted on the memory in such a way that they become associated with high levels of physiological arousal and anxiety—an evolutionary mechanism intended to help the individual identify and elude similar dangers in future. As a result, individuals with PTSD, when confronted with sensory stimuli that remind them of previously encountered dangers, will try to avoid them. This gives rise to the idea of "triggers," or sensory reminders of past events. Such avoidance can be manifest in an obvious behavioral way, as when a veteran avoids Walmart because of the crowds. Or the avoidance may be experienced as a kind of emotional numbing, as when Jesse's uncle died and he was disconcerted to find that he felt no grief.

Exposure therapy rests on the principle that traumatic lessons learned in the past cannot be relearned to accurately reflect the current environment—for example, a veteran cannot learn that crowds at the Walmart in San Antonio do not pose the same threat as crowds in a marketplace in Baghdad—unless avoidance is overcome and there is sufficient exposure to the trigger that the individual "habituates."[21] Therefore, if the veteran who is frightened of crowds is forced to go to Walmart and spend some time walking around (this is a real therapeutic technique called "in vivo" exposure), two things are thought to happen. First, he will relearn that crowds do not necessarily equal danger, something he probably knew prior to Iraq. Second, the anxiety associated with crowds will be lessened because high levels of anxiety cannot be maintained forever in the absence of a perceived threat. It is not possible to stay continuously at the same high level of alert tension; over time, the body and mind habituate and relax. Relaxation training is also part of the exposure therapies, building on the theory that learning to face anxiety teaches the individual to understand that he controls his own anxiety, not vice versa.

The same essential principle is applied to dealing with memories. It is thought, under the PE model, to be the *avoidance* of painful memories that results in their uncontrolled intrusion into dreaming and waking life. Thus exposure therapy requires that the individual spend extended amounts of time revisiting traumatic memories in extreme detail, remembering the smells, sights, sounds, and thoughts that occurred at the time of the event. There are different techniques for this—for example, the story may be spoken aloud and audio-recorded or put down in writing—but a key component is that the memory be revisited again and again until the anxiety associated with it diminishes. The standard program for PE lasts between nine and twelve weeks, with one session per week.

For those swayed by the considerable scientific evidence supporting the efficacy of exposure therapy, as well as the improvements they have seen in their own patients, PE can be regarded as an incredible tool for healing. One psychologist at the trauma clinic, Dr. Alvarez, has seen Vietnam vets who have had chronic PTSD for forty years suddenly show dramatic improvement after only twelve weeks of exposure therapy—able to go to the mall or to a movie. He has heard from Vietnam vets in treatment, who said, "'I was told that I might get a little better but I'd always have the disorder.'" But now, he says, "they're in PE, doing therapy, and they're getting better." Another psychologist I spoke with, who has used these techniques among active-duty soldiers in Iraq, said results were so powerful that he has seen soldiers return to duty with no remaining symptoms. Clinicians who speak in support of exposure therapy often express relief that, after decades of mental health providers watching PTSD-diagnosed veterans fail to show significant improvement, sometimes despite years of psychodynamically driven therapy, they now have a treatment with measurable benefits to offer their patients. Both Derek and Chris had already left PTSD treatment because their symptoms no longer met the criteria for a PTSD diagnosis. They both say that Dr. Alvarez, using PE, has changed their lives.

Nor is exposure therapy a marginalized approach. In early 2008, the VA kicked off a rollout of PE (and also cognitive processing therapy, which works on similar principles and includes elements of exposure work), holding workshops all over the country to teach VA providers how to utilize these strategies in their work with PTSD.[22] The goal is to make these empirically supported treatments nationally available to veterans and to increase the level of standardization in VA mental health care. The San Antonio trauma clinic has been widely recognized as ahead of the curve in making ESTs their standard of care; the clinic's director has been asked to speak at regional conferences and provide mentorship for other VA trauma clinics attempting to follow their lead.

Nonetheless, there are those who feel that prolonged exposure is at best unproven for use with combat PTSD and at worst unethical, risking the retraumatization of already vulnerable individuals.[23] Psychodynamically inclined clinicians express a fear that the client may "decompensate," a notion suggesting that a variety of emotional reactions may result from engaging too directly with traumatic memory, ranging from a temporary loss of control to a complete psychotic break. This is a powerful concern (one clinician called the use of these therapies with recent veterans "unconscionable") and not simply a local one. After giving a talk on the debate over PE at a national conference, I was approached by a psychoanalyst who shuddered dramatically as she described the risks of talking too directly about trauma.

There is sincere trepidation behind this unease with PE, and yet this mistrust also plays into professional oppositions. At a training workshop on exposure therapies, the presiding clinical psychologist joked that (psychodynamic) "counselors" may be wary of PE because 'they like to pet their patients rather than make them suffer sometimes.' Advocates and antagonists of exposure therapy typically come from different disciplinary and generational backgrounds: individuals supporting exposure therapy tend to be younger and trained in clinical psychology or psychiatry, whereas those with reservations tend to be older and to have come from other mental health paradigms, such as social work, counseling psychology, marriage and family therapy, or psychoanalysis. There may be some amount of professional and material concern involved as well, for those expressing concern about exposure therapy are typically those who have not been trained to perform it, and vice versa.[24]

Even clinicians who support the use of PE, however, are mindful that it can require asking a great deal of patients. The same clinical psychologist who teased about 'making patients suffer' acknowledged this issue and said that she'll explain to new patients, 'Look, if you had a broken leg, the doctor might tell you that you need surgery to fix it properly so that you don't have a limp. Now the surgery may make you more incapacitated for a while, until you heal from that, but ultimately it will make you healthier and stronger than you would be without it.' She also pointed out that many of the anxiety disorders, including panic disorder and the phobias, are treated using therapies that can prompt an initial increase in anxiety, but said that she never hears complaints about this except in regard to treatment for PTSD. She related this to a sort of morality of trauma, a mind-set in which people think that trauma patients have already suffered enough.

At base, psychodynamic and CBT perspectives spring from greatly different understandings of what remembering trauma does to the self, whether luring the *mind* close to an emotional and potentially psychotic abyss or pushing the *stress response* to pass through the healthy processing of an event. Although both perspectives recognize the lasting effect that talking about trauma may have on an individual's cognitive and emotional register, the divergence between them was great enough to create friction during the trauma clinic's move toward an EST model. This necessitated that the shift occur slowly, taking place over the course of several years. Therapists who were worried about letting go of long-standing patients negotiated a gradual process of cutting back sessions—patients who had therapy once a week cut down to two to three times a month, then to a few times a year. Long-term veterans' groups (some of which had been ongoing for ten years or more) were gradually brought to a close or relocated to nonclinic facilities, like the local United Service Organization (USO). The clinic's director brought in a well-known clinical psychologist to host a training workshop on ESTs in May of 2006, preceding the national rollout by eighteen months. As of the spring of 2008, the clinic had phased out all but two of its long-term groups, both of which were aimed at the clinic's oldest population of World War II and Korea veterans.

The new roster of services looks, on the surface, much like the old. Psychiatrists still offer medication management, psychologists and social workers still offer both individual and group therapy options, and always there is the need to accommodate each veteran's individual needs. But there is an ideal pathway to the care now, a notion that patients should flow in to receive prompt care and out having regained the ability to function. Veterans who receive a diagnosis of PTSD are brought into a six-session "psycheducation class" that deals with understanding and managing their illness (called PTSD 101); then they may pass into short-term groups dealing with specific concerns such as stress or anger management. Individuals in severe distress may also receive individual therapy, either immediately upon entering the clinic or after having passed through the groups. The number of trauma clinic staff members available to provide PE and other ESTs remains limited despite increases in VA funding in recent years, and so the clinicians have experimented with trying to reorient these therapies for use in a group setting, with mixed success. Several of the clinicians have worked to bring health-outcomes research into the clinic in an attempt to continually refine treatments and services. The structure morphs as the effort to adapt continues; different providers find themselves in charge of diagnostic interviews, clinicians' schedules change as the clinic initiates evening hours to serve working veterans, and the pathway of referral changes a bit. In twenty months of observing the clinic, I found that little remained static for long.

Still, the larger shift has been in the VA's cultural paradigm for treatment of PTSD, moving from a model focused on treating it as a long-term disability to a model focused on time-limited treatment and the goal of recovery. Toward the end of my fieldwork, one of the clinicians compared the new system favorably with the post-Vietnam era, when the treatment paradigms and services were not yet in place and veterans returning home with problems were left to self-medicate on their own. His manner warmed as he noted that his colleagues, armed with the new CBT treatments and an arsenal of pharmaceuticals to support them, were now getting to see patients *get better.* For a clinician, this is the Holy Grail.

As a VA employee, on the other hand, he understood that the idea of a "recovery model" raises some potential for controversy. The notion of recovery can be taken so far as to mean losing one's PTSD diagnosis, and if there is any one issue most likely to upset some visible minority of the frustrated veterans we first met in the audience of the veterans' forum, it is the idea of *not* having PTSD. There are a variety of complex reasons for this, but one of the most important can be summed up in a single word: compensation.

Issues around compensation for service-related disabilities invariably seem to invite controversy. The basic system of VA compensation works like this. Veterans are evaluated for health problems both upon leaving the military (which, just to make things confusing, has a disability evaluation and compensation system separate from the VA's) and upon entering the VA system. For example, when Chris faced early retirement from the military, he was given a full medical examination that identified him as having service-related functional impairment related to PTSD, depression, and shrapnel wounds sustained in Afghanistan. Once he registered with the VA, he began another series of appointments when his primary care provider referred him to specialists for further evaluation.

Once any physical and/or mental health conditions have been identified that are—and this is important—understood to be a *direct result* of military service, a veteran may start the process of submitting a compensation claim to the VA. Usually this will initiate an additional health evaluation (or series of evaluations if there are several conditions under consideration) called a compensation and pension (C&P) exam, which provides independent confirmation of the original diagnosis. The medical records compiled from these evaluations are then submitted along with documentation of the veteran's service to the Veterans Benefits Administration (VBA)—which, by the way, operates separately from the Veterans Health Administration, which oversees all VA hospitals and clinics.

If the VBA decides that the claim shows sufficient evidence that a health condition is real and service-related, the veteran will be awarded a disability rating of between 0 and 100 percent. A zero percent rating means that the veteran is eligible for free VA care for that condition. A rating of 10 percent or above means that the veteran is also eligible for a tax-free monthly compensation payment, prorated according to the level of disability and the number of dependents a veteran can claim. Monthly compensation payments may range from $123 for a 10 percent disability awarded to a veteran with no dependent spouse, parents, or children, up to $3,000 for a veteran who is 100 percent disabled and has three or more dependents.[25] A single veteran may receive compensation for multiple conditions, but no matter how disabled the individual is determined to be by each condition, his total disability can never add up to more than 100 percent. Ratings can also be given out on a temporary or permanent basis. Although PTSD compensation is often talked about in terms of something that can be taken away, I have yet to hear of a single instance in which PTSD compensation payments were actually revoked.

An enormous amount of federal money goes into veterans' compensation payments. By 2004, total VA disability payments for PTSD were totaling $4.3 billion annually.[26] This may help to explain why the group Veterans for Common Sense filed a lawsuit against the VA in 2007, accusing the institution of, among other things, "deliberately cheating some veterans by working with the Pentagon to misclassify PTSD claims as pre-existing personality disorders to avoid paying benefits."[27] The executive director of the group, Paul Sullivan, was quoted as saying, "The VA has betrayed our veterans." The lawsuit demonstrated how the issue of diagnosis has at times become tied up with one of veterans' rights. The suing organization did not assume, as clinicians might, that clinicians were acting only in line with professional standards or that veterans might be accurately diagnosed with a personality disorder rather than with PTSD. In the minds of the veterans involved, individuals who *should* have been diagnosed with PTSD were being diagnosed with personality disorders instead, and this was being done with malice aforethought in an attempt to save the government money.[28] Held to be complicit in this effort, VA clinicians were seen as robbing veterans of their rightful benefits, their (mis?)diagnosis constituting a betrayal.

In truth, the issue of diagnosis, when viewed alongside concerns over compensation and veterans' rights, becomes clear as mud. From a professional perspective, clinicians view diagnosis as an act of discernment and expertise. The *DSM* sets out a list of symptoms that, in their presence and severity, indicate whether someone does or does not meet the criteria for a diagnosis of PTSD. Yet making a diagnosis is not a simple task. Clinicians at the trauma clinic talk in great detail about the lengths they go to in the effort to ensure that a diagnosis is appropriate, using nationally accepted assessment measures and a process of weeding out other possible diagnoses (referred to as "ruling-out") and of determining whether PTSD may coexist alongside one or more other disorders. Such comorbidity is common. Among PTSD-diagnosed veterans in the San Antonio study, comorbid diagnoses included substance abuse, depression, panic disorder, bipolar depression, and schizophrenia, and several veterans had gone through multiple examinations in order to ensure that their diagnoses were correct. Clinicians described this testing process as both professionally necessary and ethically responsible, pointing out that an individual given an inappropriate diagnosis is unlikely to receive the correct treatment.

Given public debate over whether the VA is adequately responsive to veterans' needs, however, such careful assessments can also be seen in profoundly negative terms. A diagnosis of personality disorder is understood to predate combat deployment and is therefore not eligible as a service-connected disability. So though such a diagnosis may be legitimate and laudable within the world of professional psychology, it may be read from another perspective as part of a conspiracy to deprive veterans of due compensation.[29] A diagnosis within the VA system is therefore not just a matter of putting the right name to the right illness. It is an act of determining who gets access to what kinds of care and what kinds of resources, and at times it seems to occur under a public spotlight.

This was made very clear in the spring of 2008, when Norma Perez, a VA psychologist in Temple, Texas (near Fort Hood), sent an e-mail around to the rest of her staff. The text of the e-mail, which was promptly leaked to the veterans' group VoteVets.org and became the center of yet another VA scandal, included the following: "Given that we are having more and more compensation-seeking veterans, I'd like to suggest that you refrain from giving a diagnosis of PTSD straight out. Consider a diagnosis of Adjustment Disorder, R/O [rule out] PTSD. Additionally, we really don't or have time [sic] to do the extensive testing that should be done to determine PTSD."

Norma Perez's e-mail left much unsaid, which may be part of what left her so vulnerable to public censure in the weeks and months after it was made public. She wrote in clinical language, the language of her profession. When she wrote "compensation-seeking veterans," she did not clarify whether she thought these veterans were seeking compensation rightfully or fraudulently, although the fact that she was worried about giving out PTSD diagnoses would suggest that she was not convinced all compensation-seeking veterans had PTSD. She advised that clinicians offer a less severe diagnosis of "Adjustment Disorder" but also that they do so in a temporary fashion, pending a more thorough rule-out of PTSD, which requires "extensive testing" for which they did not have the time. There is the echo of a clinician's concerns here: appropriate diagnosis given after due testing and the stresses of providing care for veterans in an atmosphere of limited time and manpower.

Yet her e-mail was read by some veterans' organizations as evidence of a larger VA effort to deny veterans their rightful compensation. A member of the non-profit organization Citizens for Responsibility and Ethics in Washington, which released the e-mail jointly with VoteVets.org, was quoted as saying, "It is outrageous that the VA is calling on its employees to deliberately misdiagnose returning veterans in an effort to cut costs. Those who have risked their lives serving our country deserve far better."[30] These accusations were considered politically viable enough to warrant a vehement public denial from the secretary of the VA, James Peake, and to prompt a congressional hearing at which Norma Perez was called upon to explain and repudiate her remarks.

The Perez case is only one example of the way in which VA clinicians may be called upon to function within a wider political realm; they are asked to act in accordance with their own professional expertise while simultaneously serving as the face of a government controversy that both precedes and transcends them. They not only provide care, they must also perform it.

Accordingly, a shift in treatment paradigms at the San Antonio trauma clinic represents not simply an evolution of clinical knowledge but also a political move with potentially explosive consequences. What would happen, for example, if the exposure therapies proved to be effective on a grand scale, so that clinic staff members were able to help many veterans with PTSD to get better and transition out of continuous care? Such an outcome could provide astonishing hope that Iraq and Afghanistan veterans will suffer less than did the Vietnam generation. But it might also present a circumstance like the one in which an OEF/OIF veteran who has previously been diagnosed with PTSD walks into the San Antonio VA's Compensation and Pension office and says to the clerk filing his PTSD claim, 'I don't know. I went through Dr. Alvarez's program and I just don't really have it anymore.' This is the story that one C&P officer told Dr. Alvarez. It raises the question, will a revolution in PTSD treatment—if it proves to be successful in helping OEF/OIF veterans recover from PTSD—require a revolution in the compensation system? And if so, what then?

Clinicians I interviewed were sensitive to issues of compensation, although aware that some veterans may come to them with a desire for disability pay more compelling than their PTSD symptoms. There is discomforting, but inconclusive, evidence to show that this is the case. One recent study found, upon reviewing the medical records of veterans with PTSD, that "[m]ost veterans' self-reported symptoms of PTSD become worse over time until they reach 100% disability, at which point an 82% decline in use of VA mental health services occurs."[31] So either some veterans are exaggerating symptoms until they achieve the highest possible level of compensation or they are just giving up on VA care (which is a real possibility; it is only recently that treatment to recovery has begun to seem an attainable goal). It should be noted that the same study found *no change* in veterans' corresponding use of medical health services. Although none of the San Antonio veterans admitted to flat out faking symptoms, a handful did acknowledge that they were seeking treatment only in hopes of supporting their compensation claims.[32] Clinicians are fully aware that some minority of veterans come to them seeking compensation more than treatment, but this was not a concern on which they seemed to spend a lot of energy. One psychiatrist told me, 'I err in [the veterans'] favor,' adding, 'I'm here to serve them. I'm not a detective.'

Beyond the more obvious question of sincere distress versus exaggerated or wholly manufactured distress, several staff members raised concerns about the impact of compensation on veterans' lives, for better and for worse. Several mentioned their concern for older veterans with PTSD, many of whom may have been on disability for decades, and who they fear would be left broke and unemployable if their compensation were revoked. Others speculated that perhaps lifelong compensation is not always the best thing for veterans with PTSD, particularly younger veterans, suggesting that the perpetual promise of a monthly payment may inhibit some from seeking out employment that could be fulfilling and empowering. Perhaps identifying as a disabled veteran is a poor exchange for seeing oneself as recovered and well. Clinicians are ethically bound to practice in accordance with professional standards, but there must be moments when a checklist of symptoms seems a poor guide through the quagmire of a PTSD diagnosis.

As PE and like therapies become the gold standard of care in the VA, the coming years should begin to reveal whether they will change our understanding of PTSD. If the recovery model proves viable, it will not only radically challenge widespread views of PTSD as a lifelong disorder, never shed once acquired, but will also demand a reconfiguration of the existing system for PTSD-related compensation. This in turn is likely to prompt a political battle over America's financial obligations to its veterans. If, on the other hand, the new emphasis on evidence-based treatments fails to produce a marked change in the quality of life for veterans with PTSD, the results may look all too familiar. We may see decline among this generation's PTSD-diagnosed veterans, who may begin to slip through the cracks, living as enduring reminders of the psychological cost of war. Although the outcome of this drama remains uncertain, it will be largely played out in the space between PTSD-diagnosed veterans and the clinicians who treat them, relationships that can themselves be tense.

One afternoon when I was interviewing a psychiatrist at the trauma clinic, the patient in the next office began shouting furiously at his clinician. The sudden disturbance prompted a hush throughout the clinic as those within hearing waited to see whether the conflict would escalate. It was quickly over; the man calmed down and the appointment continued. Strangely enough, when the clinician who was the object of the man's frustration later told me about the event, he did so in the process of describing how warm and appreciative he finds his PTSD patients. He said that despite the fact that the veterans he treats may have issues with anger, and may at times be frustrated by their experiences with the VA, they are pretty good at what he called "splitting." They may complain that the VA asks them to go to too many appointments or takes too long to schedule referrals or fails to resolve their compensation claims, but they tell him, 'I know that's not your fault, Doc.'

The clinician seemed to be suggesting that, despite the at times tense and politicized backdrop, veterans and clinicians at the VA trauma clinic manage for the most part to create a separate peace, if occasionally a wary one.[33] This was consistent with what I heard from veterans as well. Although PTSD diagnosis, treatment, and compensation remain hotly contested in and around the VA, these debates often remain behind the scenes in everyday clinic interactions, interactions that themselves play a profoundly important role in shaping many veterans' experiences with PTSD. Families and military personnel can and do offer up a wide array of powerful messages about PTSD, but mental health clinicians are the understood experts, and their views carry great weight. Distressed veterans who come to the trauma clinic in search of help have much incentive to listen to their clinicians, and clinicians, as individuals who have chosen a healing profession, describe a deep commitment to providing the best possible care for their veteran patients. Clinicians may themselves be veterans or the sons and daughters of veterans, and many of them expressed satisfaction at being able to provide care for those who have served their country.

Of course, veterans were not blandly accepting of VA clinicians' expertise on the subject of PTSD; on the contrary, it was not unusual to find them expressing partial or complete objection to a clinician's viewpoint or treatment suggestion. For example, at a certain point I began running into PTSD-diagnosed veterans and clients of the trauma clinic who, like the psychodynamic clinicians before them, expressed serious reservations about exposure therapy.

In later interviews I conducted, the issue of having to talk about trauma came up regularly, with veterans expressing a range of responses to the idea of probing so intently into what seemed to be dangerous memories. Some, like Chris, were initially hesitant about the idea, only to become more comfortable as the treatment went forward. "When Dr. Alvarez [first] told me about it," he says, "I was like, 'I'm outta here.' I thought we were going to shoot fireworks or go to a gun range. I didn't know what exposure therapy meant." Even when Dr. Alvarez explained to him what the therapy would entail, he remained skeptical. "'Fuck that,'" he said, "'There's no way.'"

In the end, however, Chris agreed to try it. He says that if you listen to the audiotapes made in his individual sessions, you can hear that he starts off "with a real edge. Dr. Alvarez's coaxing things out of me. And I'm talking about really minor stuff—things that aren't even traumatic but that I was having nightmares about. Then into this phase that was very emotional, where I'd be sobbing for fifteen to twenty minutes. Then into this phase where I'm talking about the most gruesome awful things, and I can remember every detail—what I was wearing, the smell, everything such clear…diarrhea of the mouth, just vomiting into the tape."

On the whole, he says, "It was very difficult and then it got very easy. Three, four months. Each week I would go from one to the next, and I would think about them, talk about it, listen to it for a few days, and then start thinking about the one for [my appointment] next Friday. So it went real slow at first, then I got good at being able to bring these things up and stop repressing them."

Some veterans, in other words, found their initial resistance to exposure therapy was resolved over time, often with some "coaxing" from their providers.[34] Others (like Adam, whose experience with treatment is described in chapter 8) refused outright to do exposure work; a few found the idea so intolerable they left VA care altogether and sought treatment in the private sector. One veteran who was studying for his master's degree in social work told me that he "disagreed" with exposure therapy and would not continue treatment, although he would not explain why. From a clinical perspective, this kind of resistance can be a matter for concern, given that exposure therapy is now part of the VA's standard of care for PTSD treatment (although other options are available). Beyond the difficulties of ensuring prompt access to care, treatment noncompliance and dropout are regular problems among OEF/OIF veterans nationwide.[35] One recent study found that fewer than 10 percent of OEF/OIF veterans with a new PTSD diagnosis completed the recommended number of treatment sessions within the first year following their diagnosis.[36] The resistance of some veterans to exposure therapy is interesting, too, in light of the fact that tensions at the clinic over the shift toward evidence-supported therapies at times became visible to patients. Several psychodynamic clinicians I interviewed reported having discussed their concerns about exposure therapy with patients. A handful of the newer providers reported hearing from veterans that they had postponed seeking care at the VA because a former VA clinician who now maintains a private practice had spoken negatively about exposure therapy to their Vietnam-era fathers. One veteran reported that this clinician had said that exposure therapy was experimental and that veterans were being used as guinea pigs; another reported something similar on the last session before he stopped coming to therapy at the trauma clinic. And so conflicts that began between clinicians had the potential to leak out into encounters with veterans, affecting their view of particular therapies and, ultimately, their willingness to engage in them.

Given the distrust of civilians expressed by some veterans, it may be that clinicians who are not veterans themselves, as many of the providers at the trauma clinic are not, are especially likely to encounter clients who respond to treatment suggestions with some suspicion. During one group session at the trauma clinic, an unknown veteran walked uninvited into the room and stood at the back, loudly challenging the clinicians to tell him whether they had ever been in combat and, when they said they had not, yelling that they 'didn't know shit.'[37] The implication was that they had no business teaching veterans how to deal with combat if they had never encountered it themselves.

Challenges to the trauma clinic's new reliance on evidence-supported treatments, then, fell into the realm not only of veterans' existing distrust of the VA but also of professional conflicts over who knows best how to treat what and clinicians' claims to know what treatments are best for veterans. Both of these debates reflect concerns over "authoritative knowledge," the question of whose knowledge holds most authority when a conflict arises.[38] Where trust is lacking—as may be the case in any health-care setting but particularly in one as politicized as the VA—the question of who knows the truth about best practices in PTSD treatment is liable to take on an added level of conflict, with very real potential to influence how veterans make decisions in their pursuit of mental health care.

NAVIGATION

Identity and Social Relations in Treatment Seeking and Recovery

Over the course of these pages, I have offered a portrait of how veterans of Iraq and Afghanistan experience combat PTSD as they move across time and a series of cultural environments, each of which adds another layer of memories, frustrations, and expectations to their understanding of themselves and their illness. We have, however, not yet heard veterans articulate how they understand what has happened to them, what is at stake for them in their journeys, and where they imagine themselves ending up.

The anthropologist Arthur Kleinman has described what he calls "illness narratives," the tales and accounts through which people make meaning from illness and the suffering that may accompany it.[1] In his writings, Kleinman evokes the many layers of meaning that are embedded in such narratives—social, moral, symbolic—and suggests that to talk about illness narratives only as passively told stories is to miss their true importance, which lies in the active role they play in contouring the very form of human illness and the lives of which it is a part. Jerome Bruner has similarly written about what he calls "acts of meaning," going perhaps a step beyond Kleinman to argue that "the lives and Selves we construct" are themselves an outcome of the meaning-making process.[2]

As I hope has become clear by now, we do not simply *speak* of meaning. We enact it in the things we do and feel, the choices we make, and the lives we work to create. Similarly, the way we understand illness, the meanings we ascribe to it, and the narratives we tell about it are all active in a very real sense.[3] They shape how we seek out health care and support, how we decide whether to participate in recommended treatments or abandon them, whether we feel shame in having an illness or take pride in how we meet the challenge it presents. The way we understand illness and its meanings *makes things happen;* it shapes actions, distress, and even the possibility of healing.

In this way the stories that veterans with PTSD tell are not simply narratives thick with meaning; they are also maps, navigational charts for those crossing wide oceans of life and loss. They are detailed, depicting the social, cultural, political, and economic forces with and against which veterans with PTSD must orient in charting a successful course to that most longed-for of destinations: a satisfactory life. For all their shared elements, these maps are deeply individual, incorporating personal details of history and experience and idiosyncratic understandings of PTSD itself. They chart past, present, and future and change over time.

Revisiting three veterans—Chris, Adam, and Derek—gives us the opportunity to see how their own maps were drawn and where their efforts at navigating life and illness have taken them.

For Chris, treatment has meant a combination of medications (Seroquel, Wellbutrin, and Trazodone) and a period of group therapy, followed by individual therapy with Dr. Alvarez using prolonged exposure and cognitive behavioral therapies. Of group therapy, Chris says, "I had to go to classes with these other guys, with Dr. Alvarez." When he first began going, he still was not sure he had PTSD. "I just thought I was weak." Hearing other veterans describe symptoms eerily similar to his own made him realize, "Wow. I'm not the only one."

Of exposure therapy, Chris says, "I had to sit and basically recite what happened down there, downrange [while deployed], into a tape recorder and listen to it over and over again." It was difficult at first. "I was always on edge," he says. "The nightmares would keep coming. Everything just started flooding forward. I was sleeping maybe two to three hours a night. I wouldn't take the medication because it—I didn't tell this to my doctor—but it felt like [the trauma] was coming out. I realized that I could process these things if I was thinking about them, but if I wasn't thinking about them I couldn't process them."

Over the course of his treatment for PTSD and depression, he gained enough control over his symptoms that he felt able to leave therapy. He stopped taking Seroquel, which interfered, he said, with his ability "to think creatively." By our last meeting, he was also tapering off of the antidepressant Wellbutrin, hoping to be free of his medications. He has also incorporated his psychologist's teachings on cognitive restructuring, a technique of training oneself to correct negative patterns of thinking, into his thought process. "It becomes a constant, constant check, what am I thinking? Is this an accurate thought? What is the truth of what is happening here? I've been able to apply that for my own psychological well-being. So instead of internalizing things I've been able to compute things a little more rationally, and I think that's been able to help with things I had wrong with me long before I went to Afghanistan."

He has come to see PTSD as the outcome of "not processing things that are either too terrifying or because you feel weak or you had a moment of what you feel was cowardice." I described in chapter 3 how deeply ashamed Chris was of his first firefight. His delay in firing and the indignity of his fear remain a significant part of the trauma that has haunted him. This is what he didn't want to remember. This is what eats away at him. "The reason I know that it causes the disorder is because when I started to listen to those tapes over and over again, I realized that the disorder itself, the symptoms I was having, went away," he explains. "So it's got to be related to that. It's just not dealing with stuff that's extreme, and how you were involved in that extreme situation."

Perhaps most strikingly, his way of perceiving the world has also changed since the treatment, coming to bear more resemblance to how he observed his surroundings before he went to war. "I'm not living in the shooting gallery that was my mind," he says. "Everywhere I went it was just," and he swivels his head back and forth as though looking to all sides, identifying imagined objects and the potential threat they pose:

"Bridge. Danger... Sniper.
"Guy walking... Bomber.
"Car pulling up fast in the rear view mirror... Bomb.
"Trash on the side of the road... Bomb.
"Pot-hole filled in freshly... Bomb."

This was how he saw the world.

Now, by contrast, he says, "It's not that constant edge. When I'd drive from my work to my house, I'd just be sweating bullets every time, you know. Because it was just like this race—this race for life. I don't feel that way anymore. It's great."

He says he is "probably 98 percent cured" of PTSD. "Other than a few nightmares here and there, or I see things and every once in a while for a half second I think I'm somewhere else. They're not crippling things. They're just things that I'll probably have to deal with the rest of my life. And if I didn't have to deal with those things, because I'm human, it would probably mean I wouldn't be human." After all the suffering he has witnessed and endured, not to hold on to these memories would seem wrong to him. He says, "They're things that I want to keep with me, just as a reminder."

His positive experience with exposure therapy has led him to become something of an advocate for PTSD treatment. "If somebody says it's not treatable," he offers, his voice hardening, "they're full of shit. They're not trying. Or they're not suffering enough, maybe. Maybe it's not that bad for them. Because when it's bad, you definitely want to be helped." His words reveal his continued reliance on a military mind-set: if therapy doesn't work, you're just not trying hard enough. Toughen up, soldier. He admits to an ongoing struggle with the diagnosis of PTSD. "It just feels weak," he says, "It still to this day feels like a cop-out. It's not a bullet to the chest." Certain experiences with other veterans, in particular an older man Chris met at the VA who tried to coach him in what symptoms he should report to get compensation for PTSD, have not lessened his sense of shame. "I didn't want to ever be that guy, you know what I mean? There's a lot of people out there that ruin it for the certifiables."

Chris's view of PTSD provides some insight into the notion of an "explanatory model," the term anthropologists use to describe an individual's culturally based understanding of a given illness.[4] Patients' explanatory models do not always include a fixed idea about their disorder, complete with a clearly identified cause and expected trajectory. Chris's perspective on PTSD exemplifies this; it is an amalgam of sometimes contradictory ideas. He sees it as evidence of some flaw in himself, a weakness, and yet also something he recognizes and accepts. He views PTSD as the outcome of trauma—traumas he has described in great detail during audiotaped therapy sessions—yet also acknowledges the role of things that troubled him long before Afghanistan. His ideas, too, are drawn from many sources: his years in the military, experiences with other veterans, psychological views of cognition and behavior, and psychiatric prescriptions for medication. He has taken up particular aspects of his treatment while rejecting others: his medications, for example, which he thought interfered with the process of the trauma's "coming out" while he was engaged in the most strenuous period of exposure therapy.[5]

Even with his PTSD under control, there are still difficulties. His wife, he acknowledges, still thinks PTSD is "something that I may use as an excuse," although he takes some responsibility for this. "The few times that I've ever tried to approach her about it, it's always at the wrong time. It's always at a time when it could be construed as an excuse. And she gets upset about that and says I'm trying to withdraw, and I can't think with my PTSD acting up." This remains an issue between them. "Part of the reason that I wanted to have treatment and get better was so that I wouldn't have that excuse." When he remembers the level of performance he expected from himself and from his enlisted men in the air force, he feels as though he can no longer live up. "I can see somebody looking from the outside—even my best friend Brent, I can see him coming here and looking from the outside and saying, 'Dude, what the hell happened to you? You were fine. When we left [Afghanistan] you were fine.' I really wasn't, but I seemed that way. I can see him being cynical. I know I shouldn't give a damn what people say, but…I don't know."

He remains humbled, too, by his inability to achieve greater financial and career success. There was a time shortly after Chris's release from the hospital when, despite working two jobs, he was unable to pay the bills and had to fall back on aid from a private veterans' organization. He was grateful for their intervention but stung that he was unable to make ends meet.[6] Many veterans found that the lack of economic and educational opportunities that had pushed them to join the military were still there after their separation, unresolved by time in the service and the skills and benefits accrued there. Many found themselves at least temporarily unemployed or underemployed, unable to provide for themselves or their families as expected.

There is no separating Chris's struggle for a postwar identity from his struggle to live up to the expectations he believes those around him might have for him. "I feel ashamed when my friends from the military call me," he says. It has gotten easier to face them since he starting working at the credit card company. Before that, he worked for a while as a shoe salesman in an upscale department store. "I was making great money, but I was still selling shoes. You know? And I could feel people, although I'm sure none of them said that, but I could hear them saying it, 'I saw this dude run headlong into enemy fire…and now he's selling shoes?!'" He shakes his head. "And that's pride once again, but that's the part of me that wishes I'd just died over there and been left a picture on the wall in the NCO club." When he has struggled with the urge to kill himself, this is part of what has tormented him. "People were like, 'But you have so much to live for— your kids!' And that's what I can't even express to people, that at that point it just doesn't matter. People who've never been suicidal…I wanted to kill myself *for* my kids! I was so miserable and depressed and ashamed and low, I didn't want them to see me."

In the end, what stands out here is that Chris's view of a life worth living— and for a man who has struggled with the desire to kill himself over a period of several years, this is a matter of some importance—is driven by notions of both identity and obligation. He imagines a life in which he sees himself as someone his children can look up to. Part of this desire involves a sense of "moving up," engaging in work that not only meets his financial needs but also allows him to retain the identity he acquired in the military, as the man who ran headlong into enemy fire. He wants to live without disappointing the expectations of his friends from that time. He is unwilling to go from heroic leader to shoe salesman; this feels like an unbearable comedown. He feels the pull of his obligations to his children but acknowledges that this has not always been enough to maintain his will to live in times of crushing distress. It has taken the help of others to keep that will in motion—his wife and children but also his friends, military leaders, and clinicians. It was this net of joined forces that caught and held him when he was falling. He is, for all their efforts and his own, still alive.

After seven months in Iraq with his marine reserve unit, Adam returned to Camp Pendleton to face the usual short period of briefings and paperwork prior to release. He was already sensing that all was not well and had begun drinking heavily almost as soon as he landed back in the United States. "I was having horrific nightmares and I wasn't sleeping. I mean I literally wasn't sleeping. I would stay awake or I would drink so much that I would pass out. And of course I would wake up an hour later and start drinking again."

He did not find the post-deployment briefings on PTSD at Camp Pendleton particularly helpful, even as they described the same problems he was already having. "The staff sergeant would stand up there and he'd read a piece of paper that says, 'If you're having a, b, c, and d, they need you to go do h, i, j, whatever.' And of course you're home, you just got home, and you're ready to go see your family, your friends. I mean, you're not *listening*. Who are we kidding here?"

Back at his home unit there was another briefing on readjustment and PTSD. In this one, the information was roughly the same but Adam says it was presented "in a manner in which it was...if you were smart enough, you understood that they were basically saying [that] whatever, you just need to suck it up. You just need to deal with it. I mean, they didn't *say* that. It was just, 'if this, then you go do this ...' It was kind of an aside almost."

He got stuck between the two messages he heard in the scheduled briefings, recognizing that his nightmares and drinking might signal a larger problem but unwilling to be the one who admitted to needing help. As platoon sergeant, he got other men in his unit to seek care, and when necessary, he says, "We physically took them to go see people. But when it came to me, I refused to. What's good for them isn't good for me, so to speak. I just felt like it was weak. I was supposed to be stronger and bigger and meaner, and I was supposed to be able to deal with all those things." His resolve to tough it out lasted about six weeks. He remained depressed and unable to sleep and finally broke down and sought help from the clinic on base.

This first encounter with mental health treatment made an ugly impression. The doctor, as Adam remembers it, did not even ask how he was doing before he began berating him for seeking help at the post clinic rather than through one of the official channels: at a larger local base or through the Tricare program (which enables service members to receive health care in the civilian sector). "So that was when I lost it," says Adam. "I got up and got in his face and started just screaming and yelling at him. And he knew. He backed out and got out of the room and nothing was ever said about it." Another doctor came in then and made the same referral suggestions, more civilly, and Adam wound up seeing a local civilian psychologist. Even so, he says, "I did that very much under the radar. I didn't make a big deal out of it. I was still at that point very concerned about my career. I didn't tell my friends, I didn't tell anybody."

A few months later, Adam left the reserves for good. After a long post-deployment leave, he arrived at Friday night formation for his first weekend drill and realized within a few minutes that "it was just everything that I didn't want it to be anymore. I got out of formation and went and got a check-out sheet and left that night. That was it. I never looked back." I ask him what he meant by "everything I didn't want it to be" and he answers, "I was always very gung-ho, and I loved it and I lived for it, you know. And I just realized after having served on active duty and having been in combat—I realized the monotony of what they did in the reserve unit. And how some of those people that were higher-ups just had no clue what they were really doing. It was a circus."

Part of his dissatisfaction came from his role as an NCO, caught between the needs of the enlisted men for whom he felt responsible and the orders coming down from superior officers, which he felt compelled to obey. "I would sit in meetings and argue with people—it was my job to run interference. Wherever I could, you know, and try to keep my marines from getting wrapped up in having to do stuff that was a waste of their time." As he stood there in formation that night, debating whether to stay or whether to go, he found that he "just didn't have the heart to deal with that stuff anymore. So I got out."

He went back to school to finish the college degree he had been working on before deploying. He had regular meetings with his psychologist, who diagnosed him with PTSD and major depression, and a psychiatrist, who prescribed Zoloft for his depression and Ambien to help him sleep. His psychologist encouraged him to try a treatment called eye movement desensitization and reprocessing (EMDR), which involves combining rapid eye movement (or other stimuli) with a detailed reassessment of traumatic events. EMDR is unlike the exposure therapies in that although it requires the individual to remember traumatic events in detail, those events do not have to be written down or shared with the clinician.[7] Of EMDR, he says, "I hated it. I absolutely hated it. Looking back on it now, I feel it was way too early in my progression in PTSD to have done EMDR. Because I didn't need EMDR to bring back those memories and those feelings and sensations and all that. I could sit there and look you in the eye and talk to you for two minutes and I would have all those feelings and smells and sounds and everything right there. So I hated it. I hated EMDR with a passion." Although he continued seeing the psychologist, his frustration with the treatment reinforced his initial discomfort with care seeking.

He finished his remaining college courses within a semester and then made the move to San Antonio to begin a new job with a large construction firm. His wife was working in Santa Fe at the time, and although they saw each other every weekend, he lived alone during the week. He admits that this "probably wasn't real good for me because I didn't have anything in the refrigerator except beer and liquor, and so I drank and I drank and I drank and I drank and I worked."

He was successful in his new job despite all the drinking, building a solid professional network and earning more than $100,000 his first year. He was not getting along with his boss, however, and decided soon afterward that it was time to go into business for himself. He found a private psychologist in San Antonio who agreed to treat him without EMDR, a stipulation he put forward from the beginning. Lacking health insurance, he continued to pay out-of-pocket for the sessions he attended as often as twice a week. He estimates that he has spent somewhere in the neighborhood of $10,000 in private care over the past few years.

For all the expense, he could not make himself seek out the care for which he was eligible at the VA. The funny thing is, he got others to go. He would receive calls from his former marines, who would tell him that they couldn't sleep, they were having nightmares, etc., and he would tell them to go to the VA. But when it came to his own nightmares, he held himself to a different standard. "I just had something wrong with my head," he says. "I don't have anything wrong with me physically. I'm not worthy."

This went on for a year or so. Adam's wife found a job in San Antonio and moved into the house with him. His new contracting business got off the ground and picked up some big jobs. He applied for service connection for his PTSD and received a 50 percent disability rating within just a few months. He saw his psychologist regularly, and they discussed his problems, debated solutions, and worked on understanding and processing his memories of Iraq. He began talking more closely with some of the Vietnam veterans among his family and friends and found that they could understand what he was going through, having faced similar challenges themselves. He made gradual progress, he says, until early 2007, when things began getting steadily worse again.

On reflection, Adam credits two things with the decline. First of all, January was about the time when he began talking with David, a close friend still in the marines, about providing volunteer assistance to other veterans applying for service connection, a move that built on his own success with getting through the benefits process. Adam made contact with a local veterans group and began devoting an increasing amount of time and energy to it, volunteering there at least once a week.

Meanwhile, David returned to Iraq for his third tour. He called one day on a satellite phone to tell Adam that leadership had left him in control of a police station in a contested area, overseeing a twenty-man detail and an Iraqi police force faced with regular sniper, mortar, and rocket attacks. "So daily [David's] got marines getting wounded," Adam says. "He's not getting support. He calls the quick reaction force and it takes them thirty-five minutes to get there because they get ambushed on the way. Anyway, he has no one to talk to. So he called me, and I guess they intercepted one of the phone calls, and were going to charge him with breach of operational security."

Confronted by his superiors, David broke down and admitted he was no longer keeping it together. He was promptly given a medical evacuation out of Iraq. "And man," Adam says, "I felt such guilt for not being there. If I could have walked into the unit and said, 'I want to be there in forty-eight hours, give me a rifle and a flak jacket, I'll go'? In a heartbeat." Returned to his home in Houston, David became embroiled in a series of convoluted miscommunications between military, VA, and civilian health-care providers. Adam retold the story, thoroughly disgusted, in such exquisite detail that it might have been his own.

This was the problem he came face-to-face with in January, when he began to slip back into depression and anxiety. He was overcome by the uncomfortable parallel of becoming excited about his volunteer work at the same time he was watching his best friend's life fall apart. The guilt was too strong and was matched, he thinks, by unconscious fears. "When I say I started regressing in January," he explains, "part of that probably was me saying, 'Holy shit, you're getting positive about something. You're getting positive about life again. You can't do that.'"

He began to feel more and more depressed, and the anxiety and nightmares began again. The regression was gradual, but by August he was no longer able to keep on as he had been. Oddly enough, when it came to a crisis point, the precipitating factor was once again David, who had come for a visit. The two went out to Adam's deer lease, down in the south of the state. Adam says, "We didn't really talk about the war, per se, but we didn't have to. You know, there's just that sense." After a few days, they drove back to San Antonio, and David left the next morning, headed back home to Houston. Within hours, Adam remembers, "I was having a major, major panic attack, and I mean, I just absolutely lost it. I was just a very small short time away from committing suicide and I didn't know what to do. I didn't call anybody. I was just—I left [work] and the only thing I could think of was the VA, so I drove there." He presented himself at the psychiatric triage unit, and that was the beginning of his experience with VA health care.

In a poignant coincidence, David was checking himself into a hospital in Houston at just about the same time, having himself come unglued on the drive home. It was several days before Adam found out; neither had called the other.

It is striking that both of these men presented themselves for care on the day they separated, after a visit in which, according to Adam, they said nothing about the war itself. It was as though their shared combat experiences lingered in the space between them, and that unspoken presence was enough to undo some delicate inner balancing act. It is perhaps the more extraordinary that when I asked Adam who or what had been most helpful to him in the preceding years, he said without hesitation, "David. Before we left [for Iraq], we were friends. But I consider him to be my best friend now, and I think if you asked him he would probably say the same. David and I can sit in a room and we don't have to articulate our feelings because we know exactly how the other one is feeling. We know exactly what the other one is thinking. We're both going through very similar situations with post-traumatic stress disorder and the VA and our feelings. So we can relate to each other 100 percent."

That relationship in turn has played an important role in shaping how Adam views his own experiences. David's frustrations with VA and military health care have fed into Adam's own. They regularly compare notes. Talking about his involvement in group therapy at the VA, Adam said that he had expected to also be offered private counseling sessions, since that was what David was receiving at the VA in Houston. And although he did not say this, I cannot help but wonder whether having another combat veteran to talk with has helped Adam to deal with the persistent sting of viewing PTSD as a weakness. If he was not, in fact, stronger and bigger and meaner than the illness, then at least he was not alone. Meanwhile, upset by his own institutional encounters and those of David and other veteran buddies, Adam has become an articulate advocate for veterans' rights. He is a repository for stories of unjust treatment. He believes strongly that veterans are in the best position to help other veterans.

When I ask him about PTSD, he responds, "PTSD to me is…the reaction to the trauma that some of us experience. It's your failure to properly reintegrate into society. It's—everybody wants you to do that reintegration process. They want you to be okay. They want you to take your camos off, put your civvies on, wash 'em and put 'em in the closet. And they want you to go back to your normal life, the way that you were. And a lot of people can't do that. And so, whether you call it PTSD or anxiety disorder or whatever, you have failed to cut loose those experiences."

He sees PTSD, in other words, as the failure to do what is expected of you. It is the failure to jettison the past and make the change from military to civilian garb, a sartorial shift cloaking an equally dramatic inner change. And that, Adam says, "is the thing that people don't get. I feel like I lost my identity that I had before, predeployment. Who I was before doesn't exist anymore. And I gained a new warrior identity, and I became that. And I'm almost afraid—I'm very much afraid of letting go of that. Because now that I've been removed from Iraq and I've been removed from the time that identity changed in me, I'm afraid of the pain and suffering that's going to come with changing again."

This fear may help to explain why, amid great change, he has sought some continuity. There are marked similarities between his new role as a volunteer claims advisor and his previous responsibilities as a platoon sergeant whose job it was "to run interference." Given that his only stated regret about leaving the reserves lay in not being able to face combat with his buddies, there is a certain rightness to the fact that he has devoted himself so fully to helping other veterans face down a new challenge. Like Chris, Adam has attempted to navigate PTSD without the orienting vision of a postwar identity. Pushed to move forward with no clear goal in sight, they have both steered by their obligation to others—Chris to his children and Adam to his fellow veterans.

Even getting to this point has, Adam acknowledges, required "two years of work." He worries for "all my guys who've been home for six months and they're realizing, they're starting to acknowledge that there's an issue. It's not PTSD because 'that couldn't happen to me!' but there's an issue. They are out on the water without a sail. They're up shit creek without a paddle. They feel very much lost. And abandoned. And alone."

This concern for other veterans has become his guiding light. Now, he says, "when I talk about volunteering, all of a sudden my life has purpose and meaning. I feel very much that my purpose and meaning was to go to Iraq, and my purpose and meaning was to lead men into battle and to do the things that I did. And I didn't expect to make it home. But when you do—it's like, now what the hell do you do?" His next words come quickly: "If you consider [Iraq]—like I do, probably twenty-nine out of thirty days—to be the pinnacle of your life, then where do you go from there? And I'm sure that a lot of veterans feel that way. To them, that was it. That was everything. So now what? They have to find something meaningful and purposeful. So I think I've found that and we're moving towards it."

But as much as I would like to say here that Adam is sailing along, confident in his vision and moving steadily forward, his story is not so simple. Finding meaning and purpose has not been enough to ease his distress. He has nightmares, still, every night—often about Iraq, other times about homicidal violence here at home. His relationship with his wife remains fragile, and although he credits her with great patience and understanding, they are struggling to find common ground. He cannot share his feelings with her the way he can with David. He finds it hard to respond to her when she reaches out. He values his psychologist and the help she has given him, but his symptoms remain uncontrolled and, given his negative experience with EMDR, he remains hesitant to try other treatments.

He is a man of many talents: intelligent, capable, well-spoken, likable. He is from a prosperous family and has been successful himself, avoiding the financial problems that plague so many veterans. He has all the tools for building a good life, yet he still struggles. Applying his description of other veterans to himself, he is on the water without a sail. Up shit creek without a paddle. Having a map has not been enough to get him to shore.

From the time Derek made the trip from Walter Reed to San Antonio's Brooke Army Medical Center, the focus was on his wounded leg. For nearly a year there were repeated surgeries as the doctors attempted to pull the fragments of his lower leg together in a way that would enable him to support a prosthesis without pain. Early in his treatment, Laticia sneaked him out of the hospital one afternoon, hopped up on antibiotics and painkillers, and they drove to the courthouse to get married. When Derek jokingly asked the presiding official for a special "veterans' discount," the judge took one look at his bandages and gave them back their $50 court fee. Afterward they stopped at a gas station for Gatorade and then headed back to the hospital, where Laticia, as Derek's wife, now had the right to receive information relevant to his care. Derek still teases her, "I was on drugs when we got married."

I asked her, "At the time, how did you see him dealing with [his injury]?"

"He really...there was really no times when it was, 'Poor me,' or the sadness. It was 'Okay, what do I do now? Let's figure out what the plan is now. We can move forward from this, let's do this.' It really wasn't any type of bad attitude. Maybe a little short temper. He would get frustrated easily and he would have a little bit of a snap. Really wasn't a lot of patience. It was those type of symptoms. But not really the beating up on himself or placing the blame on anybody."

In those early days, their greatest challenge was getting Derek's physical health squared away. They spent four months living in outpatient housing at Fort Sam Houston, where they had a hotel room to share with Laticia's two little boys. Derek had to get to know them all over again after his long absence. Through a long hot summer in a crowded room, Derek says of Laticia, "Her biggest complaint was [that]...for a long time I was extra clingy. I wanted her by my side at all times. I had missed her for eight months. I had gone through being blown up three times in one day, any day can be the last one. So I was already mentally trying to figure out that I might never see her again. And then seeing that I was still here and feeling like it was on borrowed time...and it drove her nuts."

Laticia agrees. "You don't want to say—'Oh my god, he's right there.' But it was like that, 'Oh my god he's right there!' If we had been sewn at the hip, that would have been great for him. But you know that left me no extra time or personal time or kid time. It was me and him. That's how it was. He was very clingy. Very clingy."

Every time she left the room—to take the kids to the park, to go grocery shopping, to go pick up his medicines at the pharmacy—he would ask her, "Where are you going? Where are you going? Come back." When she was in the room, he wanted her next to him, where he could reach out and stroke her hand for hours on end.

"I have very sensitive skin," she says, "so the constant petting would try my…" But she cuts the sentence short, remembering how she would remind herself, "He's hurt, he just got back, that's just part of him." Even so, she found it to be a challenging transition, the move from being an independent woman caring for her children alone to caring full-time for a husband who wanted her present every minute. She got through it by drawing on a view of Derek that made these annoyances seem bearable and mundane.

"With all the things that he went through," she says, "there's [nothing] in the world that would change my outlook on the world to match his. So that the way we see each other would be the same." It wasn't simply that they were different people. She saw the differences between them as an outcome of the suffering he had gone through in Iraq, identifying it as something like what is often called post-traumatic growth. Rather than viewing him as emotionally wounded, she saw him as more caring and giving because he had lived through these things. As she says now, "He's always going to be in a higher echelon of compassion and love for me because he has gone through those experiences. And the life that he sees is completely different from how I see life. I will never be able to be on that same level with him. My thing," she concludes, "is not to let it push us apart. Not let it—he's rubbing me, he's constantly right there—and not let that put me in a way where he's annoying me or something."

And so, with this in mind, she cooked meals to help him gain back the weight he had lost. She kept track of his medicines and appointments and did her best to entertain the kids until school began again. Day by day, they pushed on through. Derek spent months at the Center for the Intrepid, Fort Sam Houston's new state-of-the-art rehabilitation facility for wounded veterans, learning to walk on his new prosthesis. He began thinking ahead to life after the military and applied to one of the local colleges. He and Laticia found an apartment off post and got the boys settled into school. Derek began attending classes, and it was then that he was forced to realize that his problems were not only those related to his injured leg. He sought out his vocational rehabilitation counselor, and she got him linked up with the VA for a PTSD assessment.

Like Chris, Derek has gone through a fairly standard course of treatment under the VA's new time-limited model. His psychiatrist put him on medication to "even out" his serotonin levels (he believes it to be Seroquel but isn't sure),[8] and he began individual therapy with Dr. Alvarez.

"It's cognitive behavioral restructuring," he explains. "So you go in and the first [session] is like a class on PTSD and how it's structured and the different phases and stages of it." The classes changed how he understood the profound sensory and emotional responses he was having to the world around him. "[Dr. Alvarez] explained that what happens is, when you're in combat, all your senses get picked up.... Fight or flight kicks in. And because we've been in [combat] so much, we bring it up and we can't bring it back down." He found it helpful "to actually cognitively understand the thought process, the reactions, to see yourself go up and then go down and to realize subconsciously that it's going to be okay."

Following the initial classes, Derek became involved in the "in vivo" aspect of PE treatment, which required spending time in scenarios that provoked a fear response. "Things like that," he says, "were my homework. Go somewhere crowded, then stay as long as you can. Once you feel like you have to leave, stay ten more minutes. My case was simple, walk the same route to class every day"—instead of varying his route, a common tactic used in combat zones to avoid attack—"and then go straight into class and sit down." The first week, he found it almost impossible. "By Friday I was more okay with it, but Monday and Tuesday I was not happy."

The second phase of the treatment, according to Derek, focused on cognitive restructuring. "You identify situations that make you nervous and you write 'being in a crowded place makes me nervous,' and then you analyze it. Is it really something you should be nervous about, and if so, keep it. Are you overreacting? Are you not overreacting? And that helps a lot, because you can see on paper, 'No, I really shouldn't be this bothered in this situation.'"

Derek learned to think critically about his anxiety, to become aware of his distress, getting in the habit of quantifying his discomfort on a scale from one to ten (one being no anxiety, ten being unbearable). The final phase focused on talking about the combat events that Derek found more troubling, revisiting "incidents," he says, "that I had repressed for over a year. I recorded them and had to listen to them daily and then had to record my anxiety level. And watch it steadily go down."

"What was that like?" I ask.

"The first two or three days it was torture. I told Dr. Alvarez, this is something I really don't want to do. I repressed this for a reason. But at the end, I think it was supposed to be an eight-week program but I finished it early. It got a lot better. Even talking to you about the situations—yeah, it brought some anxiety, but where it used to get to an eight, now it gets to a two or a three."

Laticia breaks in here to ask him, "When I listened to [the tape] with you, that one time I listened, how many times had you listened to it?"

"Three or four."

Laticia nods as she turns to me, describing her response to hearing his war stories. "The floodgates in my eyes must have opened up to full gauge because some of those stories that he told, especially about…the girl was on there, and then another one of the Iraqi army guys, and Derek holding his stomach so the blood wouldn't come out any more, like a tourniquet or what do you call it?"

"I had a field dressing on his stomach," he says.

"Just hearing some of the things that he went through," she continues, "was like a real eye-opener for me. I think if the wives would listen to that—I think it helps. But it helped me—not understand, but at least be able to look at the picture to help me understand. You can't go into the painter's mind and know what he was thinking when Monet was scribbling, but at least you can know…" She found that with understanding came greater acceptance. "So I can better see now with the crowds or not wanting to do this, or anxiety towards that. Although it's still very very *very* frustrating, I can at least kind of see it from the other side. I think I listened to about half, for about thirty minutes? And cried like a newborn baby. And then just to know that was just a couple of incidents of what he went through over there. It was an eye-opener."

Like Chris, Derek no longer goes to treatment. He says that he is much better. "I don't walk around buildings anymore. I go out in groups of people." Together he and Laticia describe visiting a local Chuck E. Cheese (the chain of giant pizza parlors with indoor arcades and jungle gyms) and how Derek, who initially refused to go inside, ended up walking in and chasing Laticia and the kids around for three hours, oblivious to the crowds.

"I had a blast," Derek admits. Laticia laughs, and he goes on, watching his wife's face. "I was running around—I must have freaked you out with all the obstacles I did."

"No, but did you take your leg off?"

"No, it got trapped in the safety net and fell off." He grins, remembering, and says, "When I chased you through the jungle gym, that was fun."

"I was laughing, but inside, I was like, 'Wow.'"

He turns to fill me in. "She came and threw this little ball at me, and tried to run down like I couldn't get her. I just moved like a snake, put her on my knee and grabbed her. It was fun, and at my appointment with Dr. Alvarez that week, I said, 'I don't know what you did, but thank you, because there's no way I would have been able to do the things I did over the past two weeks. At all.'"

"Do you see a difference in him?" I ask Laticia.

She nods. "As far as crowds and willingness to do other things and going out of the house, and shopping is so much better now. That portion is still there. I don't think he'll ever not be clingy, but I'm okay with that now. Even though it's a little frustrating, I just chalk it up to that's just who he is and it's not PTSD. He's a lot more understanding, he's a *lot* more patient now. I notice a big change. A huge change."

"There's still nightmares," Derek says.

"Still nightmares," she agrees. "Times I have to shake him. 'Wake up! Wake up!'"

"They're different now," Derek points out. "Before it was always a replay of an event in Iraq. And now it's sometimes in Iraq, sometimes it's not. Like last night I had one and I woke up confused—not anxious, not worried, not sweating. Just confused. I was in the army still, and somehow I was in Serbia. Never been to Serbia. But we were on one side, and the Serbs were on the other side and just lobbing artillery shells back and forth, and none of them were detonating. But one of them came and detonated right by me. I could feel the shock wave lift me up and put me down, and then I climbed over the sandbags and went back into another room and went to sleep."

In other words, Derek still dreams of the army, of bombs that land too close. In these new dreams, though, the bombs fail to explode. If they do go off, he finds that he can simply ride the shock wave back to sleep. He does not wake up sweating and anxious.

Like all these veterans, however, he can identify ways in which he has changed from his prewar self. For Derek, these changes have been both good and bad. He says, "I look at life differently. Sometimes I'm short-tempered and my patience is down. My stress level is almost none. I go to school and I laugh every day at the college students getting worked up about tests and papers, because as long as nobody's shooting at me? Shooting RPGs at me? I can handle almost anything. Things that used to bother and stress me out aren't that important anymore. And at the end of the day, I still go home to my family, I don't go home to some bunker out in the desert somewhere. Little things that everybody else takes for granted, I see differently now." He has traded a leg for his younger self's unnecessary worries. He values the simple blessings of life: home, family, a safe place to sleep.

I turn to Laticia and ask, "How do you think about PTSD at this point?"

She thinks about this for a moment and then answers, "I guess if I was to tell somebody what PTSD would be in the most comfortable language, I would say it's all of the aftereffects—feelings, emotions, mental thinking—that one person has after being in an intense and stressful, dangerous environment over a long period of time. All the anxiety—you have to make quick decisions, so you're impatient. All that a person carries with them even though they're not still in an environment that's stressful."

When asked whether PTSD continues to impact Derek's life, she says, "I think it's a presence. Not so severe as when he first came back, but it still affects him. I figure it's probably always going to be a presence in some sort of way, because it's something that he has to live with and deal with and constantly make an effort to overcome and change."

And so, little by little, they work toward the goals they have set for themselves. Derek looks ahead to the day when he finishes his college degree and believes he has the networks and the expertise to start his own business in advertising. When Derek is finished with school, Laticia plans to use benefits available to wives of disabled veterans and go back for her master's degree in business.[9] They have a long-term vision of life in which their kids get old enough to graduate from high school and leave the house and they can begin traveling and living more for themselves. I ask Laticia what expectations she has for Derek.

She purses her lips for a moment and looks to where he sits leaning over the desk between us, filling out the study survey. "I would say definitely the attitude he's maintained the whole way through, to hold on to that. Not get, and I don't see this ever happening, not get sucked into the fact that the government's going to—to get sucked into the fact that he can't still be productive. Because it's a part of who he is, already, and if he's going to lose that I don't see him staying true to himself." Derek gives a small smile over his survey, and from the look that passes between them, it seems this is an issue she has raised before.

Whether at her urging or out of some deeper habit, Derek shows no signs of lowering his aims for himself. There is always, for him, the memory of his Vietnam veteran father, whose own PTSD led to alcohol abuse and abandoning his family. "[My father's] experience actually helps me with that, seeing what it did to him," he reflects. "It helps keep me in the, 'I need to see somebody. I need to get help before it gets to that point.'" He was raised by his mother and grandparents to strive to be the very best, to be impatient with average standards and to work toward something greater. "I still hold myself to that standard. I expect myself to perform to a higher level."

Ironic as it may seem, some of Derek's confidence may also stem from having been wounded.[10] Both Chris and Adam spoke of how much easier they believed it would be if they had a physical wound to mark their suffering, and there may be some truth to this.[11] There is an automatic empathy that many Americans describe feeling when they see a wounded service member, particularly if they believe that wound has been suffered in the act of patriotic service. The expectations placed on physically wounded veterans may also be somewhat fewer than those placed on the invisibly wounded. Derek says of his rehabilitation group's regular visits to obstacle courses and other excursions focused on "community integration" that they give wounded veterans an opportunity to prove that "'Yeah, you may have taken away an arm or whatever, but we can still perform at the level we did.'" Their ability to perform as before is remarkable precisely because it is not expected. Derek is a wonder to sit across the table from because—bionic man that he is—he remains so resoundingly undaunted. By contrast, for those whose wounds are internal and unseen, it can be difficult to gauge the visceral reality of what, exactly, they find so daunting. Their failures are likely to be judged more harshly, and their greatest achievements may never appear as impressive as Derek's, simply because he starts with such a visible deficit. (At the same time, it is unavoidably true that he starts with a deficit.)

By virtue of his injury, Derek also has access to other wounded veterans who provide regular inspiration. PTSD is not an unusual diagnosis among the so-called wounded warriors at the Center for the Intrepid, and there is a special on-site coordinator dedicated to providing PTSD referrals to these men and women. Those who were injured earlier in the war and have made more progress with their recovery often stay involved with the center, providing an encouraging example for the newly wounded. "We have a progressive cycle," Derek explains. "When they were the veterans, they took care of us. They held our hands as we filled out the paperwork, and now it's our turn. I did the peer visiting thing and walked around the hospital when the new guys got there and showed them the leg and said, 'This is what I'm doing now.' Just to have that support—to see the guys that have already done it and to know that it's out there."

Along with the support provided by other wounded veterans, Derek has also had Laticia. Early on she told him that anything he could do, she would do with him. And so when Derek learned to ride a bicycle again, she accompanied him in cycling the 75 miles from San Antonio to Austin. It took them two days, riding 50 miles the first day and 25 the second. They tease each other about what other plans they agree to share; she is willing to ride with him to Corpus Christi (approximately 140 miles) but draws the line at swimming across San Francisco Bay to Alcatraz.

But when Derek says he could not have made it this far without her, Laticia says, "I didn't feel like I was doing anything that—that's my *husband*....The way I grew up, my mother and father were still together. Even my grandmother and grandfather, even though they fought, they were still together. They always made a way, and I think always making a way...making it seem effortless, do what you need to do."

"And that actually helped me a lot," Derek adds, "because there were many days when I came home and felt a huge burden. If there was anything that made me depressed it was that—look at all she's doing for me and I can't give it back. I can't give enough back to her to make up for it. She never once said, 'Look what I've done for you,' or 'You're lazy, why can't you do it?' And that helped a lot."

Derek has, in his great journey, been mobilized by many forces, as has Laticia. They have developed a view of PTSD together, in dialogue with each other, with Derek's care providers at BAMC and the VA, and with other wounded veterans.

They have derived responses based in their own histories, learned expectations, and hopes for the future. Laticia admits that she cannot always understand Derek's PTSD, but hearing his stories has helped her to better imagine what war must have been like, and in understanding she finds it easier to be patient. Their life is a work in progress, but it is *their* life, plural and shared. PTSD may create dislocation in the social world—it has at times created dislocation in theirs—but the social world may also be a source of healing, the ties that rebind what was torn asunder.

For every PTSD-diagnosed veteran, there is a tale to be told of his or her effort to live with PTSD. For some the goal is as immediate as treading water, making it through the day. Life with PTSD may be simply an effort to avoid drowning (picture Chris on his worst days, unable to find a justification for continuing to live). Focusing on short-term goals may allow some veterans a pause during which to peruse the horizon when unsure of the right direction. Others may cherish a more long-term vision, complete with future-oriented goals that draw them forward—a college degree, a career, starting a family. Goals may be strongly felt at one point in the journey, less so at others. Meanwhile, the intensity of trauma-related distress varies greatly among individuals and over time, adding storminess to the waters.

Veterans with PTSD encounter many shared cultural pressures, obstacles, and opportunities. These include the economic disparities that pattern military recruiting and determine who goes off to war, political controversies over veterans' health care and benefits, the social history of past wars and past veterans, lay and professional understandings of PTSD illness, and the institutional structures of the military and of mental health care within the VA. And yet each veteran's course represents some unique attempt to navigate a collision of these forces, these layers of cultural experience. Even among such a similar group of veterans as Chris, Adam, and Derek—each has PTSD following a series of traumatic events that took place during combat, each accepts his PTSD diagnosis, and each has sought professional mental health treatment at one particular VA facility—the narratives veterans tell of their experiences are highly individual. All three of these men demonstrate how veterans acquire their understandings of PTSD and embark upon certain responses in dialogue with others in their lives, particularly with clinicians, spouses, and other veterans. Each of these three examples reveals, moreover, how an individual's way of talking about PTSD may, even as it stems from a shared idea of PTSD illness, reflect his or her own particular struggle.

With so much at stake, these individual models of PTSD become more than simply an (albeit vital) exercise in meaning making; they serve, too, as maps, charting imagined futures and possible paths for interpretation and response. They propose hypothetical answers to essential questions: What will happen to me? To my family? To my goals for a good life?

Anthropologists, so well equipped to describe cultural beliefs and institutions, have often struggled with the task of explaining how humans behave in the midst of all that culture. Even in the days when culture could be observed in isolated communities that were more homogenous than any in our current age of globalization and hypermedia, it was never true that individuals all behaved the same way. Culture might create a shared ideal for behavior, a shared template for responding to challenges like those posed by illness and suffering, but it has never succeeded in making humans predictable.

One of the richer metaphors for describing how humans build a life thus "with and against culture" has been offered by Sherry Ortner with her notion of "serious games."[12] She points out the importance of individual purpose and desire in influencing how a person behaves and emphasizes the place of cultural symbols and ideals in shaping those desires. She recognizes, too, the role of what she calls "material necessity"—in other words, the financial and material resources of life and the political structures that control access to them—in closing or creating opportunities. With the image of serious games, Ortner suggests

> that people do not just enact either material necessity or cultural scripts but live life with (often intense) purpose and intention; that people are defined and redefined by their social and cultural contexts, which frame not only the resources they start with but the intentions and purposes they bring to the games of life; that social life is precisely social, a matter of relationships—of cooperation and competition, of solidarity and exploitation, of allying and betraying.[13]

In calling such games serious, she further points out how much is at stake in many of the interactions of daily life. She emphasizes the role of history and power in shaping the games that people play and also how people themselves make history with their actions, challenging and resisting power when the opportunity arises.

The metaphor of navigation that I have offered here is not unlike Ortner's notion of serious games. Navigation is simply the process of working to realize a life that is personally and culturally desirable despite all the idiosyncratic challenges of individual experience and unyielding constraints of the political, historical, economic, and cultural moment. It is accomplished by calling upon all available resources, including extraordinary creativity, the lessons of experience, the reach of social networks, and the full cultural repertoire of knowledge and action.

Ortner's particular insight is, I think, in recognizing the importance of desire in shaping how humans move through life, and with what intentions. Among this group of veterans it became vividly apparent that the power of cultural expectations to shape individual action is mediated by desire. So much of this discussion of PTSD has been focused on veterans' sense of having failed—failed to reintegrate, failed to succeed, failed to overcome—and there can be no failure without desire.

This may be the last and most important way in which culture shapes veterans' experiences of PTSD—by influencing their desire for those larger life goals with which it may interfere. These veterans are American men, and their goals are fully in line with normative priorities for men in contemporary American culture: marriage, fatherhood, career success, and the admiration of family, community, and peers. But they are also combat veterans, and they desire an identity that lives up to cultural expectations without doing any disservice to the men they became during war—men whom they often see, at least in retrospect, as being the bravest, most heroic version of themselves.[14]

To give one last example, Eduardo was, in his late forties, among the older Iraq veterans, on the tail end of a twenty-five-year army career. He came to the hospital for our interview straight from the gym, sweaty and wearing a gray T-shirt that read, "Life without MOBILIZATION—I don't think so!" His hair, cropped short on the sides, had grown too long on top, a neglected high-and-tight. I found it hard to believe him when he first told me that he had been a major in the army. He slouched too far in his chair, looked too unkempt and bedraggled. Nothing in his appearance or manner of speaking—slow, deliberate, rarely making eye contact, and then, when he did so, staring me aggressively in the face—fit with my experience of army officers (whom I have generally found to be good-humored and well-spoken). We talked for a long time that day, largely because he insisted on telling extended stories of his time in Iraq. He referred constantly to having seen combat and told me several times, rather dismissively, that it was impossible for anyone who hasn't "seen the elephant" [been in combat] to understand what it is like. And yet, relentlessly and despite his own better judgment, he kept trying to *tell* me what it had been like, as though he could wear down my ignorance with the sheer volume of his words. He spoke for something approaching four and a half hours.

Several times in our conversation, Eduardo mentioned a photograph of himself that he had found online. It was taken during his time in Iraq and captured him in the middle of a hectic workday, overseeing the implementation of a new data security initiative for the Iraqi government. In describing his struggles with post-deployment life, he kept returning to this image of himself, which he described with a proud and wistful little smile. He admitted frankly that Iraq had been the high point of his life and that he was struggling to make a life he could live with after the end of his military career. As a middle-aged man, he felt he was too old to start over and too young to retire. He was not married and had no close family, although he spoke of a handful of close male and female friends from the army. What he did have was that photograph, that tangible proof that he had been and done something great.

When I returned home after the interview, I Googled his name and the picture came up almost immediately, accompanied by a caption confirming that he was indeed a major. In the photo, he stands looking over the shoulder of a young woman soldier, examining some piece of paperwork she is holding. He is focused, intent on the task. He looks like the cool, calm center of a whirlwind, the very image of a dependable leader. He is, in this picture, almost unrecognizable from the man who had sat talking in the chair across from me. The man in the chair knew this. This was the dislocation he felt most keenly, and his efforts at navigation, which that day in my office took the form of such prolific storytelling, were aimed at bringing him back to that best possible version of himself. This was his strongest desire.

Beyond identity, there was one additional aspect of veterans' desire that was just as important, if not more so, and that was the impetus to maintain key social relationships, whether with spouses or other romantic partners, with other veterans, or with children and family. Even when I went looking for anthropological staples like institutions and political economy, for culture writ large, I found myself running again and again into the social relationships that give culture so much of its meaning. Veterans' experiences with PTSD have proven to be impossible to understand without an appreciation for the social contexts in which they are lived out. Little boys may grow up to be soldiers amid family traditions that value military service, eagerly showing off their new uniforms to family and friends whose opinions they value. Some of PTSD's most potent impact occurs when it challenges men's ability to maintain the networks they value most. As Juan—the marine who returned from the war to live alone in an empty apartment, unfurnished but for a mattress, a television, and his duffel bag—put it, "It sucks to be alone. Family, friends, the relationships you make are really important to have a good life." And so, though sleep disruption and nightmares are troubling occurrences in the post-deployment period, they remain far less devastating than a feeling of isolation from family and friends. PTSD is also social in that it creates distress far beyond the individual. There was no PTSD-diagnosed veteran whose illness affected only himself—always there were children, girlfriends, wives, parents, or friends whose lives were also affected, if only by the veteran's absence as he succumbed to the desire to retreat.

It is nothing new to say that suffering is a social process or event (there is even a subset of theory in medical anthropology devoted to "social suffering").[15] But this is again where culture meets PTSD. The desire to maintain these social relationships is a powerful mechanism by which cultural expectations are enforced in daily life. Veterans with PTSD face the responses of family members and their peers and leadership in the military uncertain as to whether their distress will be met with stigma or empathy. These fears of negative judgment, too often realized, affect how they name their troubles and seek care. It is one thing to buck a trend in the abstract—for example, for a soldier to say to himself, "To hell with weakness, I need help"—and something very different for that same soldier to imagine disgust in the eyes of his best friend upon making such a statement. Chris worried, years after the last time he had seen him, what his friend Brent might think of his PTSD diagnosis. Chris continued to judge himself against Brent's imagined response because of the importance of that relationship in his life. It is in this way that culture is embodied in the real and imagined desires of the people we see and know and love, and it is in this way that their desires can become our own. It is in this way that the distress caused by PTSD is inextricably bound up with a veteran's social and cultural networks.

We must remember, however, that it is within these same networks that many veterans find the way to navigate their distress and create resilience. I asked Derek, "Is there anything or anyone that has particularly helped you through this period of your life?" He answered, pointing at Laticia where she sat beside him, "I couldn't have done it without her. No way. Not at all."

"What'd she do that was so great?"

"She was my counselor, my financial adviser, she managed everything while I was too doped up to do anything." Laticia provided vital support, but she also provided the motivation to get up and get moving. "I have a family to take care of and support, so I can't sit there and feel sorry for myself. I never had the chance to just sit there and 'why did this happen to me?' It happened. You can't go back and change it, now we just figure out how do we take the best care of everyone."[16]

A growing number of clinicians and researchers point to the importance of these networks in understanding the onset and course of PTSD. In 2008 researchers at New York University's Institute for Trauma and Resilience went so far as to call for developing a "social ecology of PTSD," arguing for the clinical importance of "understanding how both PTSD risk and recovery are highly dependent on social phenomena."[17] More and more individuals involved in coordinating clinical and policy-level responses to PTSD are beginning to appreciate the importance of including families in treatment, in working to combat stigma, and in helping veterans to negotiate the social challenges of living with PTSD.

There is much yet to learn and discover.

CONCLUSION

In the introduction, I suggested that PTSD is best approached via a series of stories being told about war and its aftermath in contemporary America. Subsequent chapters have recounted some of the stories that PTSD-diagnosed veterans tell of military service, of combat, of coming home from war to find themselves changed, of struggling to make sense of their distress and to take action in response to it. The book has been organized around two major focal points—personal experience and cultural politics—but it should be abundantly clear by now that one cannot separate the two. Combat trauma (the personal) may occur during war (the political) but is unavoidably shaped by the meaning of the event to the individual (the personal), a meaning that is partly the product of a shared vocabulary for describing experience (the cultural).

Along the way I have suggested that it is impossible to comprehend PTSD without stopping to appreciate the stories that become labeled as traumas (Jesse's fear that he had killed an Iraqi child), as well as many of the stories that do not (Brian's burying the dead in the first Gulf War). I have presented findings that reiterate the results of many other studies, showing that combat trauma is only one of many kinds of experiences that cumulatively increase the risk of developing PTSD. Post-deployment knocks such as the inability to reintegrate into family and community life, divorce, unemployment, and so forth play an important role in exacerbating PTSD risk among recent veterans. When veterans return from war to find that what they thought would be a chance to create new post-combat lives is, in fact, far more challenging than they ever imagined—when they find themselves dislocated from their loved ones and struggling to meet their most basic expectations for self and life—these challenges make it far more difficult to muster a resilient response to the trauma of war.

Post-deployment experiences are also inexorably influenced by the way that veterans and those in their social worlds interpret and respond to the problems created by PTSD. It is one thing for a veteran and his loved ones to presume that nightmares and aggressiveness are a natural part of the return from combat; the veteran may then see these phenomena as part of a warrior's noble burden, name them PTSD, and seek treatment without shame. It is another thing entirely if the veteran returns home and judges his distress as a sign of inadequacy or meets such judgment in the eyes of his family and friends. PTSD may be a hard diagnosis to accept ("It just seems weak") or alternatively may become the acknowledgment that enables a veteran to live with himself ("I thought I was the only one"). Powerful and deep-seated, these interpretations and reactions are rooted in American cultural ideas about trauma-related suffering and mental illness and in highly gendered expectations for male emotion and behavior.

Moreover, views on combat PTSD may be complex and contradictory, shading from stigma to acceptance and back again as one moves across social settings.[1] Driven by the practical need to retain as many healthy service members as possible in a time of war and under pressure from public opinion and national media to demonstrate due concern for troops' well-being, the U.S. military has instituted a variety of measures aimed at easing the experience of readjustment and providing prompt and effective treatment for service members dealing with PTSD. Though the military's efforts have been prodigious, they have at times run up against opposing messages deeply rooted in military culture and wartime necessity. The military has spent decades creating a structure of ongoing socialization that instructs its members in the masculine values of toughness, stamina, and invincibility and that rewards those who push past their own limits to become cool and composed under fire. These values are passed on in the relationships between service members, and, in a time of war, are reinforced further by the pressures of combat, when every unit member is encouraged to believe that group survival depends upon his living up to his obligations. In the face of these powerful lessons, even the best efforts of military leadership have often proven inadequate to uproot stigmatizing ideas about PTSD. Too many service members have found themselves caught between conflicting messages: "We can help!" they hear, but also, "If you're broke, we'll kick you to the curb."

Amid this muddled scenario, official protocols for prevention and treatment in the military are inconsistently enforced, and service members may find themselves torn between differing sets of needs and expectations. This is how Chris found himself drinking into a three-year decline, punctuated by arrests and pats on the back ("He's a combat vet. We don't mess with him."), before ending up under personal escort on a plane back to the States, locked down in a psychiatric ward while the paperwork was filed for his early retirement.

Meanwhile, PTSD has taken on a wholly different set of meanings in the public forums of history, media, and national obligation. Within highly politicized debates around the role of the U.S. Department of Veterans Affairs, PTSD has become associated with the abandonment of Vietnam veterans a generation ago and with the VA's past failures to provide adequate benefits and health care. Veterans, politicians, veterans' advocates, and VA clinicians all move within this social and historical milieu, meeting in a convoluted effort to provide what is thought to be needed, whether disability pay, PTSD treatment of one kind or another, or symbolic acknowledgment of veterans' service and sacrifice. Against this backdrop, mental health clinicians conduct their own negotiations at the VA, initiating a slow shift in PTSD treatment paradigms that may over the coming decades have radical implications for how PTSD is popularly and professionally understood, shifting the model from one of chronic suffering to one of recovery and resilience. If successful, this move may have ripple effects far beyond the clinic, reverberating in both the political debate over veterans' disability compensation and the personal space of veterans' lives.

PTSD thus is an idea in flux, subject to different meanings and concerns depending on the settings and stakeholders involved: within the military as opposed to the VA, for active-duty service members as opposed to veterans, for veterans as opposed to clinicians.

Finally, there are immense cultural expectations placed on all returning male veterans to fulfill their roles as men, as partners, as fathers, as participants in the workforce, even as veterans. And it is not only these expectations that are so vital but *veterans' own desire to live up to them,* in part because of the social bonds retained if such roles are performed successfully, and the real or imagined consequences if they are left unfulfilled. Perhaps no consequence is harder for social beings to bear than the loss or slippage of personal relationships.

It is in these interactions between veterans and their social worlds, too, that the dialectic between the personal and the cultural/political is played out. Individual veterans' experiences of PTSD are shared with family and friends. Stories are passed around through social networks and the media and may at times become cautionary tales of what can go wrong for new veterans. These cautionary tales in turn become part of the cultural interpretation of PTSD, informing public understandings of what types of distress are characteristic of the illness, what its likely course will be, and what responses are most appropriate (whether seeking care or suffering in silence). These understandings become part of veterans' lives, communicated in print and on TV and in the spoken and unspoken messages of daily interaction.

These then are the fields of combat, the messy and shifting grounds on which PTSD-diagnosed veterans must navigate. And the stakes are high. Chris and Adam both continue to live one day at a time, although Chris would say he is "98 percent cured." Suicide remains all too common among recent veterans. Recovery would seem to be a real possibility, but so too is the collapse into utter despair.

From the beginning, this was primarily a study of male veterans and their experiences of combat PTSD, in part because few female veterans were seeking care at the San Antonio VA clinic at the time research was beginning, making it difficult to recruit a representative sample. However, since women now comprise some 15 percent of the armed forces and are taking on unprecedented roles and responsibilities within the modern American military—as combat medics, pilots, convoy drivers, and so on—it is impossible to ignore the question of whether and how female veterans' experience of PTSD may differ from that of men. Over the course of the study, I was able to interview seven women who had deployed to Iraq or Afghanistan, and the insights they so generously shared suggest a few points worthy of further investigation.

First of all, the women I spoke with—veterans of the army, air force, and National Guard who performed missions ranging from supply officer to working with combat stress teams—told stories of deployment that varied as much as those of the men. One woman had been a nurse in Afghanistan, and her most vivid memories were of treating wounded Afghani children. An older reservist spoke fondly of a store located just outside the Green Zone, where she spent many hours on a stool at the counter talking with the Iraqi shopkeeper. Another woman, Angela, was deployed early in the war and described the same overwhelming physical conditions as many of the men: sleeping on the ground before cots became available, extreme heat and cold, overflowing toilets, and bunking in bombed-out Iraqi army barracks festooned with anti-American graffiti. She tells of being in a completely unfamiliar environment, where you were "totally taken out of your comfort zone." All the women understood the stress of living with the knowledge that death and disaster could descend at any moment.

A number of these women also described the additional stress of having to prove themselves in a predominantly male environment, among, as Angela said, "men who don't want you." Angela completed basic training with a National Guard unit only two months before deploying and was one of the few women on her transport team. She felt the need to demonstrate over and over again that she was capable "above and beyond." She drove a forty-eight-wheel vehicle designed to tow tanks and would refuse help when a tire went flat, insisting on changing it herself: "No, get away. It's my job just like it is yours." She pushed so hard that she returned home beaten up by her own efforts, with arthritis in her hands, plantar fasciitis in her feet, and destroyed cartilage in her back. But the barriers remain. A Vietnam veteran came into the office where she now works and began joking loudly about a Vietnam-era nurse who had come up to him wanting to talk about Vietnam. "He bashed her like nothing," Angela fumes. He said that the nurse didn't know what she was talking about, that she had never gone to Vietnam. Angela thought of Vietnam nurses "that have worse PTSD than the men they were out there to treat" and of her own stubborn efforts day after day in Iraq. "I felt like telling him to get the hell out of the office."

Part of Angela's fury, and that of other female veterans, stems from how little recognition there often is of the threats they face alongside their male compatriots. Ambushes, explosions, mortar and sniper fire, the shock and grief of unit casualties—women deploying to Iraq and Afghanistan know these things all too well, but their courage, bravery, and fortitude are less conspicuously recognized and honored. The aftereffects they face, however, may be no less profound. Civilian studies have found that women are more likely than men to develop PTSD in the wake of trauma.[2] Women are more commonly exposed to many of the premilitary stressors that have been shown to shape cumulative risk for developing combat PTSD, including childhood sexual assault.[3] Certainly women's risk of sexual assault is much greater than men's and may be particularly high in an overwhelmingly male environment; between 13 and 30 percent of women veterans report having been raped during their period of service.[4] Military sexual trauma is also associated with a greater risk of developing PTSD than many other traumas, including combat exposure. War-deployed female veterans, therefore, may be at particular risk for developing PTSD.

Upon returning home, female service members often face many of the same difficulties in building a postwar life that men do. Most women who have been combat deployed for long periods will go through some period of readjustment. One woman spoke of how strange she felt in leaving the house unarmed when she first got back; she said it took months before she lost the urge to reach for her weapon as she opened the car door. Women who left the military after returning home often described a familiar sense of isolation and loss. Angela says she was an "emotional wreck" when she first got home. "A big part of it was missing the camaraderie in the unit," she explains. "You seriously become a family. Then you, 'Oh, bye.'" Like Chris or Eduardo, she had trouble coming to terms with life outside the military. As a member of the National Guard, she returned to her civilian job after deployment but soon went searching for a way to get back on active-duty rotation. "I belong in uniform," she says.

The question of how their identity as women affects female veterans is an open and fascinating one. The women I interviewed all had one thing in common: they were all proud of having shown themselves capable of doing work and facing risks widely thought to belong to the world of men. Women who join the military are no less likely than men to aspire to toughness and self-reliance; on the contrary, they may be more so, since military service may be a less socially applauded choice for women. And because so many female service members feel they have something to prove, they may be even less likely to seek help when they begin to experience combat-related psychological symptoms.

Women, too, often face different roles and responsibilities upon returning home. Although many of the men in the study were fathers who played an active role in parenting, mothers tend to remain the primary caregivers. Angela, for example, has a toddler-age son for whom she is the sole provider. Now diagnosed with PTSD, she doesn't sleep well and is "really really really short-tempered," a fact that seems to bother her largely because of how it impacts her little boy. She catches herself yelling at him, then halts midsentence: "I take a step back and say, 'What are you doing?'" Her experience of other symptoms is also interwoven with her love for her son. When she describes the classic post-deployment anxiety around going to the grocery store, she does so in terms of how vulnerable she feels as a woman with a child, knowing that, for example, if someone attacked her in the parking lot while she was buckling her little boy into his car seat, she would do anything to protect him. She used to feel invulnerable. She was an amateur boxer even before she joined the National Guard; she knows how to fight. But the old sense of safety has faded, and now she worries about the two of them living alone.

Her obligations as a mother also shape her decision making around such practical matters as care seeking and treatment options. The desire to be more patient with her son has been her motivation in getting help, but her child-care needs sometimes interfere with getting to therapy. Her psychiatrist has suggested medications for sleep, but she worries about what would happen if her son woke up in the night and she didn't hear him. Seeking care at the VA, she encounters an institution that is still learning to provide care to women. I once heard a clinician point out how few pictures of women there are on the walls of the VA hospital, noting that specialty care for obstetrics and gynecology have only recently become available in many such institutions around the country.

It seems likely that women also receive different kinds of social support during and after deployment, particularly if they begin showing signs of PTSD or other problems. I once asked an army chaplain whether he saw any impact of gender on PTSD, and he said that the biggest difference he saw was that men seemed to get a lot of support from their wives and girlfriends, whereas women's partners seemed more likely to leave. It may be that readjustment and PTSD symptoms in women appear more jarring than in men; irritation and anger are rarely thought of as conventionally feminine. At the same time, I interviewed several husbands who had been patient and adaptive in dealing with their wives' PTSD and were proud of the courage their wives had shown during deployment.

We are left with the need to be more proactive in researching and responding to the needs of women service members and veterans. Women's experiences of combat PTSD are not well understood; we simply do not yet have the information to know whether and how their needs may be distinct.

Regardless of gender, it is clear that combat PTSD brings about profound suffering for many veterans and their loved ones. In the face of such suffering, it should come as no surprise that PTSD can be hard to pin down as one thing or another: a mental illness related to psychological mechanisms of avoidance and adaptation, a loss of innocence, or a normal experience of terrible grief at witnessing horror and injustice.[5] All these things can be said to be true. There is, in other words, no single answer to the question of what PTSD is. There may be a clinical definition written in the pages of the *DSM-IV,* but that definition becomes something far more slippery when it passes out into the world, diagnosed and lived out and claimed and apologized for and made real in the discourses and engagements of everyday life.

When I have discussed my research with anthropologists, they have often asked—with an air of gentle foot tapping, as if to say, "Let's get to the crux of this now, shall we?"—whether I think PTSD really exists. At first glance, this seems like a rather simple question. Of course it exists. It is described in the pages of the *DSM,* and hundreds of other books have been written about it. Hospitals have entire clinical programs devoted to it, and there are national laws and policies detailing when and under what circumstances it is appropriate to provide compensation for it. Around the world, hundreds of thousands of individuals have been diagnosed with PTSD following combat, rape, torture, motor vehicle accidents, acts of terrorism, and other traumas. PTSD has become a dominant way of describing the psychological aftermath of trauma worldwide. So why would anyone ask whether it exists?

But this isn't exactly the question being posed. The question is, more accurately put, something like, "Do you believe that PTSD is a universal human phenomenon, or is it simply a cultural model Americans have cooked up to describe certain kinds of suffering, a model that has then managed to catch on in much of the rest of the world?" This question is actually a very good one, and stems from a conversation about PTSD that has taken place within the social sciences. Allan Young's critique of the diagnosis in the mid-1990s kicked off this debate, but it has since been taken up by other scholars exploring trauma and trauma treatment programs around the world. In his initial work Young suggested that PTSD was largely a construct in which common psychiatric symptoms were clumped together and given a new name for a variety of reasons: to provide compensation for disenfranchised veterans, to appease an American conscience uneasy with the then-recent memory of Vietnam, and in accordance with an idiosyncratic view of traumatic memory developed within professional psychiatry.[6] He argued, essentially, that the diagnosis was an imperfect product of cultural process. In Young's view, PTSD was an illness construct brought to life by clinicians in the very practices of the clinic, rather than a phenomenon describing a cross-culturally available response to trauma.

Young's critique of PTSD has been built upon by other clinicians and researchers. Derek Summerfield, an influential researcher in the United Kingdom, has argued that PTSD is a Western biomedical construct that has unclear relevance and meaning in non-Western cultures. Observing PTSD among a wide variety of groups around the world—refugees, victims of genocide, etc.—he contends that PTSD focuses rather arbitrarily on trauma as the essential cause for psychological distress when a number of other causes, such as poverty, might suit just as well.[7] Others have argued that focusing too closely on PTSD distracts attention from the needs of those with other psychiatric disorders or that it locates trauma within the individual, thereby removing focus from upstream causes of trauma—such as social inequality, war, and the greed of nations[8]—and from the most likely source of cure—reestablishing social relations.[9] Much concern has been expressed about the "medicalization" of trauma, the idea that trauma is best described in medical rather than moral terms and that it indicates something wrong with the individual rather than with the society that produced or allowed violence in the first place.[10]

PTSD has also been the subject of considerable examination by those working in cross-cultural settings. Many of these authors have expressed doubt as to whether locally specific ways of describing trauma might be of more use to, say, Sudanese refugees living in a camp in Kenya than a set of symptoms and criteria originally identified among combat veterans in the United States. A number of studies have provided important answers to this question by examining how individuals who appear to be struggling in the aftermath of trauma manifest such struggles in non-Western contexts.[11] The results have generally found that some subset of any given population exposed to trauma will exhibit symptoms of PTSD. They may be more likely to exhibit some symptoms than others, and may *also* exhibit symptoms that are more in line with local ways of expressing distress.[12] For example, the psychiatrist Devon Hinton and his colleagues have found that a significant number of traumatized Cambodian refugees meet diagnostic criteria for PTSD (56% of those reporting to a psychiatry clinic, in one study)[13] but may also exhibit more culturally specific symptoms such as sleep paralysis, tinnitus, and neck-focused symptoms.[14]

All together these studies demonstrate that even in settings where traumatized individuals have not been exposed to Western notions of trauma or PTSD, a subset of people are likely to show signs of hyperarousal, avoidance, and reexperiencing. In other words, PTSD may manifest somewhat differently in different cultural settings, but there appears to be a core shared phenomenon around the globe. Trauma changes the way that some people experience themselves and the world around them, and in doing so it interferes with their ability to live a happy and fruitful life.[15]

A rapidly growing scientific literature on PTSD reveals that the mechanisms for this change involve interactions among a variety of social, cultural, biological, and psychological factors, although many of the specifics of these interactions are clear only in their broadest outlines.[16] For example, although it is widely agreed that parental PTSD increases the likelihood of PTSD among offspring, there appear to be a variety of pathways by which this occurs. A parent with PTSD is likely to pass on certain patterns of hypervigilant behavior and attitudes about the safety of the world to his or her children.[17] In addition, a PTSD-diagnosed parent may pass on a genetic predisposition to the disorder, such that offspring who are exposed to traumatic events may be more likely to develop PTSD.[18] Recent work by Rachel Yehuda and colleagues also indicates that there may be epigenetic factors involved in shaping PTSD risk. Their research suggests that maternal PTSD may contribute heavily to shaping a child's risk because endocrine conditions in the mother's body during pregnancy influence the developing fetus's physical and emotional responsiveness to environmental stimuli.[19]

This book's focus on social and cultural factors related to PTSD risk and recovery in returning veterans should not be taken as a dismissal of the role of physiological pathways in shaping PTSD. On the contrary, I think the clinical and scientific research being conducted on PTSD is of the utmost importance, and has the potential to inform broader understandings of how the human body and mind respond to stress and threat in the environment. Chris, for example, spoke of urinating on himself when first under fire in Afghanistan. This is not an uncommon response to the first time in combat—nor is it an uncommon response to threat across the animal world[20]—but still, not everyone experiences such a profound physiological response to conditions of extreme threat. There is great individual variety in such responses, and much of this variety is driven by the sorts of physiological differences currently under scientific exploration. I am convinced, however, that these explorations remain incomplete without an appreciation for how culture shapes both the environment (e.g., life in the military, gendered role expectations) and the individual response to it (e.g., experiencing anxiety and thinking of it as weakness).

Ronald Simons's work on startle responses provides one case study of how the integrated analysis of cultural and biological factors can result in key insights into the workings of human illness. Simons has spent much of his career studying startle syndromes around the world, focusing in particular on the phenomenon of *latah* in Malaysia.[21] *Latah* is a condition that occurs among those who naturally startle more actively than others, perhaps jumping visibly at unexpected noises when those around them might only look up. However, it also provides a sort of game for some Malaysian villagers, who may—upon noticing that someone has a stronger than usual startle reaction—begin startling that individual over and over again, sneaking up behind him or her and setting off loud noises or giving a sudden poke or strike. Over time, the *latah* (for the term describes the person with the condition as well as the condition itself) develops a more and more extreme response. Although both men and women may become *latahs,* the vast majority are women, for the simple reason that villagers are more likely to go around startling women than they are men. Villagers explained this difference to Simons by saying that men might be more likely to become angry and strike back. And so it is that a basically physiological experience becomes culturally elaborated, named and subject to local norms for gender and behavior. It may even be that a *latah*'s increasingly violent responses have some basis in the individual's understanding of what it means to be *latah*. Would she startle quite so dramatically if she weren't expecting/expected to?

Similarly, it remains true that although PTSD undoubtedly has strong physiological underpinnings, some veterans who describe PTSD symptoms may do so, either consciously or unconsciously, on the basis of communicated ideas about what PTSD is supposed to look like. A psychiatrist I know told me of hearing a story in medical school about how, in the early days of PTSD research, a VA hospital in Washington, D.C., began to see a record number of veterans walking in with blankets slung over their shoulders. One of the doctors at the hospital became so curious about this that he finally asked one of the blanket-wielding veterans, "Excuse me, but may I ask why you're carrying that blanket?" "It's my survival quilt," the man replied. This odd response failed to settle the doctor's mind until he heard from a colleague about a new study on PTSD being conducted at the hospital. Flyers for the study had been printed up and requested the participation of veterans who felt they had, among other things, "survivor guilt." Only there had been a typo, and "guilt" was spelled "quilt." Hence the blankets.

The point of the story is supposed to be that these veterans were faking what they thought was a PTSD symptom because they wanted to be identified with PTSD (either to participate in the study or for some other reason). This story is probably apocryphal, and the fact that this psychiatrist heard it in medical school says as much about the nature of clinical training as it does about PTSD.

But it does reflect a widespread appreciation that veterans may have a number of reasons for wanting to be labeled with PTSD. They may want to participate in a study for which they'll receive compensation. They may find that PTSD provides what clinicians call "secondary gain," offering some social or psychological or financial benefit that comes along with the diagnosis and that may be satisfactory enough to make it desirable despite the additional baggage of its stigma. Veterans might want to identify with having been in combat (whether or not they actually have been), because combat is one experience that is held to be sound proof of one's heroism. There are other kinds of gain as well. One psychologist I interviewed described a veteran he had treated several years back: every time the veteran began to describe his PTSD symptoms, the wife would take his hand between hers and stroke it with a worried expression on her face. Her loving concern could also be understood as providing secondary gain.

Beyond secondary gain, there are also veterans who may experience a generalized psychological distress that manifests in the form of PTSD simply because after all those military briefings and cautionary tales and articles in the news, PTSD is the example of distress they have come to know best. They may have learned to pay attention to PTSD-like symptoms more than to symptoms reflecting depression or anxiety or even the ordinary, nonpathological misery of everyday life.[22] There are, in short, many reasons why American veterans may express PTSD the way they do. Still, even with all the caveats, the domestic and cross-cultural evidence suggests that PTSD is best understood as a universal phenomenon with important local and individual variations. Individuals may come to PTSD for a wide variety of voluntary, involuntary, conscious, and unconscious reasons, but the illness itself reflects something common in the human experience.

Nevertheless, for those who rightfully critique the illness category of PTSD as an imperfect entity—identifying problems with the diagnostic criteria, limitations of the disorder for describing the range of human experience, and so forth—it seems useful to propose a series of criteria by which it should be judged. To my mind, the essential question is this: does the construct of PTSD provide a way of describing a particular experience of human suffering that acknowledges, helps to identify, and provides a means of offering support and healing for that experience? I believe that most of those who have debated the nature of PTSD would agree that what matters are the following:

1. That those whose lives have been disrupted by trauma have access to a name (or names) for their experience that provides respectful acknowledgment of their suffering
2. That there be a name and definition for trauma-related suffering that helps to distinguish between those who are in the process of healing and those

who have gotten caught up somewhere along the way, making it possible to identify and provide help to those who are not healing in the way they would like to be

3. That this name and definition be flexible enough to recognize that such suffering may look somewhat different in different social and cultural settings, because humans are vastly heterogeneous

4. That this name and definition be constructed in such a way that they leave room for identifying effective means by which to aid in healing. And since clinicians are sometimes made uncomfortable by mushy social science words like "healing," let me also say it this way: that the name and definition be constructed in such a way that people who are suffering after trauma can be helped to suffer *less*. This is, after all, the goal of naming illness in human life: to use that name to find ways to minimize suffering.

When these goals are kept in mind, it strikes me that PTSD can be considered as useful an illness construct as any other, although it remains very much a work in progress, in terms of both social meanings and scientific understanding. It is inevitable that PTSD will continue to be politicized and socially contested simply because it is so closely linked with issues of suffering and culpability. It raises questions like, who is suffering? Who is responsible for that suffering? What are the appropriate responses to such suffering? Whose responsibility is it to make sure those responses are meted out as intended? Because attitudes toward suffering, responsibility, and culpability are foundational elements of culture, these concerns, too, are likely to be understood differently across cultural worlds.[23]

All this, of course, raises the question of how the United States will deal with the distress of veterans who have returned from the wars in Iraq and Afghanistan. On August 31, 2010, President Barack Obama announced that Operation Iraqi Freedom was officially over. Troop reductions in Afghanistan are expected to begin in 2011. It seems as though these wars may be winding down, but it is impossible to know what threats American service members will face in the years to come. Meanwhile, the toll of combat-related psychological distress continues to grow among OEF/OIF veterans, although its visibility comes and goes with the news cycles. The issue breaks through occasionally, as when Kentucky's Fort Campbell closed down all operations for three days to conduct a massive antisuicide campaign among its much-deployed soldiers, eleven of whom had committed suicide in the preceding five months.[24] But no matter how frequent the news reports, the burden of these wars has not, thus far, been a shared one. They have been paid for by the American people as a whole, but they have been largely fought and sacrificed for by military families and communities, leaving too many of the rest of us able to ignore the daily cumulative consequences. For now, the image of the service member who is left physically or psychologically injured by war remains a powerful one in the American psyche. Despite the presence of considerable stigma around PTSD, I think most Americans, in the abstract at least, are sympathetic toward service members and their postwar needs. Their support-the-troops attitude has held strong thus far. The question remains, however, whether Americans will continue in their commitment to the troops ten years from now, when the wars will (one can only hope) be long finished, and when the health-care, educational, and other resources required by veterans may begin to seem—as they have after prior wars—like too much of a burden. Veterans with PTSD can at times present as unsympathetic figures. As the perceived glory of their service fades into the past, it can become too easy to focus on the anger and aggression associated with their illness.

It is impossible to know now how many veterans of Iraq and Afghanistan will end up with a PTSD diagnosis. As of August 2009, more than 120,000 OEF/OIF veterans had already received a provisional PTSD diagnosis, and the number continues to rise.[25] Although our understanding of the relationship between PTSD and suicide remains limited, many have watched the U.S. Army's steadily increasing suicide rates over the past several years and read this as evidence of untreated or undiagnosed PTSD.[26] In addition to the toll of human suffering, the burden upon national health care and benefits resources is likely to be immense. In the five years between 1999 and 2004, the number of veterans awarded disability compensation for PTSD increased by 79.5 percent (compared with an average 12.2% increase across all disabilities).[27] It is clear that PTSD and related health concerns will present a significant challenge over the coming decades for veterans, their families, the military, and the VA.

It is also clear that nearly all veterans of Iraq and Afghanistan will experience some amount of "readjustment" after long deployments away from their families. However, the U.S. military has moved in what seems a positive direction by stepping up its efforts to educate service members about readjustment and coping strategies for managing it. Deployment does take a profound toll on families, and it should be expected that service members returning home will require time to reacclimate both to their families and to the conditions of a noncombat environment. The challenges of life in contemporary America are profoundly different from those in a combat zone, and individuals who have spent a year or more adapting to Iraq may find it hard to manage in San Antonio (or New York or Albuquerque or Peoria). This may be a particular challenge if they are simultaneously going through a process of reintegrating with family and friends, grieving losses endured during deployments, or making new meaning of a world in which the devastations of combat can occur. But the fact that this process may be difficult should not be taken as an indication that the service member or veteran has PTSD; he or she may just need time to make peace with a new and ever-changing reality. Certainly, the majority of those who go through some period of reacclimating to life at home manage to accomplish the task and should not be weighed down by the stigma or pathology of a diagnosis when facing an opportunity for resilience and even personal growth.

Of all the veterans I interviewed, not one ever said to me, 'I wish I'd never heard of Iraq or Afghanistan.' All of them valued their time in the combat zone, if only because of what it taught them about life and purpose and love and loss, about what extraordinary things are possible when one is stretched to the very limit. It will be important to remember this over the long run and to maintain the expectation that, with appropriate support and opportunities, most veterans will flourish in their time after service. We must acknowledge the reality that readjustment is a process, and find ways to normalize the experience; some evidence suggests that individuals who go through the military's programs in this vein—Battlemind, for example—report fewer symptoms of anxiety and PTSD after deployment.[28]

More recently, there has been growing discussion of whether and to what degree PTSD may be overdiagnosed among recent veterans.[29] During 2007–8, the question of overdiagnosis was widely debated in both military and VA circles, even as it was recognized that PTSD was also probably being underdiagnosed in certain groups—for example, among active combat troops serving in Iraq and among those undergoing repeat deployments.[30] In early 2009, the science writer David Dobbs brought these questions to national attention with an article in *Scientific American* in which he argued that the *DSM* criteria used to define PTSD were so broad as to result in "rampant overdiagnosis"; he suggested that normal problems of readjustment were being mislabeled as PTSD, creating unnecessary disability in PTSD-diagnosed veterans.[31] It seems likely that Dobbs is correct and some amount of overdiagnosis is occurring, although it is at this time impossible to say how much, and I would argue that this overdiagnosis results as much from the pressure placed on VA clinicians to "serve our veterans" as from flawed *DSM* criteria. As long as the diagnosis of PTSD results in the awarding of financial disability compensation, there will be those who seek out a diagnosis unnecessarily. And as long as VA clinicians are under political pressure to provide care whose "quality" is measured by media interviews with unsatisfied veterans rather than by broader and more objective criteria (such as veterans' health outcomes and overall patient satisfaction), they will be more likely to award a diagnosis where none is needed.

This is and will remain a tricky political issue, precisely because of the access to treatment and compensation made available to veterans given a PTSD diagnosis. Those brave enough to take on this issue in the public forum will need to strive for a balance of sensitivity and specificity, working to ensure that the criteria for diagnosing PTSD are sufficiently sensitive to catch all those who are in need of additional treatment and support, while not overdiagnosing the illness among those who are functioning well. This is an issue of cost-effectiveness, but more important, it is an issue of avoiding either neglect or learned helplessness. Combat PTSD can be a devastating and even fatal condition, and veterans must receive the care they need to overcome its ravages. But PTSD has the potential to become an identity as well as an illness, and this is not always to the good.

Despite the daunting scale of these challenges and at the risk of sounding like an optimist, I am made greatly hopeful by two things. First, resilience, that adaptive ability to continue functioning after stress or trauma, is far more common than PTSD. Only a minority of those exposed to trauma develop PTSD, and so it is reasonable to expect that most OEF/OIF service members will return home and do very well. To date, it remains unclear to what degree resilience is a *trait*, an inborn or acquired characteristic, and to what degree it is a *process*, a series of cognitive, psychosocial, and/or physiological adaptations. However, there is a lively research movement afoot to explore just exactly how resilience works, and it may be that these studies will offer new insight into ways that we might learn to teach resilient coping strategies, behaviors, and attitudes.[32]

The second thing that makes me hopeful is that the cumulative evidence suggests PTSD is responsive to a number of the newer treatments, such as certain medications and the exposure-based cognitive behavioral therapies, although the widespread effectiveness of these treatments for combat veterans has yet to be tested. For myself, I can say that witnessing the recovery of individuals like Chris and Derek has been extraordinarily moving, and I can only hope that the immeasurable effort both clinicians and veterans are putting into these treatments will pay off. Given the political and professional debates involved in such a task, it will be a challenge to shift the model for PTSD illness from one of chronic disability to one of recovery. But if this should come to pass in such a way that most PTSD-diagnosed veterans themselves feel truly better off—with their symptoms in remission, perhaps, if not full recovery—the benefits for quality of life would be entirely worth the battle.

At the same time, clinical treatments, though an essential part of the picture, should not be seen as the only venue for helping to minimize the impact of PTSD on veterans and service members in the coming decades. Actions at all levels—from steps taken by individuals to national policy measures—have the potential to make an important difference in the well-being of those returning from Iraq and Afghanistan. Here is a short list of approaches that should be prioritized:

A. Recommendations for preventing combat PTSD

1. *Provide support for resilience research.* Although resilience in the wake of traumatic events has remained underexplored,[33] there is evidence to suggest that educational, pharmacologic, and psychosocial interventions may all have an important role to play in increasing resilience among service members deployed to combat zones.[34] Further research in these areas has the potential to go a long way toward developing programs aimed at minimizing the impact of trauma exposure on service members' health and well-being over the life course.

2. *Continue to focus on efforts to lessen stigma in the military.* The stigma against PTSD remains frequent and destructive. It encourages shame, deters healthy sharing and processing of emotions, and interferes with care seeking. Ongoing efforts aimed at reducing the stigma of PTSD can be strengthened by making it a stated goal for every service member to support mission readiness and the well-being of the group through positive self-care. Many veterans in the PDS study described deciding to seek care out of a sense of obligation to family members; active-duty service members also acknowledged that, once psychological distress began to interfere with their ability to function, they became less able to contribute to their unit's well-being. Since service members and veterans are already motivated by a strong sense of duty to others, antistigma efforts should include communicating an ideal of strength that emphasizes prompt care seeking as a way of remaining fit and ready to meet one's obligations to unit and family. By reframing the military's cultural emphasis on toughness and stamina in different terms—replacing an ethos of grin and bear it with one aimed at maintaining optimal fitness over time—such efforts will be better equipped to counteract existing stigma, while encouraging service members to seek care before problems spin out of control.

3. *Provide support for research on military families.* Families face their own difficulties with long deployments, and much can be done to minimize their struggles by providing adequate social, clinical, and institutional support. Clinicians and researchers have made great strides in this area over the past several years, but there is still a need for evidence-based programs aimed at supporting families during long deployments. Family problems arising during deployment, besides threatening the well-being of spouses, children, and other family members, can also erupt into conflicts that inhibit

service members' post-deployment readjustment. Programs tailored to build positive coping and communication strategies within the family may therefore have the potential to support post-combat resilience as well as family well-being.[35] These programs should strive to provide education on what readjustment may mean for family relations and how best to help service members struggling in the readjustment period.

B. Recommendations for minimizing the severity of combat PTSD

1. *Improve veterans' and service members' access to appropriate mental health care.* San Antonio is home to one of the best veterans' health-care systems in the country, with health outcomes rated in the top 10 percent across the United States. Not all veterans, however, have access to such care. Many of them, particularly those who live in rural or underserved areas, may have to travel long distances to access the resources available, making it impossible or impractical to attend the multiple appointments necessary to establish and maintain adequate treatment.[36] Likewise, service members' access to mental health care while on active or reserve duty appears to be inconsistent, varying by service branch, service location, and local leadership's goals and priorities. Achieving consistent access to quality care for all veterans and service members must remain a top priority.

2. *Continue to support research on therapeutic and pharmacological treatments for PTSD.* Although there has been tremendous growth in this area over the past two decades, the coming years will present an unprecedented opportunity to evaluate how effective current treatments are in addressing combat PTSD in real-life clinical settings, as a growing number of veterans and service members find their way into care. Despite the challenges of caring for all of those flooding into mental health clinics, clinicians and researchers must make it a priority to evaluate the treatments on offer in order to continue the process of identifying and refining best practices. This research focus should extend to the continued investigation of basic mechanisms in the onset and maintenance of PTSD in hopes that accumulating knowledge will illuminate new methods for preventing and treating the disorder.

3. *Support research on gender and PTSD, as well as the needs of female veterans.* Because women's roles in the military have changed so rapidly since the 1990s, our current understanding of how experiences of combat PTSD may differ for men and women lags behind the need to provide the best possible care to all veterans. What does seem clear is that the military and VA are not yet fully equipped to provide top-quality care to women and must develop more focused outreach and treatment programs to serve female veterans, taking into account needs like child care for those attending medical

appointments (something that would be an enormous help to many male veterans as well). Both the military and the VA have, at various times, gone out of their way to applaud the contribution of women in the service, and yet this positive recognition of women's contribution has not yet come to be taken for granted, either within these institutions or within the communities that surround them. We must continue to acknowledge and express our appreciation for the vital role that female service members play in the contemporary military and the risks they take in doing so and to make this a habit at every level of society—within families, locally, and nationally.

4. *Invite families to be involved in treatment.* The findings of this study suggest that families who have a solid (clinical) understanding of PTSD's symptoms and causes may be more sympathetic toward the veteran and more likely to develop positive coping strategies that minimize the impact of PTSD.[37] Some clinicians have also begun to argue for involving spouses and other family members more directly in PTSD treatment.[38] Movement in this area will require additional research on family attitudes toward PTSD, which has been relatively scarce until recently, and will provide opportunities for formulating and evaluating partner-focused treatment as well as health promotion and literacy programs.

5. *Involve veterans of all ages in outreach efforts.* Veterans I spoke with were often reliant on other veterans—whether close friends, family members, or former superiors—in making sense of their struggles with PTSD and in selecting options for coping and care seeking. Both the military and the VA have made efforts to take advantage of these naturally occurring networks to encourage appropriate care seeking and other self-care behaviors—the military by educating service members on how to recognize PTSD in others and the San Antonio VA by including video testimony from veterans who have completed treatment in their orientation seminars for newly PTSD-diagnosed veterans. These are excellent beginnings, but more can be done to involve local veterans in outreach and educational efforts, building on the unique bonds between veterans and helping to address issues of trust that are especially relevant for veterans with PTSD. This strategy has the added benefit of empowering veterans to have a voice within local care networks, thus fostering more positive relations between veterans and the institutions intended to serve them.

6. *Continue to invest in dual-diagnosis treatment and research for veterans with comorbid PTSD and substance abuse concerns.* Mental-health-care providers have historically insisted that PTSD-diagnosed patients attain sobriety before beginning PTSD treatment. The VA has recently acknowledged that this strategy may actually be counterproductive, as veterans often engage

in alcohol and drug use in an attempt to manage their PTSD symptoms. Efforts are being made to address this problem through programs aimed at treating PTSD and substance abuse simultaneously[39] and by hiring providers at VAs across the nation to serve as specialized dual-diagnosis coordinators for veterans with PTSD and substance abuse problems. However, there is evidence to suggest that individuals with comorbid PTSD and substance disorders may be less responsive to many of the treatments effective for those with PTSD alone.[40] Additional research will be necessary to develop practice guidelines attuned to the unique needs of these veterans.

7. *Remain committed to the goals of patient-centered care.* The organizing tenets of a patient-centered-care model are widely considered an essential part of the VA's remarkable transformation over the past few decades, a shift that has taken the nation's largest health system from providing mediocre to providing top-ranked care. Under this model, the focus is placed on centering control in the hands of the individual patient (rather than the provider) and on extending care beyond the clinic into the patient's home and community, striving to provide a seamless network of care that is responsive to all of a patient's needs (e.g., both mental health and substance abuse).[41] One of the findings of the San Antonio study has been that Latino and non-Latino veterans do not necessarily vary greatly in their experiences of PTSD; to assume otherwise may well interfere with a provider's ability to be responsive to the needs of the individual patient. As more research explores the needs of particular groups with PTSD (e.g., Latinos, women, sexual assault survivors), it will be essential to incorporate the knowledge gained into treatment practice without ever losing sight of the fact that every person's experience of PTSD is unique.

C. Recommendations for decreasing the impact of combat PTSD on families

1. *Include family-level outcomes in PTSD treatment research.* One concern that arises in taking an anthropological view on the PTSD literature is how frequently studies focus solely on the well-being of the individual with PTSD. This is a predictable outcome of the biomedical perspective, which tends to view disease as a product of dysfunction in the individual body. However, an overly single-minded focus on the individual can deflect attention from the very important ways in which PTSD may be both shaped by and a detriment to social relations.[42] One simple way to broaden this perspective is by encouraging researchers to regularly include measures of family members' physical, social, and mental well-being in PTSD research.

2. *Prioritize the safety of all family members.* Although family violence appears to be a concern for only a minority of PTSD-diagnosed veterans, this is a

topic that calls out for more investigation than it has received until now. Preliminary findings of the San Antonio study suggest that family violence committed by PTSD-diagnosed veterans may fall into patterns that do not entirely fit the classic batterer paradigm and that a better understanding of these patterns may be essential to helping veterans and their spouses take steps to prevent violence and ensure the safety of all family members.[43]

D. Recommendations for supporting resilience at the national and community levels

1. *Extend education and outreach to include those in law enforcement, non-VA health-care settings, and other key points of contact for veterans in the community.* The military and VA are not the only institutions that encounter struggling veterans. PTSD-related phenomena like aggression, suicide, and substance abuse all put veterans at risk of high-stakes encounters with law enforcement, the judicial system, and health-care providers outside the VA. Providing education on PTSD to those who serve as key points of contact in the community can reduce the likelihood of unnecessary conflict and enable more effective decision making about appropriate responses, including referrals to treatment. Efforts aimed at education and outreach in the larger community can also work to decrease stigma by disseminating more accurate information about PTSD and counteracting negative stereotypes. In addition, spreading information about treatment options and the possibility of recovery throughout the community provides another means of making such information available to veterans themselves.

2. *Continue to support the troops.* Americans on the whole have continued to express support for service members serving overseas, despite considerable protest as to the handling of the wars in Iraq and Afghanistan. As a nation we learned the hard way after Vietnam that turning against those who fight our wars only drives their suffering underground, making it harder for them to share and process the memories that may torment them, with sometimes disastrous results. Maintaining our support for the troops plays an important role in encouraging a healthy and productive reintegration for all veterans and also in keeping the public eye on those who would cut corners in providing exceptional resources and health care to veterans and service members. Public opinion is a vital force in leveraging change when change is necessary.

3. *Expect that all combat veterans and other trauma survivors will remain resilient after a period of normal readjustment and that those with PTSD will recover. Convey these expectations.* As important as it is to ensure that all service members and veterans have adequate access to quality mental

health care, it is equally important that Americans not come to believe that PTSD is an inevitable outcome of combat or an inevitable source of disability when it arises. The majority of those exposed to trauma, even combat, will not develop PTSD. They may struggle with readjustment and need to process their experiences internally and in conversation with others, but they will never be made unable to function by their experiences. Among those who do develop PTSD, the emphasis should remain on providing access to evidence-based treatments and on working toward full recovery. Daniel Moerman has written about the extraordinary power of what he calls the "meaning effect"—that poorly understood process by which human beings get sick or well according to their expectations of what will happen to them.[44] Science has proven time and time again that it is possible to make people well with a placebo, just as it is also possible to make them sick with what is called a nocebo.[45] This expectation of recovery and resilience should be made structural as well as cultural; in other words, the expectation of recovery should be incorporated into military and VA systems of benefits and compensation as well as into popular and professional understandings of resilience and PTSD. This will require a considerable overhaul of the current system and should take into account the actual progress that OEF/OIF veterans with PTSD are able to make in reestablishing their lives. There are no easy answers for how to do this, but the current system should be stripped of provisions that encourage veterans to remain chronically disabled when they need not be while leaving those who are truly disabled with all the support they require.[46]

It should be taken as the basis for tremendous hope that nearly all of these recommendations are already in motion.

I have lately found myself drawn to the art of earlier wars, including Robert Service's poems of World War I and the 1946 movie *The Best Years of Our Lives,* which has perhaps the most well-rounded portrayal of combat veterans struggling with readjustment and PTSD ever brought to film. It is widely known that Erich Maria Remarque wrote *All Quiet on the Western Front* in the wake of his own experiences in World War I, but it is less often remembered that he published a sequel to that book in 1930, entitled *The Road Back.* The challenges depicted in it, of soldiers returning home to find that life is not as they left it, would seem familiar to readers. They tell of dislocation, nightmares, suicide, estranged relationships, and the uneasy bonds between veterans. Reflecting on the unsettled strife of postwar soldiers, Remarque wrote,

We thought to build us houses, we desired gardens with terraces, for we wanted to look out upon the sea and to feel the wind, but we did not think that a house needs foundations. We are like those abandoned fields full of shell holes in France, no less peaceful than the other ploughed lands about them, but in them are lying still the buried explosives, and until these shall have been dug out and cleared away, to plough will be a danger.[47]

There is, in his words, the wistful hope for a life that will have in it all the good and necessary things—for Remarque, a house, a garden, a view to the sea. Perhaps for veterans like Chris and Tony and Adam, the list would include marriage and family, satisfying work, and a sense of oneself as a man to be proud of. But Remarque captures, too, that sense of what barriers the war has created for the fulfillment of dreams. Fields cannot be fertile if riddled with shells.

For the men in these pages, the struggle to manage PTSD is the struggle to build a life worth living. To do so, they must navigate the grinds of money and work and institutional resources. They must weave and maintain the many-threaded fabric of close relationships. And they must find acceptable ways to understand themselves as men with PTSD amid the many possible versions of PTSD available to them. They may be distracted along the way by grief, regret, fury at their own deep knowledge of tragedy, and a transformed way of experiencing the world. But there can be no higher stakes, and so their struggle continues—until they slip and fall under the weight of the burden they carry, fulfill the quiet triumph of finding some manageable peace, or come to a place where they can, at the least, put the burden down to rest for a while.

There is no way to undo PTSD, just as there is no way to undo trauma. There is no way to give Derek back his leg or to bring Chris's lost friends back to life. These men will be forever changed by their experiences, and so—perhaps—it should be, for them and the tens of thousands of veterans like them. But if it should also prove possible to minimize the power of trauma to disrupt the course of their lives and the lives of their wives and children, that would be a victory indeed.

Notes

INTRODUCTION

1. Accepted spellings also include post traumatic stress disorder and posttraumatic stress disorder.

2. VHA Office of Public Health and Environmental Hazards 2009.

3. This is a classic area of scholarship within medical anthropology, particularly within the literature on social suffering (e.g., Bourdieu and Accardo 1999; Das et al. 2001; Das et al. 2000; Kleinman 1986; Kleinman, Das, and Lock 1997b) and critical phenomenology (e.g., Biehl 2005; Desjarlais 1997; Good 1994).

4. Yehuda 2002, 108.

5. This question reflects the experience-near approach of phenomenological anthropology, which I relied upon in conceptualizing the ideas developed here (e.g., Csordas 2002; Jackson 1998; Kleinman and Seeman 2000). Given that combat PTSD in this current context results directly from state-level violence, my viewpoint is also critical in its attempt to bring together historical, political economic, and interpretive perspectives (Desjarlais 1997; Good 1994). This analysis owes considerable debt to the anthropologies of violence and suffering more generally (Dickson-Gomez 2003; Feldman 1991; Hinton et al. 2005; Kleinman, Das, and Lock 1997b; Nordstrom 1997; Robben and Suarez-Orozco 2000; Scheper-Hughes 1992).

6. NEPEC 2009.

7. The study protocol was reviewed and approved by the Emory University Institutional Review Board, the University of Texas Health Science Center at San Antonio Institutional Review Board, and the South Texas Veterans Health Care System Research and Development Committee, as well as several other committees representing patients, employees, and other stakeholders.

8. The study was described as follows on the consent form: "The purpose of this research is to explore how post-deployment stress and post-traumatic stress disorder (PTSD) are talked about and understood by veterans and their families, by local mental health and other professionals, and by military and civilian community members in the San Antonio area. This research is also intended to learn more about what it is like for veterans and their families to live with post-deployment stress and/or PTSD, and what sorts of experiences make it easier or more difficult to live with post-deployment stress and/or PTSD."

9. Veterans entered the PDS study through one of three routes, the first of which was clinician referral. Mental health and primary care clinicians provided information about the study to patients they thought might be interested; these patients then had the option of contacting me directly to request further information. The second means was through study announcements in psychoeducation groups. When invited by clinicians, I would briefly visit the group, make a two-minute announcement about the study, and leave behind a sign-up sheet for anyone interested. When the clinicians then passed the sheet along to me, I would contact those who had left their name and contact information, provide additional information about the study, and schedule a meeting with anyone who desired to participate. The third method was through recruitment flyers that were hung at

the VA and several affiliated clinics in the San Antonio area and also at local colleges and universities. Veterans responding to flyers could contact me directly by phone or e-mail, at which point we discussed the study and their eligibility and interest. Group announcements and recruitment flyers were the most frequently reported means of entry into the study. Family members were recruited either via participating veterans or by recruitment flyers. Clinicians and community members were identified via purposive and convenience sampling and contacted directly by me.

10. Measures included seven sections of the Deployment Risk and Resilience Inventory (DRRI) (King, King, and Vogt 2003); the Post-Traumatic Checklist—Military Version (PCL-M)(Gray, Bolton, and Litz 2004; Magruder et al. 2004); the World Health Organization Disability Assessment Scale, Version II (WHODAS-II), which has been utilized previously to establish levels of disability among mentally ill populations (Alonso et al. 2004); the twenty-five-item Hopkins Symptom Checklist (HSCL-25), which is a commonly used measure of depression and anxiety among traumatized populations (Carlsson, Mortensen, and Kastrup 2005; Sabin et al. 2003); and the Brief Acculturation Rating Scale for Mexican Americans, Version II (ARSMA-II) (Cuéllar, Arnold, and Maldonado 1995).

11. Gutmann 1997; Sabo and Gordon 1995.

12. Jakupcak et al. 2006; Lorber and Garcia, 2010; Seal et al. 2010.

13. Unfortunately, this portrayal also leaves out the experiences of men whose partners are men. Although one man who identified himself as gay did participate in the study, his concern for privacy was such that he did not feel comfortable addressing how he felt PTSD had affected his relationship with his partner.

14. Study participants (n=133) were divided into four groups: sixty-two veterans, twenty-one family members, twenty-eight clinicians, and twenty-two community members. Although participants were counted and treated as distinct study groups, the life roles they actually played were often overlapping. Thus those who were interviewed as veterans might also be family members, clinicians might also be veterans, etc. All participants provided informed consent; those in the veterans' group completed signed and witnessed consent forms, while all other participants gave verbal consent only.

15. Kleinman 1988a.

16. Dobbs 2009.

17. Michalowski and Dubisch 2001.

18. Gutmann and Lutz 2009.

19. It may be that this will change over time. As the wars continue and public opinion around them shifts, and as these veterans gain distance from their own experiences in combat, it may be that the politics of war will become more central to their PTSD illness narratives. Susie Kilshaw (2004) has shown how veterans' narratives of war-related illness may shift over time, and her work seems to support this possibility.

CHAPTER 1

1. Of sixty-two participants in the veterans' group, thirty-two reported having been born in Texas. Of these, fifteen individuals were born or raised in San Antonio, while seventeen came from elsewhere in Texas. For the purpose of avoiding repetition, I will refer to veterans in the PDS study as simply "veterans" from here on out. For clarity's sake, if I am describing a larger group of veterans, such as all Iraq/Afghanistan veterans in the United States, I will say so directly.

2. For example, Fort Sam Houston has a long history of providing medical training for army medics and other health providers. In 2005, the Department of Defense's (DOD's) Base Closure and Realignment Commission recommended that Brooke Army Medical Center and Wilford Hall be merged to form the San Antonio Military Medical

Center. The combined facilities will in the future provide medical training for all medics and other health professionals across the armed forces.

3. Brookings Institution 2003. A note on terms used throughout: I will generally use "white," "Latino," and "African American" to refer to ethnicities common in the United States. There is a legitimate concern about use of the term "white," as it speaks to race rather than ethnicity; nonetheless, this is the most frequent term in use, and the possible alternatives, such as "Euro-American" or "Caucasian," are themselves imperfect. I have selected "Latino" rather than "Hispanic" because it speaks to cultural heritage rather than language (since, of course, not all Latinos speak Spanish). "African American" seemed most appropriate here as none of those I will be discussing are themselves from Africa or the Caribbean, which might have argued for more general use of the term "black."

4. USCB 2007.

5. All text in double quotes is taken directly from the transcripts of recorded interviews. All study participants completed informed consent and were then asked whether they would mind if the interviews were audio-recorded; most had no problem with this and the interviews of those who said they would not mind were recorded. Text in single quotes is drawn from unrecorded interviews or observations, signaling conversations reconstructed from detailed notes. Interview quotes have been edited primarily for length, although I have also taken the liberty of removing pausing phrases such as "like," "you know," etc., where they recur with some frequency. In certain cases I have corrected minor mistakes in grammar if I felt these created unnecessary confusion. Some edits have been made for the purpose of removing identifying names or facts. I have used brackets to indicate places where it seemed necessary to include additional information to clarify a quote.

6. NPP 2009.

7. Galtung 1969.

8. I'm associating this youthful desire with young men and masculinity here because Brian and some of the other veterans do. However, as a little girl, I was obsessed with Tom Wolfe's *The Right Stuff* and wanted to be a navy test pilot even more than I wanted to be a ballerina. We should perhaps be hesitant to link the desire for adventure too closely with masculinity.

9. The primary exception I found to this generalization was among those who joined up in the wake of the attacks on September 11, 2001. A small group of veterans described enlisting 'because of 9/11.' Upon further discussion, however, these men usually revealed that they were already in the process of enlisting at the time or that they had some previous link to the military, such as ongoing participation in the reserves or an ROTC program at their high school. I clarify this point not to undercut the patriotism of those who enlisted but rather to give proper weight to the complexity of their decision-making process.

CHAPTER 2

1. Each of the key informants returned to throughout the book represents a composite of several individuals. After much consideration, it became clear that no simple change of identifying facts (dates, places, occupations, etc.) would be sufficient to honor the spirit of the confidentiality agreement made when study participants and I spoke in interviews together. Instead, I have disguised these individuals by creating a composite of several identities while working to remain true to the integrity of the original stories. This tactic has the additional benefit of offering maximum depth and complexity (by representing a variety of experiences) alongside minimum confusion (by avoiding an endless string of names and offering a more substantial portrait of particular individuals). Each of these composites in turn represents a particular pattern of approaches to the experiences of

deployment, life after deployment, and PTSD that emerged in the larger set of veterans' interviews; each was selected for its ability to articulate and represent these common concerns and perspectives.

2. Since much of this book is drawn from the interviews conducted in this office, it is worth noting that it was a fairly small room, and although it was big enough for the desk and two or three chairs, it lent itself to the kind of intimacy that can arise when two individuals have nothing to distract them from the business of conversing with each other. By the time they came into the room, veterans had already spoken with me by phone or in person and knew that the purpose of the study was to better understand their experiences of deployment and post-deployment, a purpose we discussed in greater detail as they completed the informed-consent process. Although there were a series of demographic questions and a long survey to get through during the interview, my goal as an interviewer was always to create a respectful space in which veterans could feel comfortable telling their stories as they thought best.

3. Although PDS study data include information on traumas reported by veterans who completed the survey, I did not probe for more detailed descriptions in our conversations. If a memory began and was left half told and then abandoned, I let it rest. Alternatively, I never asked about the good stories, about the best memories a veteran might have of the military. What I did ask were things like "What was your day-to-day life like in the military?" "In Iraq?" Prompted by such general questions, these were some of the stories that emerged.

4. Dickson-Gomez 2003; Englund 1998; Fassin and d'Halluin 2007; Henry 2006; Kleinman, Das, and Lock 1997b; Robben and Suarez-Orozco 2000; Zarowsky 2004.

CHAPTER 3

1. Driving is an important source of frustration and distress for many OEF/OIF veterans. Three veterans who had undergone PTSD treatment were interviewed on video in an effort by the local VA's trauma clinic to use veterans' own success stories and testimonials to improve retention rates in treatment. All three, unprompted, mentioned how difficult they had found driving prior to their treatment.

2. In theory, triggers might also be associated with positive feelings, although I never heard the word used that way by clinicians. But Derek, for example, came to associate the sound of helicopters with protection while he was in Iraq, and he joked that if he could just get a recording of Black Hawks to play by his bed at night he would "sleep like a baby."

3. Service 1916, 135.

4. *MedlinePlus* 2009.

5. *Dictionary.com* 2009.

6. Ibid.

7. S. J. Johnson et al. 2007.

8. Zoroya 2008.

9. Gibbs et al. 2007.

10. Veterans in this study reported deployments ranging from three to eighteen months at a time.

11. Finley, Pugh, and Jeffreys 2010.

12. The U.S. Air Force Core Values are Integrity First, Service before Self, and Excellence in All We Do, http://www.usafa.af.mil/core-value. The U.S. Navy (including the Marine Corps) Core Values are Honor, Courage, and Commitment, http://www.navy.mil/navydata/cno/DON_Core_Values_Charter.pdf.

13. One can, of course, debate whether the military constitutes a separate culture (I find it interesting that I was asked this question by military personnel on more than one occasion) or whether all service members subscribe with equal devotion to Core Values.

From my perspective, it is less useful to say that the military is a distinct culture than to recognize that it offers a very powerful set of cultural influences.

14. Bonanno 2004; Bonanno et al. 2007; Butler et al. 2009.

15. Tedeschi and Calhoun 2004.

16. APA 2000.

17. Breslau et al. 1998.

18. Kessler et al. 1995; Perkonigg, Storz, and Wittchen 2000.

19. Milliken, Auchterlonie, and Hoge 2007. One may find many reasons to dispute these figures—not least because it is a widely accepted fact (particularly among military epidemiologists) that personnel returning from deployment underreport PTSD symptoms. However, the essential point is borne out—far more people are exposed to trauma than develop PTSD.

20. Fontana and Rosenheck 1994; Johansen et al. 2007; Ozer et al. 2003.

21. This text is taken directly from the Deployment Risk and Resilience Inventory, subscale A, developed by King et al. (2006) and used as a measure of stressful life experiences in this study. See also King, King, and Vogt 2003.

22. Hourani, Yuan, and Bray 2003.

23. Milliken, Auchterlonie, and Hoge 2007.

24. Combat exposure was measured utilizing the Deployment Risk and Resilience Inventory Combat Exposure subscale. L. A. King et al. 2006.

25. By comparison, Milliken and his coauthors, in their study (2007) of eighty-eight thousand soldiers returning home, found that only 54 percent had witnessed someone being wounded or killed, and only about a quarter of the sample had fired their weapons.

26. Weathers et al. 1993.

27. With a one-tailed Pearson correlation score of .355, significant at the 0.01 level.

28. Starr 2009.

29. Chedekel and Kauffman 2008.

30. Suicide Risk Management and Surveillance Office 2008.

31. Ahern et al. 2004; Bonanno et al. 2007; Taft et al. 1999.

32. Fontana and Rosenheck 1994.

33. Dirkzwager, Bramsen, and Van der Ploeg 2003; L. A. King et al. 1998; Solomon 1987; Stretch 1985.

34. Keane et al. 1985; D. W. King et al. 2006.

35. Matsakis 1988; Elbogen et al. 2008; Glenn et al. 2002; Marshall, Panuzio, and Taft 2005.

36. Goff et al. 2007.

37. Dirkzwager et al. 2005; Dekel, Solomon, and Bleich 2005.

38. The period of time since relationship failure is not standard, and may have occurred anytime since the return from deployment, which ranged from four months to several years.

39. There is a significant inverse correlation between current PTSD symptoms and reported social support since the return home.

40. L. A. King et al. 1998.

41. Geertz 1973.

42. Ibid., 6.

CHAPTER 4

1. Jakupcak et al. 2009. Of fifty OEF/OIF veterans in the PDS study (including those with and without a diagnosis of PTSD), fourteen (29%) reported having had thoughts of ending their lives during the week before our interview.

2. Emphasis in the original.

3. Hogg 2008.

4. An earlier *New York Post* editorial had claimed that the "stereotype [of the Vietnam vet] was also a news-media lie to begin with" and that the "myth of the dysfunctional vet that began with Vietnam has been created and spread, in large measure, by groups bitterly opposed to all U.S. military action" (as quoted in Kolb 2006). In the debate that ensued, the central question remained: Was the *New York Times* article simply resurrecting the post-Vietnam wacko-vet myth in an effort to discredit the wars in Iraq and Afghanistan? Or was this important coverage of the suffering experienced and inflicted by combat veterans?

5. *Economist* 2009.

6. This perception of PTSD as associated with violence can also affect how episodes of violence committed by veterans, including violence in the home, are interpreted by those involved. Finley ct al., 2010. If that violence is understood to be "the result of PTSD," spouses and partners may feel that it is not the veteran's fault or is otherwise outside his control, with important implications for their safety-seeking behaviors.

7. Marshall, Panuzio, and Taft 2005; Straus and Gelles 1990.

8. Byrne and Riggs 1996; Sherman et al. 2006; Taft et al. 2005.

9. Jordan et al. 1992.

10. Elbogen et al. 2008; O'Donnell et al. 2006. In addition, PTSD related to combat as opposed to other traumas appears to increase the risk of partner violence. Prigerson, Maciejewski, and Rosenheck 2001.

11. PTSD may at times be seen as a justification for violence. One woman I interviewed told me flat out that if a veteran has PTSD and is violent at home, "It's not the same as domestic violence. It's really not because a lot of times these guys really don't realize they're doing it."

12. Mahalik et al. 2003.

13. Ibid.; Tager and Good 2005.

14. Jakupcak et al. 2006.

15. Irritability has also been discussed as an alternative to showing depressive symptoms among men. Magovcevic and Addis 2005.

16. Female veterans, of course, have their own experience of the intersection between gender and PTSD; for additional discussion of this, please see the conclusion.

17. Addis and Mahalik 2003; Good et al. 2006; Magovcevic and Addis 2005.

18. Mejia 2005.

19. Ibid.; Lorber and Garcia, 2010.

20. Thompson and Pleck 1986.

21. For an interesting study of masculinity among veterans with Gulf War Illness, see Susie Kilshaw's *Impotent Warriors* (2008).

22. Pole et al. 2005; Ruef, Litz, and Schlenger 2000.

23. Ortega and Rosenheck 2000; Ruef, Litz, and Schlenger 2000.

24. Alegria et al. 2008.

25. Arthur Kleinman explains this and many other difficulties with mental health research in his classic *Rethinking Psychiatry* (1988b).

26. There is a rich literature on these issues within anthropology, of which one very interesting example is Vilma Santiago-Irizarry's *Medicalizing Ethnicity: The Construction of Latino Identity in a Psychiatric Setting* (2001).

27. Bremner and Brett 1997; Pole et al. 2005; van der Kolk et al. 1996.

28. E.g., Guarnaccia et al. 1996; Marshall and Orlando 2002; Rubel, O'Nell, and Collado 1984; Ruef, Litz, and Schlenger 2000. Such explanations, despite anthropological warnings against essentializing culture and ethnicity in the clinical setting (e.g., Kleinman

1988a; Rubel and Garro 1992), have been put forward without analysis of how *ataque de nervios, susto,* or even PTSD is understood or experienced by Latino veterans.

29. Alfredo Mirandé (1997) has a useful chapter outlining the historical context of machismo in Mexican culture.

30. Arciniega et al. 2008; Mirandé 1997.

31. For two excellent discussions of this issue, see Gutmann 1996 and Mirandé 1997.

32. Mirandé 1997, 66.

33. Rubel 1966. Similar examples can be found in the ethnographic work of Matthew Gutmann (1996) and Mirandé (1997).

34. In addition to asking veterans to identify their own ethnicity, I also asked them to complete a locally developed acculturation scale, the Brief Acculturation Rating Scale for Mexican Americans (Cuéllar, Arnold, and Maldonado 1995). Although acculturation is a much and rightly critiqued concept (Abraida Lanza et al. 2006), this was intended to provide additional detail on aspects of daily life related to cultural heritage and environment, such as Spanish/English language use and ethnicity of close friends. When examined statistically, acculturation was not significantly associated with PTSD severity.

35. Garcia et al., forthcoming.

36. In the study we also suggest that dedication to success may promote behaviors, like going out in public, that function as a kind of low-level exposure therapy and inhibit a cycle of increasing dysfunction. Exposure therapy is explained in chapter 7.

37. Dohrenwend et al. 2008; see also Lewis-Fernandez et al. 2008.

38. Marshall, Schell, and Miles 2009.

39. Lorber and Garcia, 2010.

CHAPTER 5

1. Dean 1997.

2. Ibid.

3. Shephard 2001.

4. Many of those Victorian ladies famous for swooning on couches were said to have hysteria, an epidemic whose dramatic ebb and flow stands as a historical example of how cultural ideas about illness can get inside the brain and body, influencing the manifestation of physical or emotional distress.

5. Shephard 2001.

6. Rivers 1920, 1. Italics mine.

7. Young 1995.

8. From this unresolved legacy arose the British army's habit of lumping together all war neuroses in the early part of World War II, drawing on a list that grew to include shell shock, hysteria, neurasthenia, disordered action of the heart (DAH, a heart condition not unlike soldier's heart), and not yet diagnosed (nervous), which was a loose diagnosis that gave military physicians a temporary catch-all category for potential war neurosis cases (Shephard 2001). Although war neurosis was a more common diagnosis than shell shock by the end of World War I, this should not be taken as a victory for advocates of the psychological model for combat trauma. In the years following the war, two key figures—W. H. R. Rivers and Abram Kardiner—would produce their own biological explanations for the "psychoneuroses," becoming part of the surge of biological psychiatry that, although subordinate to the psychoanalytic tradition in the coming decades, would resurface during the Vietnam era to provide much of the frame for PTSD as we know it today (Young 1995).

9. Shephard 2001, 25.

10. Shephard 2001.

11. Chermol 1985; Shephard 2001.

12. Shephard 2001, 29. See also Young 1995 for a detailed discussion of diagnostic taxonomy during this era.

13. Shephard 2001.

14. Roberts 2006.

15. Shephard 2001.

16. Ibid.

17. Ibid.

18. HQDA 1994.

19. HQDA 1994; Wanke 1999.

20. Shephard 2001.

21. Wanke 1999.

22. Shephard 2001.

23. Pols and Oak 2007; Wanke 1999.

24. Wanke 1999.

25. Shephard 2001.

26. Wanke 1999.

27. Ibid.

28. Nisbet 1945; Wanke 1999.

29. Shephard 2001.

30. Rochefort 1997.

31. Wanke 1999.

32. HQDA 1994.

33. CSOC 2003; Hamre 1999.

34. MHAT 2003, E-6.

35. Hamre 1999; HQDA 1994; MHAT 2003.

36. Hamre 1999; HQDA 1994.

37. The increasing use of pharmaceuticals by military personnel during combat deployments has been the subject of some media controversy (Thompson 2008), although the data on this issue remain scattered. I have been unable to locate reliable statistics on how many military personnel serving in Iraq or Afghanistan are currently taking psychoactive medications. The use of such medications during combat raises important questions as to the potential impact on service members' experiences of trauma and the processing of emotion and memory in the aftermath of traumatic events, but investigations in this area remain fledgling.

38. HQDA 1994; MHAT 2003. Four of the clinicians I interviewed for the PDS study had each spent a year providing mental health care in Iraq. One of them expressed consternation that very little research had been done examining the most effective therapeutic treatments for combat stress during deployment (several new studies are now under way). His impression was that the status quo was based on anecdotal evidence rather than formal research and that changes were generally decreed from the top down by interested leadership rather than based on the accumulation of clinical evidence. This critique comes in interesting contrast to recent efforts at the VA clinic described in chapter 7, which have relied on the use of an evidence-based model to restructure care for PTSD.

39. Shephard 2001.

40. Ibid.

41. Lifton [1973] 1992, 35.

42. Lifton [1973] 1992; Shephard 2001; Young 1995.

43. Scott 1993.

44. Goodwin and Guze 1996.

45. Young 1995.

46. Ibid., 114.

47. Young 1995.

48. Quoted ibid. 1995, 117. Because it was defined among veterans, most of whom had been out of the service for years, PTSD described a phenomenon quite different from that which had brought earlier psychiatrists to write about shell shock and combat fatigue— the diagnosis bore more resemblance to old sergeant's syndrome than to the acute cases that first garnered attention in World War I (Young 1995).

49. This was not the first time civilians had been susceptible to a PTSD-like phenomenon; see Young's (1995) discussion of "railway spine." And this acceptance has not been without continuing controversy. For an articulate critique, see Summerfield 1999.

50. Kessler et al. 1995.

51. Herman 1992.

52. Shmotkin, Blumstein, and Modan 2003. It is perhaps ironic that PTSD as a diagnosis began with veterans and ebbed outward toward civilian forms of trauma, whereas the most effective treatments for PTSD were pioneered among civilian patients and only later brought into the VA.

53. Tanielian et al. 2008.

CHAPTER 6

1. Starr 2002.

2. A LexisNexis Academic search of newspaper articles containing the words "post-traumatic stress disorder" among major U.S. and world newspapers found 83 articles in 2002, 90 in 2003, 69 in 2004, 66 in 2005, 82 in 2006, 97 in 2007, and 197 in 2008.

3. Gettleman 2003. Pogany worked in intelligence and was deployed to serve with a Special Forces unit in September 2003. On his second night in Iraq, a nearby U.S. patrol was ambushed and returned to the compound with Iraqi prisoners and several wounded. Pogany heard the trucks pulling in and left his bedroom to find a disarray of ambulances, Humvees, and people screaming. Smelling blood, he looked down and saw a body bag, which two men opened to reveal the corpse of an Iraqi man whose torso had been torn apart by gunfire. Nearby were five handcuffed Iraqi prisoners, one with a severe leg wound, and a young U.S. soldier sitting at a table, shaking and pale (Warner 2005). Pogany returned to his room but became nauseated and vomited a half hour later. He was panicked and trembling, and when finally able to sleep, he had nightmares of the room exploding; he woke to find that the nightmare was continuing as a hallucination. Still shaking the next morning, Pogany sought out the team sergeant and was told to "get himself together," "act like a soldier," and "go away and think about what he was saying, because it could lead to serious complications for his career" (ibid.). Pogany's weapons were confiscated. The next day he again approached the sergeant and requested help, after which he was sent to Tikrit and held on suicide watch. After several days, he was visited by a chaplain, who told him the nightmares and trembling were normal and took him to the nearby COSC unit. There an army psychologist also told Pogany his reaction was normal but recommended to his superiors that Pogany be given short-term care with the CSC unit. Instead, Pogany was called before his superior officers and berated for his behavior, then told he would be immediately shipped home to Colorado (ibid.).

Once home, Pogany was stripped of his job, personal weapon, and security clearance and charged with cowardly conduct under Article 99 of the Uniform Code of Military Justice, the first such charge since 1968 (ibid.). Pogany continued to experience symptoms of panic, confusion, and depression but chose to fight the charges rather than accept the military equivalent of a plea bargain. Charges were first diminished to dereliction of duty and then later dropped entirely. Pogany was found to have suffered brain damage and a probable episode of acute psychosis following Lariam toxicity resulting from the malaria prophylaxis he had been given prior to deployment (McHugh 2004).

4. Priest and Hull 2007a.

5. DOD 2007.

6. Given the stigma around psychological issues in the military, it seems reasonable to question whether the fallout would have been as severe if the problems had not been identified first among physically, visibly wounded service members before being linked to those who were psychologically wounded as well.

7. Priest and Hull 2007b.

8. Press 2007.

9. Pulitzer 2008.

10. Stop-loss—a policy placing involuntary extensions on service members' terms of service—was implemented in 2004 following recognition that the army was insufficiently staffed to maintain a ground war on two fronts (Iraq and Afghanistan). Under this policy, active-duty and reserve soldiers whose contracts had expired and who had planned to leave the army were forced to serve a full additional deployment of up to fifteen months. Officials claimed that the measure protected units from attrition occurring right before combat deployment, thus helping units to retain seasoned members at the time they were needed most, putting "the best fighting force on the battlefield" (Squitieri 2004). However, the policy's implementation was widely criticized, with detractors calling the policy a "back-door draft" (*Chicago Tribune* 2004; White 2004).

11. At the same time, the military's health-care resources were being taxed as they had not been since Vietnam. New medical technologies enabled physicians to save a much higher percentage of wounded service members. Mortality rates among those injured have dropped dramatically, with the unprecedented survival rate leaving the military struggling with the necessity of caring for very seriously injured service members.

12. MHAT 2003. The team released its report in March of 2004 in what would become the first in a series of annual MHAT reports documenting elevated rates of psychological symptoms among service members serving in Iraq and Afghanistan. The initial MHAT report found that 23 percent of soldiers surveyed in Iraq reported moderate or severe stress or emotional or family problems, with 17 percent of the sample screening positive for depression, anxiety, or traumatic stress. Of those who screened positive, only 27 percent reported having received attention from a health professional or chaplain; even among those expressing a desire for help, only 32 percent had received any. It is difficult to compare these numbers with those from prior wars, as combat-zone mental health surveillance has improved considerably over the past few decades.

13. Another study conducted at roughly the same time found that among soldiers returning from Iraq who screened positive for a possible mental disorder, 65 percent feared being seen as weak, and 59 percent worried that their units would have less confidence in them (Hoge et al. 2004).

14. MHAT 2003.

15. This change was the result of increasing controversy over the draft during the Vietnam era. Catherine Lutz (2001, 167) has written, "As the war ended, the military had to change in the face of massive refusals to soldier, and the potential recruit's now pressing suspicion that an army job entailed more than career training."

16. The recession of 2008–9 seemed to lessen the problem of recruitment for at least some branches of the U.S. Armed Forces. Army National Guard recruitment was up sufficiently in 2009 to allow the Guard to begin trimming signing bonuses and educational benefits that had skyrocketed in 2005 in an attempt to meet a twenty-thousand-soldier shortfall (Vanden Brook 2009).

17. O'Hara 2006; White 2004. One article in the British newspaper *The Observer* told of how "[e]xhaustion and combat stress are besieging U.S. troops in Iraq" and claimed,

"As desertions and absences increase, the military is struggling to cope with the crisis" (Beaumont 2007).

18. Hoge et al. 2004.

19. HQDA 1994, 8–9.

20. The U.S. military represents such a massive and complex institution (or set of institutions, depending on one's perspective) that I am not able to offer a more comprehensive overview of these efforts.

21. Richie 2008.

22. CDP 2009.

23. See also Milliken, Auchterlonie, and Hoge 2007.

24. "Battlemind Training I: Transitioning from Combat Home," brochure developed by the Walter Reed Army Institute of Research Land Combat Study Team.

25. MHAT 2008. In thus educating soldiers about this post-deployment transition or readjustment period, the army is explicitly working to normalize combat behaviors and reactions that clinicians often call by another name: symptoms. Among the phenomena that Battlemind materials describe are hypervigilance, emotional withdrawal, and inappropriate anger and aggression, all of which clinicians might well describe as symptoms of PTSD. Chaplains and army clinicians give several reasons for this different way of framing things, focusing in particular on trying to minimize the anxiety that service members may feel upon returning home to find readjustment more difficult than they might have expected. Chaplain and military clinicians express hope that these experiences will be less alarming if anticipated and understood within a framework of what is normal. In addition, by using the Battlemind workshops as an opportunity to talk about danger signs, these providers work to educate soldiers about when it is time to seek out added help, usually in the form of professional mental health care.

26. Richie 2008.

27. Ibid.

28. The Battlemind program for Spouses focuses on identifying a series of behaviors—taking control of household and family affairs, avoiding discussion of deployment, and so forth—and reframes them in the context of the environment soldiers lived in during deployment. For example, one Battlemind brochure describes how soldiers in combat "Controlled their emotions in order to be successful in missions." The brochure goes on to list how this tendency toward emotional control may create conflict if carried over into the home environment, noting that "Spouse or Soldier expectations for emotional or physical intimacy might not be met upon return." Suggestions are then given for helping to work through this aspect of the post-deployment transition. Spouses are urged to "Be patient," while soldiers are cautioned to "Appreciate the difference between sex and intimacy." https://www.battlemind.army.mil/assets/files/spouse_battlemind_training_post_deploy ment_brochure.pdf.

29. Anna Simons (1999) has noted that this has not always been the case, however, as seen in World War II–era works by Benedict, Mead, and Bateson, among others.

30. Barrett 1996; Burke 2004; Frese and Harrell 2003; Hawkins 2001; Katz 1990; A. Simons 1997, 1999.

31. Gill 1997.

32. Bar and Ben-Ari 2005; Ben-Ari 1989, 1998; Kanaaneh 2005; Kaplan and Ben-Ari 2000; Lomsky-Feder and Ben-Ari 1999.

33. Agostino 1998.

34. Connell, [1995] 2005.

35. A. Simons 1997; Tiger 1999. One wonders what will happen to our understanding of the importance of "male bonding" in combat as more and more women are recognized for their role in modern warfare.

36. Katz 1990.

37. Goffman 1961.

38. Bourke 1999; Burke 2004; Grossman 1995.

39. E.g., Agostino 1998; Barrett 1996; Burke 2004; Karner 1998; Katz 1990.

40. Kanaaneh 2005; Kaplan and Ben-Ari 2000; Kohn 2004; Mrozek 1987; Gilmore 1990.

41. Jakupcak et al. 2006.

42. Agostino 1998; Arkin and Dobrofsky 1990; A. Simons 1997.

43. Though male gender and masculinity provide one perspective on examining soldiers' experiences in deployment and readjustment, there is no one single masculinity or warrior ethos, even within the relative cultural homogeneity of the U.S. Armed Forces (Mrozek 1987). Barrett (1996), for example, has deconstructed the idea of a monolithic masculinity within the contemporary navy, demonstrating that the most highly valued elements of a "manly" performance vary considerably by operational specialty. Whereas aviators value aggressiveness, courage, and autonomy, surface warfare officers emphasize the authoritative command of combat operations, technical expertise, discipline, and coolness under pressure. In contrast, supply officers accentuate their control over the movement of information and goods and, lacking the opportunity to demonstrate their prowess under fire, may invest additional energy in seeking higher rank, thus proving themselves through upward mobility. Barrett's findings do not refute the idea of a hegemonic masculinity within the navy—he notes that aviators most closely approach the ideal of emotional discipline, audacity, and technical mastery—but rather elucidate how men construct and perform alternative models of gendered excellence *in relation* to such hegemony.

44. However, there has been some wonderful scholarship in this area, such as Faris 1976; Katz 1990; and A. Simons 1997, 1998.

45. For more on the important role played by other service members in veterans' lives, please see chapter 9.

46. Of course, the very idea of military socialization seems to suggest something that happens during military service. Though this is true, many of these men were also the sons, nephews, or grandchildren of veterans, men who had grown up around military men and been instilled with military values from early childhood.

47. These examples likely reflect differences between the army and air force in terms of cultural values and the structural pressures placed on each branch. They also appear to be consistent with local variations in mission focus, attitudes toward mental health, and commanders' leadership styles.

CHAPTER 7

1. The line is taken from President Abraham Lincoln's second inaugural address, given in March of 1865.

2. There are separate outpatient and inpatient services available locally for veterans with non-PTSD-related mental illness.

3. This statistic is repeated so widely that it has gained the status of a social fact, although I have been unable to locate any data to support its veracity. In 1990 one study estimated that according to population-based mortality studies, fewer than nine thousand Vietnam veterans had committed suicide, although claims ranging from fifty to a hundred thousand Vietnam veteran suicides were already circulating by the late 1980s (Pollack et al. 1990). The authors also found that relative risk for suicide among Vietnam veterans studied (as compared with other Vietnam-era veterans, nonveterans, and men in the general U.S. population) ranged from 0.93 to 1.46 but never came remotely close to the

estimated sixfold increase in suicide among Vietnam veterans that would be required to meet the extraordinarily high numbers claimed. Bullman and Kang (1995) did report that among Vietnam veterans in the Agent Orange registry, veterans with PTSD were more likely to die of suicide, single-vehicle motor accidents, accidental poisoning, and other accidents than were other veterans or men in the general population. In contrast, Boyle and Decoufle (1988) found that in a sample of eighteen thousand Vietnam-era veterans matched with men from the general U.S. population, there was no apparent increase in suicide risk among veterans, although there was an 8 percent increase in motor vehicle mortality among those who had actually served in Vietnam. In other words, the data seem to support the conclusion that although suicide rates among Vietnam veterans have historically been higher than among other veterans and nonveterans, they are unlikely to have been nearly as high as suggested by claims of fifty thousand or more veteran suicides.

4. Hamilton 2007.

5. Michalowski and Dubisch (2001) offer a rich analysis of the meanings of the Vietnam war in contemporary America. Eric Dean (1992) has challenged the idea that the Vietnam veteran was unusually neglected, arguing that this is instead a myth that has worked greatly to the benefit of Vietnam veterans.

6. Gawande 2004.

7. Ephron and Childress 2007.

8. Longman 2007, 1.

9. Shephard 2001.

10. Longman 2007, 14.

11. During this period the VA was headed by Omar Bradley, who initiated its close relationship with medical schools by offering VA hospitals as training sites for interns and residents (Longman 2007).

12. Longman 2007, 15.

13. Ibid.

14. NCQA 2004.

15. McAuliffe 2007.

16. Frieden 2009.

17. IOM 2007.

18. I was fortunate enough to interview many of these clinicians, as well as a dozen other non-VA clinicians working in the San Antonio area (total n=28). Both VA and non-VA clinicians were incredibly generous with their time in supporting this research. I have changed names and other identifying features.

19. For example, Bryant et al. 2008; Creamer and Forbes 2004; Foa, Dancu et al. 1999; Foa, Hembree et al. 2005; Foa and Rauch 2004; Foa, Zoellner et al. 2002; Glynn et al. 1999; IOM 2007; Mason et al. 2002; Rauch et al. 2009; Resick et al. 2002; Schnurr et al. 2007; Slagle and Gray 2007; Taylor et al. 2003.

20. *Time* 2010.

21. Those familiar with the concept of "desensitization" will recognize the exposure therapies for their roots in this older technique. Edna Foa was herself trained in desensitization in the 1960s but has continued to refine the original model over the past several decades.

22. Rauch et al. 2009.

23. Most of the research on PE to date has been conducted on survivors of rape or other single, noncombat trauma events. This explains the concern that PE may prove less effective among survivors of the ongoing and cumulative trauma often associated with combat. One recent study, however, found that PE is an effective treatment among combat veterans, with effect sizes comparable to those of previous findings in veteran

and nonveteran populations (ibid.). Additional studies are ongoing among active-duty military and veteran populations.

24. Certainly this perception of trauma as something potentially dangerous—damaging not only to live through but also to discuss too closely—is in certain ways in harmony with lay models of trauma in American society.

25. Figures based on Veterans Compensation Benefits Rates Tables as of December 2008, the most recent date for which information was available. Up-to-date information on benefits tables is available from the U.S. Department of Veterans Affairs website, http://www.vba.va.gov/bln/21/Rates/comp01.htm.

26. Frueh et al. 2007; IOM 2007.

27. Yen 2007.

28. This bears similarity to Briggs's (2004) analysis of explanations of a cholera epidemic and the role of political economy in shaping public discourses.

29. Ibid.

30. Lee 2008.

31. Frueh et al. 2007.

32. I also didn't ask, either directly or indirectly.

33. There are rare exceptions to this. Shots were fired one night in 2007 through a window at the San Antonio VA clinic, although the culprit was never identified. There are very occasional threats made against the VA or particular VA employees, although this is not unusual in mental health care more generally.

34. One would imagine this is to some degree an outcome of burgeoning trust in that relationship (e.g., Battaglia, Finley, and Liebschutz 2003).

35. There appear to be a number of reasons for treatment dropout among OEF/OIF veterans, a phenomenon that clinicians I spoke with at a recent national VA conference said they were seeing all over the country. These veterans tend to be young and are often involved in the early stages (and heavy obligations) of their family, educational, and career lives. Several of the clinicians had polled veterans about their reasons for treatment dropout, and veterans reported feeling that they didn't have enough time to attend sessions and/or had scheduling conflicts.

36. Seal et al. 2010

37. This event was described to me by both of the clinicians involved and two of the veterans who had been at the session. One of the clinicians opined that the disruption, perhaps ironically, seemed to strengthen rather than weaken the group's rapport.

38. Jordan 1996.

CHAPTER 8

1. Kleinman 1988a.

2. Bruner 1990, 138.

3. These issues have also been explored by Daniel Moerman (2002) in his work on the meaning effect.

4. Kleinman 1988a.

5. It is unclear whether Chris received this idea from a clinician, although he did admit that he had not told his provider about his decision to stop taking the medication. Nonetheless, this idea reflects a concern among some psychiatrists and psychologists that certain types of medications—especially sedatives like the benzodiazapines—may interfere with the processing of trauma during exposure therapy. This has yet to be demonstrated in clinical trials, although there is evidence that the combination of benzodiazepines with psychotherapy in the treatment of panic disorder is less effective at bringing about long-term symptom reduction than psychotherapy alone (Spiegal and Bruce 1997; Watanabe, Churchill, and Furukawa, 2009). Many clinicians believe the sedation effects thought to

interfere with habituation in treatment for panic disorder may also reduce the efficacy of exposure therapy for PTSD because the two treatments rely on similar principles.

6. Chris's feelings here run parallel to the findings of Susan Faludi (1999) in her work on changing expectations for American men in the mid-twentieth century. Faludi describes how American manhood has increasingly been defined by the expectation that men will be financially successful, even as a changing national economic structure and social norms have increasingly deprived working- and even middle-class men of career opportunity. Many men's expectations for themselves, and those placed upon them by others, may be founded on unrealistic assessments of the available prospects.

7. Silver, Rogers, and Russell 2008. The evidence for EMDR's effectiveness remains controversial and less conclusive than that for PE and CPT (IOM 2007). Nonetheless, one of EMDR's strongest recent proponents has published an interesting analysis of the treatment's outsider status within the field of professional psychology, arguing that it is professional bias and resistance to change, rather than a lack of evidence, that perpetuate the controversy around EMDR (Russell 2008).

8. Seroquel (quetiapine) is one of the atypical antipsychotic drugs commonly used to treat PTSD. Although there are no published reports on its effectiveness for use with PTSD based upon randomized clinical trials, there is some open-label evidence for its effectiveness in diminishing intrusive symptoms when used alongside selective serotonin reuptake inhibitor (SSRI) antidepressants (Ahearn et al. 2005). It has also been shown to reduce symptoms among combat veterans whose PTSD has psychotic features (Pivac and Kozaric-Kovacic 2007).

9. Under section 301 of Public Law 109-461, effective December 23, 2006, the spouse or child of an individual who is determined by the VA to have a permanent and total disability that is service-connected and who is to be discharged from the service because of this disability may be eligible for educational assistance. For more information, see the DEA program, http://www.gibill.va.gov/GI_Bill_Info/benefits.htm.

10. Zohar and his colleagues have debunked the myth that wounded soldiers are less likely to develop PTSD because they have a visible injury and receive more compassion (Zohar et al. 2008). I would still speculate, however, that wounded soldiers may find it easier to *recover* from PTSD, given the additional supports and reduced stigma they often face. This question calls for further research.

11. A 2009 neuroimaging study found that participants demonstrated a more compassionate response when learning of another person's physical injury than they did when hearing of social or psychological distress. The authors of the study, who included famed neuroscientist Antonio Damasio, found that watching a video of a tennis star breaking her ankle, for example, triggered a stronger response in the brain than did an audiorecording of how cerebral palsy had led a woman to give up hope of ever marrying (Immordino-Yang et al. 2009). Not only was the compassion response to the second story slower to begin, but it actually triggered a different series of neural pathways than did the tennis injury. In other words, there may be something fundamentally different between the human response to physical pain and that to emotional pain and suffering.

12. Ortner 1999.

13. Ibid., 23.

14. This may be particularly true for those who joined the military when they were still too young to have developed an adult identity other than that learned in the service.

15. Das et al. 2001; Das et al. 2000; Kleinman, Das, and Lock 1997b.

16. The impact of social relationships on health is also an area of increasing focus in psychological and epidemiological research more generally. Studies conducted over the past several decades point to an important role for social relationships in shaping morbidity and mortality across the life span (Seeman 1996; Seeman and Crimmins 2001).

Social integration has been associated with decreased mortality by coronary heart disease independent of other risk factors (Orth-Somer, Rosengren, and Wilhelmsen 1993; Vogt et al. 1992). Social integration and support have also been associated with differential disease severity, as in studies showing an inverse association between instrumental and emotional support and the extent of coronary atherosclerosis (Blumenthal et al. 1987; Seeman and Syme 1987) and linking social integration to improved recovery outcomes following myocardial infarction and stroke (Berkman, Leo-Summers, and Horwitz 1992; Colantonio, Kasl, and Ostfeld 1992; Ruberman et al. 1984). Social ties have also been found to affect mental health outcomes, with a number of studies identifying a protective effect for social support in preventing depression (George 1989) and PTSD (Brewin, Andrews, and Valentine 2000; Ozer et al. 2003).

With further study has come a growing appreciation for the complexity of the relationship between sociality and health as it has become clear that, whereas positive aspects of social relationships may have a protective health effect, negative aspects may have a counterposed detrimental effect on health (Abbey, Abramis, and Caplan 1985; Burg and Seeman 1994; Schuster, Kessler, and Aseltine 1990), particularly in relationships characterized by criticism, conflict, and demands for assistance (Kessler, McLeod, and Wethington 1985). Moreover, positive and negative aspects of social ties appear to occur independently of one another (Finch et al. 1989; Schuster, Kessler, and Aseltine 1990), suggesting that their effects may not be mutually exclusive and should be separately accounted for. Although the mechanisms by which social relationships may affect physical and mental health remain understudied, Seeman and Crimmins (2001) point out that the two most promising pathways appear to be (1) via the social learning influence of family, peers, and other members of the social environment on health behaviors and (2) via a direct impact of social relationships on physiological states and mechanisms, such as immune function and neuroendocrine activity.

17. Charuvastra and Cloitre 2008.

CONCLUSION

1. Readers familiar with Unni Wikan's *Managing Turbulent Hearts: A Balinese Formula for Living* (1990) will recognize the underlying influence of her theory of "crisscrossings," describing how individuals shift their performances of self as they move across physical and social space. She notes that individuals adjust their performance across social settings—presenting themselves differently within the home, for example, than they may in the street—but that the requirements of each setting are a reflection most importantly of the other people present. Neighbors present within the home, therefore, may transform even "home" space into "street" space, although this will depend at least in part on the characteristics of the relationships between neighbors. Thus she demonstrates that self-performance, a necessary component of working to meet cultural expectations, is profoundly shaped by social relationships, imagined judgments, and the social creation of physical space. This is certainly true for veterans, whose physical moves across the spaces of home and family, the military, and the VA are profoundly social in their implications.

2. Gill, Szanton, and Page 2005; Seedat, Stein, and Carey 2005.

3. Wolfe 1996.

4. Yaeger et al. 2006.

5. Gutmann and Lutz 2009.

6. Young 1995.

7. Summerfield 2000a, 2000b.

8. Silove 2005.

9. Englund 1998. A larger part of the anthropological work related to trauma has focused on trauma and suffering rather than PTSD specifically (e.g., Bourdieu and Accardo

1999; Das et al. 2001; Das et al. 2000; Fassin and d'Halluin 2007; Henry 2006; Kleinman and Desjarlais 1995; McKinney 2007; Robben and Suarez-Orozco 2000; Zarowsky 2004).

10. Kleinman 1995.

11. E.g., Cardozo et al. 2004; Hinton, Chhean, Pich, Pollack et al. 2006; Hinton et al. 2003; Monmartin et al. 2003; Van Ommeren et al. 2001.

12. I.e., idioms of distress (Nichter 1981; Rechtman 2000).

13. Hinton, Chhean, Pich, Pollack et al. 2006.

14. Hinton, Chhean, Pich, Hofmann, and Barlow 2006; Hinton et al. 2005.

15. E.g., Bremner et al. 1993; Bremner and Vermetten 2001; Charney 2004; De Jong 2005; Fontana and Rosenheck 1994; Konner 2007; Yehuda 2002; Yehuda et al. 2004; Yehuda et al. 1993.

16. E.g., Bremner et al. 1993; Bremner and Vermetten 2001; Charney 2004; De Jong 2005; Fontana and Rosenheck 1994; Konner2007; Yehuda 2002; Yehuda et al. 2004; Yehuda et al. 1993.

17. Dekel and Goldblatt 2008.

18. Kilpatrick et al. 2007.

19. Yehuda et al. 2008.

20. Sapolsky 1998.

21. R. C. Simons 1996.

22. This is consistent with the understanding of somatic modes of attention (Kirmayer and Young 1998).

23. Kleinman, Das, and Lock 1997a; Sundar 2004.

24. Press 2009.

25. VHA Office of Public Health and Environmental Hazards 2009.

26. One nationwide study of suicide among veterans found that a comorbid diagnosis of PTSD and depression actually predicted lower rates of suicide than did a diagnosis of depression alone; however, this study considered a cohort of veterans during the years 1999–2004, prior to the military's suicide increase (Zivin et al. 2007). It is unclear whether active PTSD may be in some part responsible for the increasing suicide rate among more recent veterans.

27. Frueh et al. 2007.

28. MHAT 2008.

29. Dobbs 2009; Frueh et al. 2007.

30. Tanielian et al. 2008.

31. Dobbs 2009.

32. E.g., Bonanno 2004; Johnson et al. 2008; Sammons and Batten 2008; Tusaie and Dyer 2004.

33. Bonanno 2004; Tusaie and Dyer 2004.

34. Bonanno 2004; Davidson et al. 2005; Williams et al. 2008.

35. Finley et al. 2010.

36. Elhai et al. 2004.

37. The implication here is that—as Janis Jenkins found in her research on expressed hostility among families of those with schizophrenia (1991)—family attitudes may increase the struggling member's psychological distress, in turn increasing the amount of probable impact on role function and family life.

38. Erbes et al. 2008; Monson, Fredman, and Adair 2008; Rotunda et al. 2008.

39. Desai et al. 2008; Rotunda et al. 2008.

40. Corrigan and Cole 2008.

41. Perlin, Kolodner, and Roswell 2004.

42. Monson, Taft, and Fredman 2009.

43. Finley et al., 2010.

44. Moerman 2002.

45. Hahn 1998.

46. Dobbs's article (2009) proposes a model based on the Australian compensation system, which provides veterans with lifetime medical care and a small stipend but structures PTSD-related compensation using a step-down model that reduces coverage slowly over a period of years.

47. Remarque 1930, 292.

References

Abbey, A., D. J. Abramis, and R. D. Caplan. 1985. "Effects of Different Sources of Social Support and Social Conflict on Emotional Well-being." *Basic and Applied Social Psychology* 6:111–129.

Abraida Lanza, A. F., A. N. Armbrister, K. R. Florez, and A. N. Aguirre. 2006. "Toward a Theory-Driven Model of Acculturation in Public Health Research." *American Journal of Public Health* 96 (8): 1342–1346.

Addis, M. E., and J. R. Mahalik, J. R. 2003. "Men, Masculinity, and the Contexts of Help Seeking." *American Psychologist* 58 (1): 5–14.

Agostino, K. 1998. "The Making of Warriors: Men, Identity, and Military Culture." *Journal of Interdisciplinary Gender Studies* 3 (2): 58–75.

Ahern, Jennifer, Sandro Galea, William G. Fernandez, Bajram Koci, Ronald Waldman, and David Vlahov. 2004. "Gender, Social Support, and Posttraumatic Stress in Postwar Kosovo." *Journal of Nervous & Mental Disease* 192 (11): 762–770.

Ahearn, E. P., M. Mussey, C. Johnson, A. Krohn, and D. Krahn. 2005. "Quetiapine as an Adjustive Treatment for Post-Traumatic Stress Disorder: An 8-week Open-Label Study." *International Clinical Psychopharmacology* 21:29–33.

Alegria, M., G. Canino, P. E. Shrout, M. Woo, N. Duan, D. Vila et al. 2008. "Prevalence of Mental Illness in Immigrant and Non-Immigrant U.S. Latino Groups." *American Journal of Psychiatry* 165 (3): 359–369.

Alonso, J., M. C. Angermeyer, S. Bernert, R. Bruffaerts, T. S. Brugha, H. Bryson et al. 2004. "Disability and Quality of Life Impact of Mental Disorders in Europe: Results from the European Study of the Epidemiology of Mental Disorders (ESEMeD) Project." *Acta Psychiatrica Scandinavica* 109 (Supplementum 420): 38–46.

APA (American Psychiatric Association). 2000. *Diagnostic and Statistical Manual of Mental Disorders.* 4th ed., text revised [DSM-IV-TR]. Washington, D.C.: American Psychiatric Association.

Arciniega, G. M., T. C. Anderson, Z. G. Tovar-Blank, and T. J. G. Tracey. 2008. "Toward a Fuller Conception of Machismo: Development of a Traditional Machismo and Caballerismo Scale." *Journal of Counseling Psychology* 55 (1): 19–33.

Arkin, W., and L. R. Dobrofsky. 1990. "Military Socialization and Masculinity." In *Making War, Making Peace: The Social Foundations of Violent Conflict*, ed. F. M. Cancian and L. W. Gibson, 68–78. Belmont, CA: Wadsworth.

Bar, N., and E. Ben-Ari. 2005. "Killing, Humanity, and Lived Experience: Israeli Snipers in the Al-Aqsa Intifada." *Third World Quarterly* 26 (1): 133–152.

Barrett, F. 1996. "The Organizational Construction of Hegemonic Masculinity: The Case of the U.S. Navy." *Gender, Work, and Organization* 3 (3): 129–142.

Battaglia, T., E. Finley, and J. Liebschutz, J. 2003. "Survivors of Intimate Partner Violence Speak Out: Trust in the Patient-Provider Relationship." *Journal of General Internal Medicine* 18:617–623.

Beaumont, P. 2007. "Fatigue Cripples U.S. Army in Iraq." *Observer*, August 12.

Ben-Ari, E. 1989. "Masks and Soldiering: The Israeli Army and the Palestinian Uprising." *Cultural Anthropology* 4:372–389.

———. 1998. *Mastering Soldiers: Conflict, Emotions, and the Enemy in an Israeli Military Unit.* New York: Berghahn.

Berkman, L. F., L. Leo-Summers, and R. Horwitz. 1992. "Emotional Support and Survival after Myocardial Infarction: A Prospective, Population-Based Study of the Elderly." *Annals of Internal Medicine* 117:1003–1009.

Bibeau, G. 1997. "Cultural Psychiatry in a Creolizing World: Questions for a New Research Agenda." *Transcultural Psychiatry* 34 (1): 9–41.

Biehl, J. 2005. *Vita: Life in a Zone of Social Abandonment.* Berkeley: University of California Press.

Blumenthal, J. A., M. M. Burg, J. Barefoot, R. M. Williams, T. Haney, and G. Zimet. 1987. "Social Support, Type A Behavior, and Coronary Artery Disease." *Psychosomatic Medicine* 49:331–340.

Bonanno, G. A. 2004. "Loss, Trauma, and Human Resilience: Have We Underestimated the Human Capacity to Thrive after Extremely Aversive Events?" *American Psychologist* 59 (1): 20–28.

Bonanno, G. A., S. Galea, A. Bucciarelli, and D. Vlahov. 2007. "What Predicts Psychological Resilience after Disaster? The Role of Demographics, Resources, and Life Stress." *Journal of Consulting and Clinical Psychology* 75 (5): 671–682.

Bourdieu, P., and A. Accardo, eds. 1999. *The Weight of the World: Social Suffering in Contemporary Society.* Stanford: Stanford University Press.

Bourke, J. 1999. *An Intimate History of Killing.* London: Granta Books.

Boyle, C. A., and P. Decoufle. 1988. "Postdischarge Mortality from Suicide and Motor-Vehicle Injuries among Vietnam-era Veterans." *New England Journal of Medicine* 317 (8): 506.

Bremner, J. D., and E. Brett. 1997. "Trauma-Related Dissociative States and Long-Term Psychopathology in Post-Traumatic Stress Disorder." *Journal of Traumatic Stress* 10 (1): 37–49.

Bremner, J. D., S. M. Southwick, D. R. Johnson, R. Yehuda, and D. S. Charney. 1993. "Childhood Physical Abuse and Combat-Related Posttraumatic Stress Disorder in Vietnam Veterans." *American Journal of Psychiatry* 150 (2): 235–239.

Bremner, J. D., and E. Vermetten. 2001. "Stress and Development: Behavioral and Biological Consequences." *Development and Psychopathology* 13:473–489.

Breslau, N., R.C. Kessler, H. D. Chilcoat, L. Schultz, G. C. Davis, and P. Andreski. 1998. "Trauma and Posttraumatic Stress Disorder in the Community: The 1996 Detroit Areas Survey of Trauma." *Archives of General Psychiatry* 55:626–632.

Brewin, C. R., B. Andrews, and J. D. Valentine. 2000. "Meta-Analysis of Risk Factors for Post-Traumatic Stress Disorder in Trauma-Exposed Adults." *Journal of Consulting and Clinical Psychology* 68 (5): 748–766.

Briggs, C. 2004. "Theorizing Modernity Conspiratorially: Science, Scale, and the Political Economy of Public Discourse in Explanations of a Cholera Epidemic." *American Ethnologist* 31 (2): 163–186.

Brookings Institution. 2003. "San Antonio in Focus: A Profile from Census 2000." Report. Washington, DC: Brookings Institution Center on Urban and Metropolitan Policy.

Bruner, J. 1990. *Acts of Meaning.* Cambridge, MA: Harvard University Press.

Bryant, R. A., M. L. Moulds, R. M. Guthrie, S. T. Dang, J. Mastrodomenico, R. D. V. Nixon et al. 2008. "A Randomized Controlled Trial of Exposure Therapy and Cognitive Restructuring for Posttraumatic Stress Disorder." *Journal of Consulting and Clinical Psychology* 76 (4): 695–703.

Bullman, T. A., and H. K. Kang. 1995. "Posttraumatic Stress Disorder and the Risk of Traumatic Deaths among Vietnam Veterans." *Journal of Nervous and Mental Disease* 182 (11): 604–610.

Burg, M. M., and T. E. Seeman. 1994. "Families and Health: The Negative Side of Social Ties." *Annals of Behavioral Medicine* 16:109–115.

Burke, C. 2004. *Camp All-American, Hanoi Jane, and the High-and-Tight: Gender, Folklore, and Changing Military Culture.* Boston: Beacon.

Butler, L. D., C. Koopman, J. Azarow, C. Blasey, J. C. Magdalene, S. DiMiceli et al. 2009. "Psychosocial Predictors of Resilience after the September 11, 2001 Terrorist Attacks." *Journal of Nervous and Mental Disease* 197 (4): 266–273.

Byrne, C. A., and C. A. Riggs. 1996. "The Cycle of Trauma: Relationship Aggression in Male Vietnam Veterans with Symptoms of Posttraumatic Stress Disorder." *Violence and Victims* 11:213–225.

Cardozo, B. L., L. Talley, A. Burton, and C. Crawford. 2004. "Karenni Refugees Living in Thai-Burmese Border Camps: Traumatic Experiences, Mental Health Outcomes, and Social Functioning." *Social Science and Medicine* 58 (12):2637–2644.

Carlsson, J. M., E. L. Mortensen, and M. Kastrup. 2005. "A Follow-Up Study of Mental Health and Health-Related Quality of Life in Tortured Refugees in Multidisciplinary Treatment." *Journal of Nervous and Mental Disorders* 193 (10): 651–657.

CDP (Center for Deployment Psychology). 2007. "Welcome to the Center for Deployment Psychology." http://deploymentpsych.org/.

Charney, D. S. 2004. "Psychobiological Mechanisms of Resilience and Vulnerability: Implications for Successful Adaptation to Extreme Stress." *American Journal of Psychiatry* 161 (2): 195–216.

Charuvastra, A., and M. Cloitre. 2008. "Social Bonds and Posttraumatic Stress Disorder." *Annual Review of Psychology* 59:301–328.

Chedekel, L., and M. Kauffman. 2008. Army Sees Record Number of Suicides in Iraq. *Hartford Courant,* May 30, 2008. http://www.courant.com/news/nationworld/hc-soldiersuicides0530.artmay30,0,2294117.story.

Chermol, B. H. 1985. "Wounds without Scars: Treatment of Battle Fatigue in the U.S. Armed Forces in the Second World War." *Military Affairs* 49 (1): 9–12.

Chicago Tribune. 2004. "'Stop Loss' Continues." September 27.

Colantonio, A., S. V. Kasl, and A. M. Ostfeld. 1992. "Depressive Symptoms and Other Psychosocial Factors as Predictors of Stroke in the Elderly." *American Journal of Epidemiology* 136:884–894.

Connell, R. W. [1995] 2005. *Masculinities.* 2nd ed. Cambridge: Polity Press.

Corrigan, J. D., and T. B. Cole. 2008. "Substance Use Disorders and Clinical Management of Traumatic Brain Injury and Posttraumatic Stress Disorder." *JAMA* 300 (6): 720–721.

Creamer, M., and D. Forbes. 2004. "Treatment of Posttraumatic Stress Disorder in Military and Veteran Populations." *Psychotherapy: Theory, Research, Practice, Training* 41 (4): 388–398.

CSOC. 2003. "Frequently Asked Questions on Combat Stress." In *C. S. O. C. California National Guard Resources Services Division,* ed., Combat Stress Operational Control.

Csordas, T. J. 2002. *Body/Meaning/Healing.* New York: Palgrave Macmillan.

Cuéllar, I., B. Arnold, and R. Maldonado. 1995. "Acculturation Rating Scale for Mexican Americans-II: A Revision of the Original ARSMA Scale." *Hispanic Journal of Behavioral Sciences* 17 (3): 275–304.

Das, V., A. Kleinman, M. Lock, M. Ramphele, and P. Reynolds, P. 2001. *Remaking a World: Violence, Social Suffering, and Recovery.* Berkeley: University of California Press.

Das, V., A. Kleinman, M. Ramphele, and P. Reynolds. 2000. *Violence and Subjectivity.* Berkeley: University of California Press.

Davidson, J. R. T., V. M. Payne, K. M. Connor, E. B. Foa, B. O. Rothbaum, M. A. Hertz-berg et al. 2005. "Trauma, Resilience, and Saliostasis: Effects of Treatment in Post-Traumatic Stress Disorder." *International Clinical Psychopharmacology* 20:43–48.

Dean, E. T. 1992. "The Myth of the Troubled and Scorned Vietnam Vet." *Journal of American Studies* 26 (1): 59–74.

——. 1997. *Shook over Hell: Post-Traumatic Stress, Vietnam, and the Civil War.* Cambridge, MA: Harvard University Press.

De Jong, J. T. V. M. 2005. "Comment: Deconstructing Critiques on the Internationalization of PTSD." *Culture, Medicine, and Psychiatry* 29:361–370.

Dekel, R., and H. Goldblatt. 2008. "Is There Intergenerational Transmission of Trauma? The Case of Combat Veterans' Children." *American Journal of Orthopsychiatry* 78 (3): 281–289.

Dekel, R., Z. Solomon, and A. Bleich. 2005. "Emotional Distress and Marital Adjustment of Caregivers: Contribution of Level of Impairment and Appraised Burden." *Anxiety, Stress, and Coping* 18 (1): 71–82.

Desai, R. A., I. Harpaz-Rotem, L. M. Najavits, and R. A. Rosenheck. 2008. "Impact of the Seeking Safety Program on Clinical Outcomes among Homeless Female Veterans with Psychiatric Disorders." *Psychiatric Services* 59 (9): 996–1003.

Desjarlais, R. R. 1997. *Shelter Blues: Sanity and Selfhood among the Homeless.* Philadelphia: University of Pennsylvania Press.

Dickson-Gomez, J. 2003. "The Sound of Barking Dogs: Violence and Terror among Salvadoran Families in the Postwar." *Medical Anthropology Quarterly* 16 (4): 415–438.

Dictionary.com. 2009. "Dislocation." http://dictionary.reference.com/browse/dislocation.

Dirkzwager, A. J. E., I. Bramsen, and H. M. Van der Ploeg. 2003. "Social Support, Coping, Life Events, and Posttraumatic Stress Symptoms among Former Peacekeepers: A Prospective Study." *Personality and Individual Differences* 34:1545–1559.

Dirkzwager, A. J. E., I. Bramsen, H. Ader, and H. M. van der Ploeg. 2005. "Secondary Traumatization in Partners and Parents of Dutch Peacekeeping Soldiers." *Journal of Family Psychology* 19 (2): 217–226.

Dobbs, D. 2009). "Soldiers' Stress: What Doctors Get Wrong about PTSD." *Scientific American,* April.

DOD (Department of Defense). 2007. "Secretary Gates on Walter Reed Leadership Change." Press release, March 1. http://www.defenselink.mil/Releases/Release.aspx?ReleaseID=10564.

Dohrenwend, B. P., J. B. Turner, N. A. Turse, R. Lewis-Fernandez, and T. J. Yager. 2008. "War-Related Posttraumatic Stress Disorder in Black, Hispanic, and Majority White Vietnam Veterans: The Roles of Exposure and Vulnerability." *Journal of Traumatic Stress* 21 (2): 133–141.

Economist. 2009. "Take Heart: PTSD Sufferers Deserve a Medal." February 26.

Elbogen, E. B., J. C. Beckham, M. I. Butterfield, M. Swartz, and J. Swanson. 2008. "Assessing Risk of Violent Behavior among Veterans with Severe Mental Illness." *Journal of Traumatic Stress* 21 (1): 113–117.

Elhai, J. D., S. N. Baugher, R. P. Quevillon, J. Sauvegeot, and B. C. Frueh. 2004. "Psychiatric Symptoms and Health Service Utilization in Rural and Urban Combat Veterans with Posttraumatic Stress Disorder." *Journal of Nervous and Mental Disease* 192 (10): 701–704.

Englund, H. 1998. "Death, Trauma and Ritual: Mozambican Refugees in Malawi." *Social Science and Medicine* 46 (9): 1165–1174.

Ephron, D., and S. Childress. 2007. "How the U.S. Is Failing Its War Veterans." *Newsweek,* March 5.

Erbes, C. R., M. A. Polusny, S. MacDermind, and J. S. Compton. 2008. "Couple Therapy with Combat Veterans and Their Partners." *Journal of Clinical Psychology: In Session* 64:972–983.

Faludi, S. 1999. *Stiffed: The Betrayal of the American Man.* New York: Perennial.

Faris, J. H. 1976. "The Impact of Basic Combat Training: The Role of the Drill Sergeant." In *The Social Psychology of Military Service,* ed. N. L. Goldman and D. R. Segal, 13–24. Beverly Hills: Sage.

Fassin, D., and E. d'Halluin. 2007. "Critical Evidence: The Politics of Trauma in French Asylum Policies." *Ethos* 35 (3): 300–329.

Feldman, A. 1991. *Formations of Violence: The Narrative of the Body and Political Terror in Northern Ireland.* Chicago: University of Chicago Press.

Finch, J. F., M. A. Okun, M. Barrera, A. J. Zautra, and Reich, J. W. 1989. "Positive and Negative Social Ties among Older Adults: Measurement Models and the Prediction of Psychological Distress and Well-Being." *American Journal of Community Psychology* 17 (5): 585–605.

Finley, E. P., M. Baker, M. J. V. Pugh, and A. Peterson. 2010. "Patterns and Perceptions of Intimate Partner Violence Committed by Returning Veterans with Post-Traumatic Stress Disorder." *Journal of Family Violence.*

Finley, E. P., M. J. V. Pugh, and M. Jeffreys. 2010. "'Talking, Love, Time': Two Case Studies of Positive Post-Deployment Coping in Military Families." *Journal of Family Life.*

Foa, E. B., C. V. Dancu, E. A. Hembree, L. H. Jaycox, E. A. Meadows, and G. P. Street. 1999. "A Comparison of Exposure Therapy, Stress Inoculation Training, and Their Combination for Reducing Posttraumatic Stress Disorder in Female Assault Victims." *Journal of Consulting and Clinical Psychology* 67 (2): 194–200.

Foa, E. B., E. A. Hembree, S. P. Cahill, S. A. M. Rauch, D. S. Riggs, N. C. Feeny, et al. 2005. "Randomized Trial of Prolonged Exposure for Posttraumatic Stress Disorder with and without Cognitive Restructuring: Outcome at Academic and Community Clinics." *Journal of Consulting and Clinical Psychology* 73 (5): 953–964.

Foa, E. B., and S. A. M. Rauch. 2004. "Cognitive Changes during Prolonged Exposure versus Prolonged Exposure plus Cognitive Restructuring in Female Assault Survivors with Posttraumatic Stress Disorder." *Journal of Consulting and Clinical Psychology* 72 (5): 870–884.

Foa, E. B., L. A. Zoellner, N. C. Feeny, E. A. Hembree, and J. Alvarez-Conrad. 2002. "Does Imaginal Exposure Exacerbate PTSD Symptoms?" *Journal of Consulting and Clinical Psychology* 70 (4): 1022–1028.

Fontana, A., and R. Rosenheck. 1994. "Posttraumatic Stress Disorder among Vietnam Theater Veterans. A Causal Model of Etiology in a Community Sample." *Journal of Nervous and Mental Disease* 182 (12): 677–684.

Frese, P. R., and M. C. Harrell, eds. 2003. *Anthropology and the United States Military: Coming of Age in the 21st Century.* New York: Palgrave Macmillan.

Frieden, T. 2009. "VA Will Pay $20 Million to Settle Lawsuit over Stolen Laptop's Data." *CNN.com,* January 27. http://www.cnn.com/2009/POLITICS/01/27/va.data.theft/index.html?iref=newssearch.

Frueh, B. C., A. L. Grubaugh, J. D. Elhai, and T. C. Buckley. 2007. "US Department of Veterans Affairs Disability Policies for Posttraumatic Stress Disorder: Administrative Trends and Implications for Treatment, Rehabilitation, and Research." *American Journal of Public Health* 97 (12): 2143–2150.

Galtung, J. 1969. "Violence, Peace, and Peace Research." *Journal of Peace Research* 6 (3): 167–191.

Garcia, H. A., E. P. Finley, W. Lorber, and M. Jakupcak. 2010. "A Preliminary Study of the Association between Traditional Masculine Behavioral Norms and PTSD Symptoms in Iraq and Afghanistan Veterans." *Psychology of Men and Masculinity.*

Gawande, A. 2004. "Casualties of War—Military Care for the Wounded from Iraq and Afghanistan." *New England Journal of Medicine* 351 (24): 2471–2475.

Geertz, C. 1973. *The Interpretation of Cultures:* New York: Basic Books.

George, L. K. 1989. "Stress, Social Support, and Depression over the Life Course." In *Aging, Stress, Social Support, and Health,* ed. K. Markides and C. Cooper, 241–267. London: Wiley.

Gettleman, J. 2003. "Soldier Accused as Coward Says He Is Guilty Only of Panic Attack." *New York Times,* November 6. http://www.commondreams.org/headlines03/1106–04.htm.

Gibbs, D. A., S. L. Martine, L. L. Kupper, and R. E. Johnson. 2007. "Child Maltreatment in Enlisted Soldiers' Families during Combat-Related Deployments." *JAMA* 298:528–535.

Gill, J. M., S. L. Szanton, and G. G. Page. 2005. "Biological Underpinnings of Health Alternations in Women with PTSD: A Sex Disparity." *Biological Research for Nursing* 7:44–54.

Gill, Lesley. 1997. "Creating Citizens, Making Men: The Military and Masculinity in Bolivia." *Cultural Anthropology* 12 (4): 527–550.

Gilmore, David D. 1990. *Manhood in the Making: Cultural Concepts of Masculinity.* New Haven: Yale University Press.

Glenn, D. M., J. C. Beckham, M. E. Feldman, A. C. Kirby, and M. A. Hertzberg. 2002. "Violence and Hostility among Families of Vietnam Veterans with Combat-Related Posttraumatic Stress Disorder." *Violence and Victims* 17 (4): 473–489.

Glynn, S. M., S. Eth, E. T. Randolph, D. W. Foy, M. Urbaitis, L. Boxer et al. 1999. "A Test of Behavioral Family Therapy to Augment Exposure for Combat-Related Posttraumatic Stress Disorder." *Journal of Consulting and Clinical Psychology* 67 (2): 243–251.

Goff, B. S. N., J. R. Crow, A. M. J. Reisbig, and S. Hamilton. 2007. "The Impact of Individual Trauma Symptoms of Deployed Soldiers on Relationship Satisfaction." *Journal of Family Psychology* 21 (3): 344–353.

Goffman, E. 1961. *Asylums: Essays on the Social Situation of Mental Patients and Other Inmates.* New York: Anchor Books.

Good, B. J. 1994. *Medicine, Rationality, and Experience: An Anthropological Perspective.* Cambridge: Cambridge University Press.

Good, G. E., L. H. Schopp, D. Thomson, S. Hathaway, T. Sanford-Martens, M. O. Mazurek et al. 2006. "Masculine Roles and Rehabilitation Outcomes among Men Recovering from Serious Injuries." *Psychology of Men and Masculinity* 7 (3): 165–176.

Goodwin, D. W., and S. B. Guze. 1996. *Psychiatric Diagnosis.* 5th ed. New York: Oxford University Press.

Gray, M. J., E. E. Bolton, and B. T. Litz. 2004. "A Longitudinal Analysis of PTSD Symptom Course: Delayed-Onset PTSD in Somalia Peacekeepers." *Journal of Consulting and Clinical Psychology* 72 (5): 909–913.

Grossman, D. 1995. *On Killing: The Psychological Cost of Learning to Kill in War and Society.* Boston: Little, Brown.

Guarnaccia, P. J., M. Rivera, F. Franco, and C. Neighbors. 1996. "The Experiences of Ataques de Nervios: Towards an Anthropology of Emotions in Puerto Rico." *Culture, Medicine, and Psychiatry* 20:343–367.

Gutmann, M. C. 1996. *The Meanings of Macho: Being a Man in Mexico City.* Berkeley: University of California Press.

——. 1997. "Trafficking in Men: The Anthropology of Masculinity." *Annual Review of Anthropology* 26:385–409.

Gutmann, M., and C. Lutz. 2009. "Becoming Monsters in Iraq." *Anthropology Now* 1 (1): 12–20.

Hahn, R. A. 1998. "The Nocebo Phenomenon: Concept, Evidence, and Implications for Public Health." In *Understanding and Applying Medical Anthropology,* ed. P. J. Brown, 138–143. Mountain View, CA: Mayfield.

Hamilton, T. 2007. "VA Care Vet Backlash." *San Antonio Express News,* August 5.

Hamre, J. J. 1999. Department of Defense Directive No. 64905. In *Combat Stress Control Programs,* ed. Department of Defense.

Hawkins, J. P. 2001. *Army of Hope, Army of Alienation: Culture and Contradiction in the American Army Communities of Cold War Germany.* Westport, CT: Praeger.

Henry, D. 2006. "Violence and the Body: Somatic Expressions of Trauma and Vulnerability during War." *Medical Anthropology Quarterly* 20 (3): 379–398.

Herman, J. 1992. *Trauma and Recovery: The Aftermath of Violence—From Domestic Abuse to Political Terror.* New York: Basic Books.

Hinton, D. E., D. Chhean, V. Pich, S. G. Hofmann, and D. H. Barlow. 2006. "Tinnitus among Cambodian Refugees: Relationship to PTSD Severity." *Journal of Traumatic Stress* 19 (4): 541–546.

Hinton, D. E., D. Chhean, V. Pich, M. H. Pollack, S. P. Orr, and R. K. Pitman. 2006. "Assessment of Posttraumatic Stress Disorder in Cambodian Refugees Using the Clinician-Administrered PTSD Scale: Psychometric Properties and Symptoms Severity." *Journal of Traumatic Stress* 19 (3): 405–409.

Hinton, D. E., C. Hsia, K. Um, and M. W. Otto. 2003. "Anger-Associated Panic Attacks in Cambodian Refugees with PTSD: A Multiple Baseline Examination of Clinical Data." *Behavior Research & Therapy* 41 (6): 647–654.

Hinton, D. E., V. Pich, D. Chhean, M. H. Pollack, and R. J. McNally. 2005. "Sleep Paralysis among Cambodian Refugees: Association with PTSD Diagnosis and Severity." *Depression and Anxiety* 22 (2): 47–51.

Hoge, C. W., C. A. Castro, S. C. Messer, D. McGurk, D. I. Cotting, and R. L. Koffman. 2004. "Combat Duty in Iraq and Afghanistan, Mental Health Problems, and Barriers to Care." *New England Journal of Medicine* 351 (1): 13–22.

Hogg, J. 2008. "Does the New York Times Hate Veterans?" Iraq Veterans Against the War. http://ivaw.org/membersspeak/does-new-york-times-hate-veterans.

Hourani, L. L., H. Yuan, and R. M. Bray. 2003. "Psychosocial and Health Correlates of Types of Traumatic Event Exposure among U.S. Military Personnel." *Military Medicine* 168 (9): 736–743.

HQDA (Headquarters, Department of the Army). 1994. *Leaders' Manual for Combat Stress Control.* Washington, DC: Headquarters, Department of the Army.

Immordino-Yang, M., A. McColl, H. Damasio, and A. Damasio. 2009. "Neural Correlates of Admiration and Compassion." *Proceedings of the National Academy of Sciences* 106 (19): 7687–7688.

IOM (Institute of Medicine). 2007. *Treatment of Posttraumatic Stress Disorder: An Assessment of the Evidence.* Washington, DC: Institute of Medicine, National Academy Press.

Jackson, M. 1998. *Minima Ethnographica: Intersubjectivity and the Anthropological Project.* Chicago: University of Chicago Press.

Jakupcak, M., J. W. Cook, Z. Imel, A. Fontana, and R. A. Rosenheck. 2009. "Posttraumatic Stress Disorder as a Risk Factor for Suicidal Ideation in Iraq and Afghanistan War Veterans." *Journal of Traumatic Stress* 22 (4): 303–306.

Jakupcak, M., T. L. Osborne, S. Michael, J. W. Cook, and M. McFall. 2006. "Implications of Masculine Gender Role Stress in Male Veterans with Posttraumatic Stress Disorder." *Psychology of Men and Masculinity* 7 (4): 203–211.

Jenkins, J. H. 1991. "The 1990 Stirling Award Essay: Anthropology, Expressed Emotion, Schizophrenia." *Ethos* 19:387–431.

Johansen, Venke A., Astrid K. Wahl, Dag Erik Eilertsen, and Lars Weisaeth. 2007. "Prevalence and Predictors of Post-Traumatic Stress Disorder (PTSD) in Physically Injured Victims of Non-Domestic Violence." *Social Psychiatry and Psychiatric Epidemiology* 42:583–593.

Johnson, D. C., M. A. Polusny, C. R. Erbes, D. King, L. King, B. T. Litz et al. 2008. "Resilience and Response to Stress: Development and Initial Validation of the Response to Stressful Experience Scale (RSES)." Paper presented at the second annual Marine Corps Combat and Operational Stress Control (MCCOSC) Conference, San Diego.

Johnson, S. J., M. D. Sherman, J. S. Hoffman, L. C. James, P. L. Johnson, J. E. Lochman et al. 2007. "The Psychological Needs of U.S. Military Service Members and Their Families: A Preliminary Report." APA Presidential Task Force on Military Deployment Services for Youth, Families and Service Members. http://www.ptsd.ne.gov/publications/military-deployment-task-force-report.pdf.

Jordan, B. 1996. "Authoritative Knowledge and Its Construction." In *Childbirth and Authoritative Knowledge: Cross-Cultural Perspectives,* ed. R. Davis-Floyd and C. Sargent, 55–79. Berkeley: University of California Press.

Jordan, B. K., C. R. Marmar, J. A. Fairbank, W. E. Schlenger, R. A. Kulka, R. L. Hough et al. 1992. "Problems in Families of Male Vietnam Veterans with Posttraumatic Stress Disorder." *Journal of Consulting and Clinical Psychology* 60 (6): 916–926.

Kanaaneh, R. 2005. "Boys or Men? Duped or 'Made'? Palestinian Soldiers in the Israeli Military." *American Ethnologist* 32 (2): 260–275.

Kaplan, D., and E. Ben-Ari. 2000. "Brothers and Others in Arms: Managing Gay Identity in Combat Units of the Israeli Army." *Journal of Contemporary Ethnography* 29 (4): 396–432.

Karner, T. X. 1998. "Engendering Violence in Men: Oral Histories of Military Masculinity." In *Masculinities and Violence,* ed. L. Bowker, 197–232. London: Sage.

Katz, P. 1990. "Emotional Metaphors, Socialization, and Roles of Drill Sergeants." *Ethos* 18 (4): 457–480.

Keane, T. M., W. O. Scott, G. A. Chavoya, D. M. Lamparski, and J. A. Fairbank. 1985. "Social Support in Vietnam Veterans with Posttraumatic Stress Disorder: A Comparative Analysis." *Journal of Consulting and Clinical Psychology* 53 (1): 95–102.

Kessler, R. C., J. D. McLeod, and E. Wethington. 1985. "The Costs of Caring: A Perspective on the Relationship between Sex and Psychological Distress." In *Social Support: Theory, Research and Applications,* ed. I. Sarason and B. R. Sarason, 491–506. Dordrecht, Neth.: Martinus Nijhoff.

Kessler, R. C., A. C. Sonnege, E. Bromet, M. Hughes, and C. Nelson. 1995. "Posttraumatic Stress Disorder in the National Comorbidity Study." *Archives of General Psychiatry* 52 (12): 1048–1060.

Kilpatrick, D. G., K. C. Koenen, K. J. Ruggiero, R. Acierno, S. Galea, H. S. Resnick et al. 2007. "The Serotonin Transporter Genotype and Social Support and

Moderation of Posttraumatic Stress Disorder and Depression in Hurricane-Exposed Adults." *American Journal of Psychiatry* 164:1693–1699.

Kilshaw, S. 2004. "Friendly Fire: The Construction of Gulf War Syndrome Narratives." *Anthropology and Medicine* 11 (2): 149–160.

———. (2008). *Impotent Warriors: Perspectives on Gulf War Syndrome, Vulnerability, and Masculinity.* New York: Berghahn Books.

King, D. W., L. A. King, and D. S. Vogt. 2003. *Manual for the Deployment Risk and Resilience Inventory (DRRI): A Collection of Measures for Studying Deployment-Related Experiences of Military Veterans.* Boston: National Center for PTSD.

King, D. W., C. T. Taft, L. A. King, C. Hammond, and E. R. Stone. 2006. "Directionality of the Association between Social Support and Posttraumatic Stress Disorder: A Longitudinal Investigation." *Journal of Applied Social Psychology* 36 (12): 2980–2992.

King, L. A., D. W. King, J. A. Fairbank, T. M. Keane, and G. A. Adams. 1998. "Resilience-Recovery Factors in Post-Traumatic Stress Disorder among Female and Male Vietnam Veterans: Hardiness, Postwar Social Support, and Additional Stressful Life Events." *Journal of Personality and Social Psychology* 74 (2): 420–434.

King, L. A., D. W. King, D. S. Vogt, J. Knight, and R. E. Samper. 2006. "Deployment Risk and Resilience Inventory: A Collection of Measures for Studying Deployment-Related Experiences of Military Personnel and Veterans." *Military Psychology* 18 (2): 89–120.

Kirmayer, L., and A. Young. 1998. "Culture and Somatization: Clinical, Epidemiological, and Ethnographic Perspectives." *Psychosomatic Medicine* 60 (4): 420–430.

Kleinman, A. 1986. *Social Origins of Distress and Disease.* New Haven: Yale University Press.

Kleinman, A. 1988a. *The Illness Narratives.* New York: Basic Books.

———. 1988b. *Rethinking Psychiatry: From Cultural Category to Personal Experience.* New York: Free Press.

———. 1995. *Writing at the Margin: Discourse between Anthropology and Medicine.* Berkeley: University of California Press.

Kleinman, A., V. Das, and M. Lock. 1997a. Introduction. In *Social Suffering,* ed. A. Kleinman, V. Das, and M. Lock, ix–xxv. Berkeley: University of California Press.

Kleinman, A., V. Das, and M. Lock, M., eds. 1997b. *Social Suffering.* Berkeley: University of California Press.

Kleinman, A., and R. Desjarlais. 1995. "Violence, Culture, and the Politics of Trauma." In Kleinman 1995, 173–189.

Kleinman, A., and D. Seeman. 2000. "Personal Experience of Illness." In *The Handbook of Social Studies in Health and Medicine,* ed. Gary L. Albrecht, Ray Fitzpatrick, and Susan C. Scrimshaw, 230–242. Thousand Oaks, CA: Sage.

Kohn, A. 2004. *Shooters: Myths and Realities of American's Gun Cultures.* Oxford: Oxford University Press.

Kolb, R. K. 2006. "Portraying Contemporary War Vets in Popular Culture." *VFW Magazine,* April.

Konner, Melvin. 2007. Trauma, Adaptation, and Resilience: A Cross-Cultural and Evolutionary Perspective. In *Understanding Trauma: Integrating Biological, Clinical, and Cultural Perspectives,* ed. L. J. Kirmayer, R. Lemelson, and M. Barad. New York City: Cambridge University Press.

Lawrence, Q. 2009. "'Colbert Report' Broadcasts from Iraq." *Morning Edition,* NPR. June 11. http://www.npr.org/templates/story/story.php?storyId=105241013&ft=1&f=1021.

Lee, C. 2008. "Official Urged Fewer Diagnoses of PTSD." *Washington Post,* May 16. http://www.washingtonpost.com/wp-dyn/content/article/2008/05/15/AR2008051503533.html.

Lewis-Fernandez, R., J. B. Turner, R. Marshall, N. A. Turse, Y. Neria, and B. P. Dohrenwend. 2008. "Elevated Rates of Current PTSD among Hispanic Veterans in the NVVRS: True Prevalence or Methodological Artifact." *Journal of Traumatic Stress* 21 (2): 123–132.

Lifton, R. J. [1973] 1992. *Home from the War: Learning from Vietnam Veterans.* Boston: Beacon Press.

Lomsky-Feder, E., and E. Ben-Ari, eds. 1999. *The Military and Militarism in Israeli Society.* Albany: State University of New York Press.

Longman, P. 2007. *Best Care Anywhere: Why VA Health Care Is Better Than Yours.* Sausalito, CA: PoliPointPress.

Lorber, W., and H. A. Garcia. 2010. "Not Supposed to Feel This: Traditional Masculinity in Psychotherapy with Male Veterans Returning from Iraq and Afghanistan." *Psychotherapy* 47 (3): 296–305.

Lutz, C. 2001. *Homefront: A Military City and the American 20th Century.* Boston: Beacon Press.

Magovcevic, M., and M. E. Addis. 2005. "Linking Gender-Role Conflict to Nonnormative and Self-Stigmatizing Perceptions of Alcohol Abuse and Depression." *Psychology of Men and Masculinity* 6 (2): 127–136.

Magruder, K., B. C. Frueh, R. G. Knapp, M. R. Johnson, J. A. Vaughan, T. Coleman Carson et al. 2004. "PTSD Symptoms, Demographic Characteristics, and Functional Status among Veterans Treated in VA Primary Care Clinics." *Journal of Traumatic Stress* 17 (4): 293–301.

Mahalik, J. R., B. Locke, L. Ludlow, M. Diemer, R. P. J. Scott, M. Gottfried et al. 2003. "Development of the Conformity to Masculine Norms Inventory." *Psychology of Men and Masculinity* 4:3–25.

Marshall, A. D., J. Panuzio, and C. T. Taft. 2005. "Intimate Partner Violence among Military Veterans and Active Duty Servicemen." *Clinical Psychology Review* 25:862–876.

Marshall, G. N., and M. Orlando. 2002. "Acculturation and Peritraumatic Dissociation in Young Adult Latino Survivors of Community Violence." *Journal of Abnormal Psychology* 111 (1): 166–174.

Marshall, G. N., T. L. Schell, and J. N. V. Miles. 2009. "Ethnic Differences in Posttraumatic Distress: Hispanics' Symptoms Differ in Kind and Degree." *Journal of Consulting and Clinical Psychology* 77 (6): 1169–1178.

Mason, J. W., S. Wang, R. Yehuda, H. Lubin, D. Johnson, J. D. Bremner et al. 2002. "Marked Lability in Urinary Cortisol Levels in Subgroups of Combat Veterans with Posttraumatic Stress Disorder during an Intensive Exposure Treatment Program. *Psychosomatic Medicine* 64:238–246.

Matsakis, A. 1988. *Vietnam Wives: Facing the Challenges of Life with Veterans Suffering Post-Traumatic Stress.* 2nd ed. Baltimore, Maryland: Sidran Press.

McAuliffe, M. 2007. "Parents of Iraq Veterans Blame VA for His Death." *Republican,* July 27, 2007. http://www.masslive.com/news/republican/index.ssf ?/base/news-2/118552490772220.xml&coll=1.

McHugh, J. 2004. "All Charges Dropped: Soldier Was Accused of Cowardice in Iraq." *Army Times.com,* August 2, 2004. http://www.armytimes.com/print.php?f=1-ARMYPAPER-275107.php.

McKinney, K. 2007. "Breaking the Conspiracy of Silence": Testimony, Traumatic Memory, and Psychotherapy with Survivors of Political Violence. *Ethos* 35 (3): 265–299.

MedlinePlus. 2009. "Dislocation." *MedlinePlus* (May 12, 2008 ed.): U.S. National Library of Medicine, National Institutes of Health. http://www.nlm.nih.gov/medlineplus/ency/article/000014.htm.

Mejia, X. E. 2005. "Gender Matters: Working with Adult Male Survivors of Trauma." *Journal of Counseling and Development* 83:29–40.

MHAT (Mental Health Advisory Team). 2003. *Operation Iraqi Freedom (OIF): Mental Health Advisory Team Report.* Fort Bliss, TX: U.S. Army Surgeon General and Headquarters of the Department of the Army.

——. 2008. *Mental Health Advisory Team (MHAT) V: Operation Iraqi Freedom 06–08: Iraq, Operational Enduring Freedom 8: Afghanistan.* Washington, DC: Office of the Surgeon, Multi-National Force—Iraq, and Office of the Command Surgeon and Office of the Surgeon General, United States Army Medical Command.

Michalowski, R., and J. Dubisch. 2001. *Run for the Wall: Remembering Vietnam on a Motorcycle Pilgrimage.* New Brunswick, NJ: Rutgers University Press.

Milliken, C. S., J. L. Auchterlonie, and C. W. Hoge. 2007. "Longitudinal Assessment of Mental Health Problems among Active and Reserve Component Soldiers Returning from the Iraq War." *JAMA* 298 (18): 2141–2148.

Mirande, A. 1997. *Hombres y Machos: Masculinity and Latino Culture.* Boulder, CO: Westview.

Moerman, D. 2002. *Meaning, Medicine, and the "Placebo Effect."* Cambridge: Cambridge University Press.

Monmartin, S., D. Silove, V. Manicavasagar, and Z. Steel. 2003. "Dimensions of Trauma Associated with Posttraumatic Stress Disorder (PTSD) Caseness, Severity, and Functional Impairment: A Study of Bosnian Refugees Resettled in Australia." *Social Science and Medicine* 57 (5): 775–781.

Monson, C., S. J. Fredman, and K. C. Adair. 2008. "Cognitive-Behavioral Conjoint Therapy for Posttraumatic Stress Disorder: Application to Operation Enduring and Iraqi Freedom Veterans." *Journal of Clinical Psychology: In Session* 64:958–971.

Monson, C., C. T. Taft, and S. J. Fredman. 2009. "Military-Related PTSD and Intimate Relationships: From Description to Theory-Driven Research and Intervention Development." *Clinical Psychology Review* 29:707–714.

Mrozek, D. J. 1987. "The Habit of Victory: The American Military and the Cult of Manliness." In *Manliness and Morality: Middle-Class Masculinity in Britain and America, 1800–1940,* ed. J. A. Mangan and J. Walvin, 220–241. New York: St. Martin's.

NCQA (National Committee for Quality Assurance). 2004. *The State of Health Care Quality: 2004.* Washington, DC: National Committee for Quality Assurance.

NEPEC (North East Program Evaluation Center). 2009. "The Long Journey Home XVII: Treatment of Posttraumatic Stress Disorder in the Department of Veterans Affairs: Fiscal Year 2008 Service Delivery and Performance." Report. West Haven, CT: North East Program Evaluation Center.

Nichter, M. 1981. "Idioms of Distress: Alternatives in the Expression of Psychosocial Distress: A Case Study from South India." *Culture, Medicine, and Psychiatry* 5:379–408.

Nisbet, R. A. 1945. "The Coming Problem of Assimilation." *American Journal of Sociology* 50 (4): 261–271.

Nordstrom, C. 1997. *A Different Kind of War Story.* Philadelphia: University of Pennsylvania Press.

NPP (National Priorities Project). 2009. *Army Recruitment in FY 2008: A Look at Age, Race, Income, and Education of New Soldiers.* Northampton, MA: National Priorities Project.

O'Donnell, C., J. M. Cook, R. Thompson, K. Riley, and Y. Neria. 2006. "Verbal and Physical Aggression in World War II Former Prisoners of War: Role of Post-traumatic Stress Disorder and Depression." *Journal of Traumatic Stress* 19 (6): 859–866.

O'Hara, V. 2006. "U.S. Forces Overstretched? Rumsfeld Says No." *All Things Considered,* NPR. January 25. http://www.npr.org/templates/story/story.php?storyId=5172183.

Ortega, A. N., and R. Rosenheck. 2000. Posttraumatic Stress Disorder among Hispanic Vietnam Veterans. *American Journal of Psychiatry* 157 (4): 615–619.

Orth-Somer, K., A. Rosengren, and L. Wilhelmsen. 1993. "Lack of Social Support and Incidence of Coronary Heart Disease in Middle-Aged Swedish Men. *Psychosomatic Medicine* 55:37–43.

Ortner, S. B. 1999. *Life and Death on Mt. Everest: Sherpas and Himalayan Mountaineering.* Princeton: Princeton University Press.

Ozer, E. J., S. R. Best, T. L. Lipsey, and D. S. Weiss. 2003. "Predictors of Post-Traumatic Stress Disorder and Symptoms in Adults: A Meta-Analysis." *Psychological Bulletin* 129 (1): 52–73.

Perkonigg, A., R. C. Kessler, S. Storz, and H.-U. Wittchen. 2000. "Traumatic Events and Post-Traumatic Stress Disorder in the Community: Prevalence, Risk Factors, and Comorbidity." *Acta Psychiatrica Scandinavica* 101 (1): 46–59.

Perlin, J. B., R. M. Kolodner, and R. H. Roswell. 2004. "The Veterans Health Administration: Quality, Value, Accountability, and Information as Transforming Strategies for Patient-Centered Care." *American Journal of Managed Care* 10 (pt. 2): 828–836.

Pivac, N., and D. Kozaric-Kovacic. 2007. "Pharmacotherapy of Treatment-Resistant Combat-Related Posttraumatic Stress Disorder with Psychotic Features." *Croatian Medical Journal* 47:440–451.

Pole, N., S. R. Best, T. Metzler, and C. R. Marmar. 2005. "Why Are Hispanics at Greater Risk for PTSD?" *Cultural Diversity and Ethnic Minority Psychology* 11 (2): 144–161.

Pollack, D. A., P. Rhodes, C. A. Boyle, P. Decoufle, and D. L. McGee. 1990. "Estimating the Number of Suicides among Vietnam Veterans." *American Journal of Psychiatry* 147 (6): 772–776.

Pols, H., and S. Oak. 2007. "War and Military Mental Health: The US Psychiatric Response in the 20th Century." *American Journal of Public Health* 97 (12): 2132–2142.

Press, A. 2007. "Veterans Affairs Secretary Resigns." NPR.org. July 17. http://www.npr.org/templates/story/story.php?storyId=12031671.

——. 2009. "Fort Campbell Troops Trained to Prevent Suicide." MSNBC. June 27. http://www.msnbc.msn.com/id/30964820/.

Priest, D., and A. Hull, A. 2007a. "Soldiers Face Neglect, Frustration at the Army's Top Medical Facility." *Washington Post,* February 18, 2007. http://www.washingtonpost.com/wp-dyn/content/article/2007/02/17/AR2007021701172.html.

——. 2007b. "The War Inside." *Washington Post,* June 17. http://www.washingtonpost.com/wp-dyn/content/article/2007/06/16/AR2007061600866.html.

Prigerson, H., P. Maciejewski, and R. Rosenheck. 2001. "Combat Trauma: Trauma with Highest Risk of Delayed Onset and Unresolved Posttraumatic Stress Disorder Symptoms, Unemployment, and Abuse among Men." *Journal of Nervous and Mental Disease* 189 (2): 99–108.

Pulitzer. 2008. Citation to the *Washington Post* for the Pulitzer Prize in Public Service Reporting. http://www.pulitzer.org/citation/2008-Public-Service.

Rauch, S. A. M., E. Defever, T. Favorite, A. Duroe, and C. Garrity. 2009. "Prolonged Exposure for PTSD in a Veterans Health Administration PTSD Clinic." *Journal of Traumatic Stress* 22 (1): 60–64.

Rechtman, R. 2000. "Stories of Trauma and Idioms of Distress: From Cultural Narratives to Clinical Assessment." *Transcultural Psychiatry* 37 (3): 403–415.

Remarque, E. M. 1930. *The Road Back*. Translated from the German by A. W. Wheen. New York: Ballantine.

Resick, P. A., P. Nishith, T. L. Weaver, M. C. Astin, and C. A. Feuer. 2002. "A Comparison of Cognitive-Processing Therapy with Prolonged Exposure and a Waiting Condition for the Treatment of Chronic Posttraumatic Stress Disorder in Female Rape Victims." *Journal of Consulting and Clinical Psychology* 70 (4): 867–870.

Richie, E. 2008. Interview on the Diane Rehm Show, NPR. April 28.

Rivers, W. H. R. 1920. *Instinct and the Unconscious: A Contribution to a Biological Theory of the Psycho-Neuroses*. 2nd ed. Cambridge: Cambridge University Press.

Robben, A. C. G. M., and M. M. Suarez-Orozco. 2000. *Cultures under Siege: Collective Violence and Trauma*. Cambridge: Cambridge University Press.

Roberts, G. 2006. "Hundreds of Soldiers Shot for 'Cowardice' to Be Pardoned." *Independent,* August 16, 2006. http://www.independent.co.uk/news/uk/this-britain/hundreds-of-soldiers-shot-for-cowardice-to-be-pardoned-412066.html.

Rochefort, D. A. 1997. *From Poorhouses to Homelessness: Policy Analysis and Mental Health Care*. Westport, CT: Auburn House.

Rotunda, R. J., T. J. O'Farrell, M. Murphy, and S. H. Babey. 2008. "Behavioral Couples Therapy for Comorbid Substance Use Disorders and Combat-Related Posttraumatic Stress Disorder among Male Veterans: An Initial Evaluation." *Addictive Behaviors* 33:180–187.

Rubel, A. 1966. *Across the Tracks: Mexican-Americans in a Texas City*. Austin: University of Texas Press.

Rubel, A. J., and L. C. Garro. 1992. "Cultural and Social Factors in the Successful Control of Tuberculosis." *Public Health Reports* 107 (6): 626–636.

Rubel, A. J., C. W. O'Nell, and R. Collado. 1984. *Susto, a Folk Illness*. Berkeley: University of California Press.

Ruberman, W., E. Weinblatt, J. D. Goldberg, and B. S. Chaudhary. 1984. "Psychosocial Influences on Mortality after Myocardial Infarction." *New England Journal of Medicine* 311:552–559.

Ruef, A. M., B. T. Litz, and W. E. Schlenger. 2000. "Hispanic Ethnicity and Risk for Combat-Related Posttraumatic Stress Disorder." *Cultural Diversity and Ethnic Minority Psychology* 6 (3): 235–251.

Russell, M. C. 2008. "Scientific Resistance to Research, Training, and Utilization of Eye Movement Desensitization and Reprocessing (EMDR) Therapy in Treating Post-War Disorders." *Social Science and Medicine* 67 (11): 1737–1746.

Sabin, M., B. L. Cardoza, L. Nackerud, R. Kaiser, and L. Varese. 2003. "Factors Associated with Poor Mental Health among Guatemalan Refugees Living in Mexico 20 Years after Civil Conflict." *JAMA* 290 (5): 635–642.

Sabo, D., and D. F. Gordon, eds. 1995. *Men's Health and Illness: Gender, Power, and the Body*. Thousand Oaks, CA: Sage.

Sammons, M. T., and S. V. Batten. 2008. "Psychological Services for Returning Veterans and Their Families: Evolving Conceptualizations of the Sequlae of War-Zone Experiences." *Journal of Clinical Psychology* 64 (8): 921–927.

Santiago-Irizarry, V. 2001. *Medicalizing Ethnicity: The Construction of Latino Identity in a Psychiatric Setting*. Ithaca: Cornell University Press.

Sapolsky, R. M. 1998. *Why Zebras Don't Get Ulcers: An Updated Guide to Stress, Stress-Related Disease, and Coping.* New York: W. H. Freeman.

Scheper-Hughes, Nancy. 1992. *Death without Weeping: The Violence of Everyday Life in Brazil.* Berkeley: University of California Press.

Schnurr, P. P., M. J. Friedman, C. C. Engel, E. B. Foa, M. T. Shea, B. K. Chow et al. 2007. "Cognitive Behavioral Therapy for Posttraumatic Stress Disorder in Women: A Randomized Controlled Trial." *JAMA* 297 (8): 820–830.

Schuster, T. L., R. C. Kessler, and R. H. Aseltine. 1990. "Supportive Interactions, Negative Interactions, and Depressed Mood." *American Journal of Community Psychology* 18:423–438.

Scott, W. J. 1993. *The Politics of Readjustment: Vietnam Veterans since the War.* New York: Aldine de Gruyter.

Seal, K. H., S. Maguen, B. E. Cohen, K. S. Gima, T. J. Metzler, L. Ren et al. 2010. "VA Mental Health Services Utilization in Iraq and Afghanistan Veterans in the First Year of Receiving New Mental Health Diagnoses." *Journal of Traumatic Stress* 23 (1): 5–16.

Seedat, S., D. J. Stein, and P. D. Carey. 2005. "Post-Traumatic Stress Disorder in Women: Epidemiological and Treatment Issues." *CNS Drugs* 19 (5): 411–427.

Seeman, T. E. 1996. "Social Ties and Health." *Annals of Epidemiology* 6:442–451.

Seeman, T. E., and E. Crimmins. 2001. "Social Environmental Effects on Health and Aging: Integrating Epidemiologic and Demographic Approaches and Perspectives." *Annals of the New York Academy of Sciences* 954:88–117.

Seeman, T. E., and S. L. Syme. 1987. "Social Networks and Coronary Artery Disease: A Comparative Analysis of Network Structural and Support Characteristics." *Psychosomatic Medicine* 49:341–354.

Service, R. 1916. *Rhymes of a Red Cross Man:* Barse & Hopkins.

Shephard, B. 2001. *A War of Nerves: Soldiers and Psychiatrists in the Twentieth Century.* Cambridge, MA: Harvard University Press.

Sherman, M. D., F. Sautter, H. M. Jackson, J. A. Lyons, and X. Han. 2006. "Domestic Violence in Veterans with Posttraumatic Stress Disorder Who Seek Couples Therapy." *Journal of Marital and Family Therapy* 32:479–490.

Shmotkin, D., T. Blumstein, and B. Modan. 2003. "Tracing Long-Term Effects of Early Trauma: A Broad-Scope View of Holocaust Survivors in Late Life." *Journal of Consulting and Clinical Psychology* 71 (2): 223–234.

Silove, D. 2005. "From Trauma to Survival and Adaptation: Towards a Framework for Guiding Mental Health Initiatives in Post-Conflict Societies." In *Forced Migration and Mental Health: Rethinking the Care of Refugees and Displaced Persons,* ed. D. Ingleby. New York: Springer.

Silver, S. M., S. Rogers, and M. Russell. 2008. "Eye Movement Desensitization and Reprocessing in the Treatment of War Veterans." *Journal of Clinical Psychology* 64 (8): 947–957.

Simons, A. 1997. *The Company They Keep.* New York: Free Press.

——. 1998. "How Ambiguity Results in Excellence: The Role of Hierarchy and Reputation in U.S. Army Special Forces." *Human Organization* 57 (1): 117–123.

——. 1999. "War: Back to the Future." *Annual Review of Anthropology* 28:73–108.

Simons, R. C. 1996. *Boo! Culture, Experience, and the Startle Reflex.* New York: Oxford University Press.

Slagle, D. M., and M. J. Gray. 2007. "The Utility of Motivational Interviewing as an Adjunct to Exposure Therapy in the Treatment of Anxiety Disorders." *Professional Psychology: Research and Practice* 38 (4): 327–337.

Spiegal, D. A., and T. J. Bruce. 1997. "Benzodiazepines and Exposure-Based Cognitive Behavior Therapies for Panic Disorder: Conclusions from Combined Treatment Trials." *American Journal of Psychiatry* 154:773–781.

Solomon, Z. 1987. "Objective Versus Subjective Measurement of Stress and Social Support: Combat-Related Reactions." *Journal of Consulting and Clinical Psychology* 55 (4): 577–583.

Squitieri, T. 2004. "Army Expanding 'Stop Loss' Order to Keep Soldiers from Leaving." *USA Today,* January 5. http://www.usatoday.com/news/nation/2004–01-05-army-troops_x.htm.

Starr, B. 2002. "Fort Bragg Killings Raise Alarm about Stress." *CNN.com,* July 27. http://archives.cnn.com/2002/US/07/26/army.wives/.

——. 2009. "Army to Report Record Number of Suicides." CNN.com, January 30. http://www.cnn.com/2009/US/01/29/army.suicides/.

Straus, M. A., and R. J. Gelles. 1990. *Physical Violence in American Families: Risk Factors and Adaptations to Violence in 8,145 Families.* New Brunswick, NJ: Transaction Books.

Stretch, R., K. H. Knudson, and D. Durand. 1998. "Effects of Premilitary and Military Trauma on the Development of Post-traumatic Stress Disorder Symptoms in Female and Male Active Duty Soldiers." *Military Medicine* 163 (7): 466–470.

Suicide Risk Management and Surveillance Office. 2008. *Army Suicide Event Report Calendar Year 2007.* Suicide Risk Management and Surveillance Office, Army Behavioral Health Technology Office.

Summerfield, D. 1999. "A Critique of Seven Assumptions behind Psychological Trauma Programmes in War-Affected Areas." *Social Science and Medicine* 48:1449–1462.

——. 2000a. "Post-Traumatic Stress Disorder in Doctors Involved in the Omagh Bombing." *British Medical Journal* 320 (7244): 1276.

——. 2000b. "War and Mental Health: A Brief Overview." *British Medical Journal* 321 (7255): 232–235.

Sundar, N. 2004. "Toward an Anthropology of Culpability." *American Ethnologist* 31 (2): 145–163.

Taft, C. T., A. S. Stern, L. A. King, and D. W. King. 1999. "Modeling Physical Health and Functional Health Status: The Role of Combat Exposure, Posttraumatic Stress Disorder, and Personal Resource Attributes." *Journal of Traumatic Stress* 12 (1): 3–23.

Taft, C. T., A. P. Pless, L. J. Stalans, K. C. Koenen, L. A. King, and D. W. King. 2005. "Risk Factors for Partner Violence among a National Sample of Combat Veterans." *Journal of Consulting and Clinical Psychology* 73:151–159.

Tager, D., and G. E. Good. 2005. "Italian and American Masculinities: A Comparison of Masculine Gender Role Norms." *Psychology of Men and Masculinity* 6 (4): 264–274.

Tanielian, T., L. H. Jaycox, T. L. Schell, G. N. Marshall, M. A. Burnham, C. Eibner et al. 2008. *Invisible Wounds of War: Psychological and Cognitive Injuries, Their Consequences, and Services to Assist Recovery.* San Diego: RAND.

Taylor, S., D. S. Thordarson, L. Maxfield, I. C. Federoff, K. Lovell, and J. Ogrodniczuk. 2003. "Comparative Efficacy, Speed, and Adverse Effects of Three PTSD Treatments: Exposure Therapy, EMDR, and Relaxation Training." *Journal of Consulting and Clinical Psychology* 71 (2): 330–338.

Tedeschi, R. G., and L. G. Calhoun. 2004. "Posttraumatic Growth: Conceptual Foundations and Empirical Evidence." *Psychological Inquiry* 15 (1): 1–18.

Thompson, E. H., and J. H. Pleck. 1986. "The Structure of Male Role Norms." *American Behavioral Scientist* 29 (5): 531.

Thompson, M. 2008. "America's Medicated Army." *Time,* June 5.

Tiger, L. 1999. *The Decline of Males: The First Look at an Unexpected New World for Men and Women.* New York: St. Martin's.

Time. 2010. "The World's Most Influential People." April 29. http://www.time.com/time/specials/packages/0,28757,1984685,00.html.

Tusaie, K., and J. Dyer. 2004. "Resilience: A Historical Review of the Construct." *Holistic Nurse Practitioner,* 18 (1): 3–8.

USCB (United States Census Bureau). 2007. "2007 Population Estimate for San Antonio City, Texas." http://factfinder.census.gov/.

Vanden Brook, T. 2009. "Surplus of Soldiers Allows Cuts by Guard." *USA Today,* May 8–10.

van der Kolk, B. A., D. Pelcovitz, S. Roth, F. S. Mandel, A. McFarlane, and J. L. Herman. 1996. "Dissociation, Somatization, and Affect Dysregulation: The Complexity of Adaptation to Trauma." *American Journal of Psychiatry* 153:83–93.

Van Ommeren, M. V., J. T. V. M. de Jong, B. Sharma, I. Komproe, S. Thapa, and E. Cardena. 2001. "Prevalence of Psychiatric Disorders among Tortured Bhutanese Refugees in Nepal." *Archives of General Psychiatry* 58:475–482.

VHA Office of Public Health and Environmental Hazards. 2009. *Analysis of VA Health Care Utilization among Operation Enduring Freedom (OEF) and Operation Iraqi Freedom (OIF) Veterans.* VHA Office of Public Health and Environmental Hazards.

Vogt, T. M. J. P. Mullooly, D. Ernst. C. R. Pope, and J. F. Hollis. 1992. "Social Networks as Predictors of Ischemic Heart Disease, Cancer, Stroke, and Hypertension: Incidence, Survival, and Morality." *Journal of Clinical Epidemiology* 45:659–666.

Wanke, P. 1999. "American Military Psychiatry and Its Role among Ground Forces in World War II." *Journal of Military History* 63 (1): 127–146.

Warner, J. 2005. "Chemical Casualties." *Boulder Weekly,* February 17. http://www.boulderweekly.com/archive/021705/coverstory.html.

Watanabe, N., R. Churchill, and T. Furukawa. 2009. *Combined Psychotherapy plus Benzodiazepines for Panic Disorder (Review).* The Cochrane Collaboration.

Weathers, F. W., B. T. Litz, D. S. Herman, J. A. Huska, and T. M. Keane. 1993. "The PTSD Checklist (PCL): Reliability, Validity, and Diagnostic Utility." Paper presented at the ninth annual meeting of the International Society of Traumatic Stress Studies, San Antonio.

White, J. 2004. "Soldiers Facing Extended Tours: Critics of Army Policy Liken It to a Draft." *Washington Post,* June 3.

Wikan, U. 1990. *Managing Turbulent Hearts: A Balinese Formula for Living.* Chicago: University of Chicago Press.

Williams, R., D. A. Alexander, D. Bolsover, and F. K. Bakke. 2008. "Children, Resilience, and Disasters: Recent Evidence That Should Influence a Model of Psychosocial Care." *Current Opinion in Psychiatry* 21:338–344.

Wolfe, J. 1996. "Post-Traumatic Stress Disorder in Women Veterans." *Women's Health Issues* 6 (6): 349–352.

Yaeger, D., N. Himmelfarb, A. Cammack, and J. Mintz. 2006. "DSM-IV Diagnosed Posttraumatic Stress Disorder in Women Veterans with and without Military Sexual Trauma." *Journal of General Internal Medicine* 21:S65–69.

Yehuda, R. 2002. "Current Status of Cortisol Findings in Post-Traumatic Stress Disorder." *Psychiatric Clinics of North America* 25 (2): 341–368.

Yehuda, R., A. Bell, L. M. Bierer, and J. Schmeidler. 2008. "Maternal, Not Paternal, PTSD Is Related to Increased Risk for PTSD in Offspring of Holocaust Survivors." *Journal of Psychiatric Research* 42:1104–1111.

Yehuda, R., J. Golier, S. L. Halligan, and P. D. Harvey. 2004. "Learning and Memory in Holocaust Survivors with Posttraumatic Stress Disorder." *Biological Psychiatry* 55:291–295.

Yehuda, R., H. S. Resnick, B. Kahana, and E. Giller. 1993. "Long-Lasting Hormonal Alterations to Extreme Stress in Humans: Normative or Maladaptive." *Psychosomatic Medicine* 55:287–297.

Yen, H. 2007. "Injured Iraq War Veterans Sue VA Head." *Washington Post*, July 24, 2007. http://www.washingtonpost.com/wp-dyn/content/article/2007/07/23/AR2007072300686.html.

Young, A. 1995. *The Harmony of Illusions: Inventing Post-Traumatic Stress Disorder.* Princeton: Princeton University Press.

Zarowsky, C. 2004. "Writing Trauma: Emotion, Ethnography, and the Politics of Suffering among Somali Returnees in Ethiopia." *Culture, Medicine, and Psychiatry* 28:189–204.

Zivin, K., M. Kim, J. F. McCarthy, K. L. Austin, K. J. Hoggatt, H. Walters et al. 2007. "Suicide Mortality among Individuals Receiving Treatment for Depression in the Veterans Affairs Health System: Associations with Patient and Treatment Setting Characteristics." *American Journal of Public Health* 97 (12): 2193–2197.

Zohar, J., A. Juven-Wetzler, V. Myers, and L. Fostick. 2008. "Post-Traumatic Stress Disorder: Facts and Fiction." *Current Opinion in Psychiatry* 21:74–77.

Zoroya, G. 2008. "Divorce Rates Rise for Soldiers, Marines." *Army Times.* December 3. http://www.armytimes.com/news/2008/12/gns_divorcerates_120308w/.

Index